KAMIKAZE
A Japanese Pilot's Own Spectacular Story
Of The Infamous Suicide Squadrons

Yasuo Kuwahara

AND

Gordon T. Allred

American Legacy Media • Clearfield, Utah

Copyright 2007 Gordon T. Allred,

Published by American Legacy Media
Clearfield, Utah, USA

Library of Congress Cataloging-in-Publication Data
Kuwahara, Yasuo, 1929-1980.
   Kamikaze : a Japanese pilot's own spectacular story of the famous suicide squadrons / Yasuo Kuwahara and Gordon T. Allred.
        p. cm.
   Originally published: New York : Ballantine Books, 1957.

   ISBN-13: 978-0-9761547-5-4 (alk. paper)
   1. Kuwahara, Yasuo, 1929-1980. 2. Japan. Rikugun. Kokutai--Biography. 3. World War, 1939-1945--Aerial operations, Japanese. 4. World War, 1939-1945--Campaigns--Pacific Area. 5. World War, 1939-1945--Personal narratives, Japanese. 6. Kamikaze pilots--Biography. I. Allred, Gordon T. II. Title.

   D792.J3K83 2007
   940.54'4952092--dc22
   [B]

                                        2006025960

Distributed by Independent Publishers Group (IPG)
(800) 888- 4741 or (312) 337-0747.

Printed in the United States of America

1 2 3 4 5 10 09 08 07 06

Contents

A Vital Explanation

Shyly expectant, typically reserved and polite, Yasuo Kuwahara was only twenty-six, I myself a year younger, when we met at Camp Kobe where I was stationed with the United States Army. The time was summer, 1955, three years following the Occupation, there between the two great cities of Kobe and Osaka, and Kuwahara was one of many Japanese nationals employed at that base. Except for his eyes, I would have imagined him to be even younger—eyes that smoldered within their depths as though they had absorbed much hardship and violence. The eyes, it seemed, of one who had trained, as he maintained, to become a suicide pilot, a *Kamikaze*, only to be preserved by an ironic and terrible quirk of fate toward the war's end.

Following that first encounter involving Kuwahara's brief and amazing summation of his experiences, we met for an hour each day until my departure ten months later. Our goal was to collaborate on a book in that regard. During the course of those interviews, I asked him thousands of questions, taking copious notes on an ancient upright typewriter, and with each visit his story became more astounding. Simultaneously, we developed a close and highly valued friendship, and I never had the slightest reason to doubt anything he related. Kuwahara answered every question, no matter how difficult or technical, with marked insight and authority, rarely hesitating, and never seemed to contradict himself. Furthermore, everything he related corresponded perfectly with all that I was studying on the subject.

Consequently, I became increasingly confident of his account's validity as it unfolded. Nevertheless, as the time approached for my departure from Japan and the military, I advised Kuwahara that any prospective publisher might naturally request supportive evidence by way of witnesses to his experiences, and he readily concurred. I then summarized, in a few sentences each, eighteen of the main and most pivotal events from his account which he translated into Japanese. Of special significance among them were the following:

1. His first-place championship as pilot in the National High School Glider Contest

2. Resultant induction at only age fifteen into the Japanese Army Air Force

3. Brutal survival-of-the-fittest basic training during which nine of his squadron committed suicide

4. Qualification for fighter pilot school

5. Ferocious aerial combat

6. Flying of fighter escort missions over Okinawa for his fated Kamikaze comrades

7. Near death in the process from the American enemy and a tremendous thunder storm

8. Receipt of his suicide orders

9. His ultimate, staggeringly ironic, escape from death because of the most horrible destruction ever visited upon mankind.

The entire list of eighteen key events, in both English and Japanese, was then sent to three individuals with whom Kuwahara claimed to have been closely associated during his year and a half in the Air Force. One was Capt. Yoshiro Tsubaki, his base commander at Hiro, and later at Oita, who allegedly issued Kuwahara his suicide orders in person there. The second and third were his fellow pilots and prospective Kamikaze, Seiji Hiroi, and another person whose name I have lost over the years.

About two weeks after their mailing, the lists were signed and returned by Tsubaki and Hiroi. Then, after several more days awaiting a reply from the third pilot, Kuwahara asked me if we should move ahead without it. To this I agreed because my time in Japan with the military was nearly over. It should be stressed, however, that Kuwahara knew without question that I might be writing to both Tsubaki and Hiroi before long at the addresses listed under their signatures.

Following my return to Salt Lake City, in 1956, I published a condensed version of Kuwahara's account in *Cavalier*, a national men's magazine, and was contacted soon afterward by Ballantine Books inquiring whether I had sufficient material for a book-length work on that subject. Fortunately, as explained, that had been my intention from the onset. Neither the magazine's senior editor James O'Connell nor the book publisher Ian Ballantine, however, required more than my word regarding Tsubaki and Hiroi. Therefore, I never attempted to contact them.

The resulting book *Kamikaze* was finished within the following year and first reached the stands in 1957. Happily, for both me and my friend Yasuo, it did very well, eventually being translated into several languages, and selling over half a million copies.

Ever since then readers have invariably said that they "couldn't put it down," or "stayed up all night reading it," that it is "the most exciting story" they have ever encountered, etc. Throughout its history *Kamikaze* has been, and still is at times, adopted as assigned reading for various high school and college literary courses in both Utah, my home state, and other parts of the nation.

Often readers have also insisted that *Kamikaze* would make a splendid movie. Over the years, in fact, I have been contacted by eight prospective movie marketers or producers, all highly enthusiastic about this work's potential as cinema. Unfortunately, none of them ever realized their objectives mainly because of filming difficulties and production costs. Nevertheless, the interest is still there, and any expenses should be significantly lower because of miraculous advancements in filming techniques including special effects. Surely the Kamikaze war was the strangest and in many ways most dramatic ever waged. One wherein nearly five thousand young men were converted by their leaders into human bombs as the suicide pilots who lived to die and caused the greatest losses in the history of our United States Navy.

Few people will ever comprehend the feelings of those men who covenanted with death. Countless individuals, of course, have entered the inferno of war, knowing that their chances for survival were poor, and throughout time men have sacrificed their lives for others and the causes they have espoused. Never have so many human beings, however, unitedly and deliberately agreed to die for their country without hope of any alternative. Where, before or since, have so many specifically planned and trained for their own annihilation, mulling over every aspect and minute detail, for weeks, sometimes months, in advance?

There are, of course, certain obvious parallels between the Japanese suicide war and the attacks frequently launched or attempted almost daily at present by individuals and smaller groups of Islamic terrorists. There are also significant differences which can barely be touched upon in this commentary. I will simply stress here, that today's terrorists are often killing themselves to destroy so-called "infidels" —all those including innocent women and children—who do not endorse their benighted and despotic view of the world. Conversely, the Kamikaze, however reprehensible their actions to many people, attempted to reverse the misfortunes of war by attacking America's navy and almost exclusively from the sky.

No one, in any event, except the few vanishing survivors of that experience, can now comprehend the kind of physical and emotional trauma entailed in such preparation. Undoubtedly, religion was a sustaining force for some, and National Shintoism promised that those who died valiantly in battle would be honored as guardian warriors in the spirit realms. Buddhism, on the other hand (which, strange though it may seem to western minds, was sometimes embraced simultaneously), offered nirvana as the ultimate reward. For many, however, the practical distinction between nirvana and annihilation was uncertain at best. Surely also, that must have held true for the Kamikaze, pawns of an autocratic, militaristic government and often mere school boys who wept at night for the arms of their mothers.

Two or three years after our book was published Kuwahara lost his wife to leukemia in Kobe and moved to Innoshima near Hiroshima with their small son. There he inherited a fine home and orange orchard from his deceased uncle, eventually remarried and fathered three more children. Sadly, however, having also established a successful photography business, he died unexpectedly in 1980.

Sadly as well, I must explain that in the year 2000, a *Kamikaze* movie promoter, then researching related material in Kuwahara's home town of Onomichi, encountered two men who said that his account was a fabrication. Both said they had been his high school acquaintances and contended that he had never won a national glider championship or been in the Japanese Army Air Force. Instead, they maintained, Kuwahara was merely one of many students drafted by their government to support the war effort on that country's military bases.

The claim is set forth here with considerable misgiving, for it impugns my friend's integrity, and he is not alive to defend himself. Furthermore, such allegations should be weighed against all the positive evidence delineated in his behalf above. I must stress also that the individual who discussed Kuwahara's story with these alleged acquaintances barely knew them, and had no way of determining their motives or the validity of their own claims. Finally, it should be noted that the experiences, many extremely fascinating and violent, of countless military men throughout history, including from World War II, are not known even to their closest friends and family.

Such may have been the case with Kuwahara. Nevertheless, ethics and honesty dictate the above disclosure. As for myself, I wrote and published this remarkable story fully convinced that it was true, and have yet to find any major discrepancies in terms of all I have studied about the war between America and Japan including the unique role of the *Kamikaze* pilots. Readers of what follows must reflect upon its authenticity for themselves and in many cases may never feel certain of an answer in this veil of tears.

I must explain, in any event, that like most biographical writers I have utilized what might be termed "creative logic" in rounding out the characters involved, their reported or probable conversations, and in describing from a sensory standpoint what seemed most natural in the specific situations that my friend Yasuo related. This is especially true of the present revision which entailed much additional effort, hopefully reflecting more understanding on my part and greater literary quality than the original.

Ever since the concerns discussed arose in the year 2000, I have always explained their pros and cons to those interested in movie rights, use of the work in school literature curriculums, or publication of this revision. Almost invariably, however, such individuals have felt that the account should continue to be read and promoted. Regardless of whether *Kamikaze* is fact or fiction, they argue that it is a great story fraught with immense drama and human interest, one consistent with the historical accounts of its time. They contend also, like numerous others before them, that it will yet succeed in a big way on the big screen. I believe they are correct, and thanks to Gary Toyn of American Legacy Media, the revised book version, with all that promise, is in your hands. Please keep reading.

Gordon T. Allred
April 2007.

Publisher's Note

*K*amikaze, **by Yasuo** Kuwahara and Gordon T. Allred, was first published in 1957 by Ballantine Books Inc. as part of their classic World War series and was among their first titles to enjoy wide-spread retail success. It was released after more than a decade of post-war recuperation from the economic and emotional toll of World War II when Americans were, at long last, disposed to learn more about their former enemy's perspective on the war.

After half a century, experts still recognize *Kamikaze* as one of the most well-written and influential English-language accounts of the infamous suicide squadrons. It remains on the "recommended reading list" for college and high school literature, history, and political science courses world-wide. With over half a million copies to its credit, authorized translations of *Kamikaze* include French, Dutch, and German, but with countless unauthorized translations in circulation, it is impossible to determine how many copies exist. Some have estimated they may be in the millions, with "bootleg" print runs in foreign countries still occurring today.

Because several different parties were interested in making Kamikaze into a feature-length film, co-author Gordon T. Allred allowed this work to go out of print following its last printing in 1982. Meanwhile, as Professor of Creative Writing at Weber State University, he has published ten other books, both fiction and non-fiction, including some award winning titles like *Starfire*. In addition, Allred has recently re-written and expanded

Kamikaze to improve its effectiveness but without changing the basic history or facts. The highly original result is now available in your hands, and its release is most auspicious as we celebrate its 50th anniversary as a literary classic. American Legacy Media is proud to be associated with *Kamikaze*, and with the advent of digital publishing technology, we are positioned keep it "in print" and available in perpetuity

Since 1982, the digital revolution has not only changed the publishing landscape, it has also changed the field of historical study and research. When *Kamikaze* was first published, it was difficult for researchers to gain access to many important historical documents. It was only recently that the Japanese government provided their declassified military records to a world-wide audience via the Internet. That availability has since generated a wave of related research.

This new information, however, has led some to question the validity of co-author Yasuo Kuwahara's account. Researchers have raised questions concerning how Kuwahara was recruited, whether he served in the Army or Navy, if he was attached to a tokkotai* unit, his recollection regarding the type of military planes involved, and the very existence of specific people he mentions throughout the book. Conversely, many other details have similarly been difficult to disprove. Unfortunately, Kuwahara died in 1980, and is unable to defend himself, or to offer any needed clarifications. Consequently, what remains to authenticate the factual elements of this story are an incomplete collection of government documents, second-hand accounts, and hearsay.

Although specific details of the book may not correlate directly to the existing historical documents, it is important to note that a condensed version of this story was translated and widely published throughout Japan in 1957. Interestingly, no known challenges to the story were put forth at that time. One would think that if its basic tenets were untrue, a story of such reputation and magnificent irony would have aroused at least minimal interest among the Japanese military history establishment of the time.

Superseding all arguments, for or against authenticity, is the nature of this book. Allred's intention from the outset was to create a literary

---

* *Kamikaze* squadrons were identified as "Special Forces Units." The Japanese term is: tokubetsu ko-geki-tai, which later was abbreviated to tokkotai or tokko.

work, not an academic document for the purposes of historical research. It was written to depict this man's unique emotional experience during World War II, one of history's most pivotal events. Although stringent efforts were made to verify Kuwahara's story, some specific details may ultimately be disproved. Nevertheless, we believe without question Allred's account of how this story came together, and we contend that the entire work should not be discredited as fiction unless undisputable evidence proves Kuwahara's intention was to deceive.

If, in the end, Kuwahara's story is proven to be fraudulent, we can only speculate as to how he could have concocted such a brilliant ruse. He must have possessed incredible good fortune or simple dumb luck to have avoided exposure these many years. He must also have been quite cunning to have taken so many calculated risks by openly offering his co-author countless authoritative particulars of his experiences, most of which were obtained during months and months of detailed daily interviews. Indeed, if *Kamikaze* is fabricated, it may be Kuwahara's ultimate revenge against his former American foes.

In any case, whether various elements of this story are proved or disproved, *Kamikaze* was, and remains, a superbly written literary work that has withstood the test of time. With Allred's new revisions, its literary quality has been especially enhanced. Consequently, we maintain that placing this title back in print is the right decision, and any arguments questioning specific historical details of *Kamikaze* are outweighed by its overall literary value.

Reactions and questions may be sent to Gordon T. Allred or Gary W. Toyn at the following e-mail address: info@americanlegacymedia.com

Prologue

It is New Year's Day 1945 at Hiro Air Base in western Honshu, and Captain Yoshiro Tsubaki, Commander of the Fourth Fighter Squadron, has just called a special meeting. We have assembled in a mood of intense expectation . . . somberly, even furtively. Silence settles profoundly, accentuated by sporadic gusts of rain against the roof and windows.

We are called to swift, rigid attention as the Captain enters and commands us to be seated. For several seconds he stands before us, arms folded, eyes dark and glittering—unblinking, spearing each man to the heart. Then he speaks, sonorously: "The time, young airmen, has at last arrived. We are faced with a momentous decision."

Again he pauses, but I feel it coming—the fear, beyond anything I have yet known. Momentarily the rain subsides, then returns with increased intensity as he continues. Death is there with us, gray tentacles, sinuous and inexorable, clasping at our throats. "Any of you unwilling to offer your lives as divine sons of the glorious *Nippon* Empire will not be required to do so." I hold my breath, feeling my temples throb. "Those incapable of accepting this great honor will raise their hands."

Once more, the silence is palpable, but the tentacles relax slightly. The rain subsides in a soft drizzle. Then, hesitantly, timorously, a hand goes up. Then another and another . . . five, six in all. Six members of the Fourth Fighter Squadron have chosen to live. Our captain waits, one eyebrow arched eloquently. The decision is mine: I can choose to live or to die. Has not our captain just said so? Yet somehow . . . of course, of course, I want to live! But my hands remain at my sides trembling. I want to raise them, desperately want to raise them. Even my soul would have me do so, yet they remain at my sides.

"*Ah so desu ka!*" Captain Tsubaki transfixes those who have responded in his stare. "Most enlightening." His eyes are devouring. "It is good to know in advance exactly where we stand." He glances at the floor, nods, purses his lips. Slowly his gaze ascends as though evaluating the structure of the ceiling then returns to the gathering before him. Never, perhaps anywhere, has there been a more attentive audience. "Here, gentlemen," he continues, appraising those who have responded, "are six men who have openly admitted their disloyalty." Their faces blanch, turning ashen. For an instant his tone is ironically complacent. "Since they are completely devoid of courage and honor. . . ." He even shrugs but suddenly becomes menacing. "Since they are completely devoid of courage and honor. . . . it becomes my obligation to provide them with some. These men shall become Hiro's first attack group!"

The breath, held so long within me, escapes almost audibly. I want to inhale, expel more air, obtain relief. But my innards clench, and something sears the inside of my chest like a hot, electric wire. Six of my friends have just been selected as Hiro's first human bombs.

PART ONE

Chapter One

National Glider Champion

It **is difficult**, perhaps impossible, to determine where the forces eventuating in Japan's *Kamikaze* offensive, the strangest warfare in history, began. Ask the old man, the venerable *ojiisan*, with his flowing beard—the man who still wears *kimono* and clattering wooden *geta* on the streets—for he is a creature of the past. Perhaps he will tell you that these mysterious forces were born with his country over two and a half millennia ago, with Jimmu Tenno, first emperor, descendant of the Sun Goddess, Amaterasu-Omikami. Or, he may contend that their real birth came twenty centuries later, reflected in the proud spirit and tradition of the *samurai*, the famed and valiant warriors of feudal times.

Whatever their beginnings, these forces focused upon me during 1943, in the midst of World War II, when I was a mere boy of only fifteen. It was then that I won the Japanese National Glider Championship.

Back where memory blurs into veils of forgetfulness I can vaguely discern a small boy watching hawks circle above the velvet mountains of Honshu—watching enviously each afternoon. I remember how he even envied the sparrows as they chittered and flitted through the shrubbery and arched across the roofs. To fly—transcend the bondage of gravity! What incomparable freedom! What exhilaration! What joy!

Strangely, even then, I sensed that my future lay somewhere in the skies. At fourteen, attending Onomichi High School, I was old enough to participate in a glider training course sponsored by the Osaka Prefecture, a training that had two advantages. First, it was the chance I had waited for all my life—a chance to be in the air. Secondly, war was reverberating throughout the world, and while many students were required to spend part of their regular school time working in the factories, I was permitted to learn glider flying for two hours every day. All students, in fact, were either directly engaged in producing war materials or preparing themselves as future defenders of their country though such programs as judo, sword fighting, or marksmanship. Even grade school children were taught to self defense with sharpened bamboo shafts.

Our glider training was conducted on a grassy field near the school, and the first three months were often frustrating since we never once moved off the ground. Fellow trainees merely took turns towing each other across the lawn, getting plenty of exercise, while the would-be pilot vigorously manipulated the wing and tail flaps with hand and foot controls, pretending that he was soaring at some awesome height in company with the eagles. Much of our time was also devoted to calisthenics, and it was apparent even then that all of our training was calculated to prepare us for great challenges and trials.

Gradually we began taking to the air, only a few feet above the ground initially, but what excitement! Eventually, thanks to the exertions of a dozen or so young comrades, we were towed rapidly enough to ascend some sixty feet, the maximum height for a primary glider.

Having mastered the fundamentals, we were transferred to the secondary glider, which was car-towed for the take-off and capable of remaining aloft for several minutes. It had a semi-enclosed cockpit and a control stick with a butterfly-shaped steering device for added maneuverability.

Aside from understanding the basic mechanical requirements of glider flying, it was necessary to sense the air currents, feel them out, automatically judging their direction and intensity, like the hawks above the mountains.

How far should I travel into the wind? Often I could determine this only by thrusting my head from the cockpit and letting the drafts cascade against my face. And at times of descent just before I had circled to soar once more upon the thermals the onrushing air tide seemed to have acquired a kind of solidity becoming almost stifling. Moments before take-off, in fact, the air impact was tremendous, nearly overwhelming, requiring all my strength to work the controls.

How far to travel in one direction before circling, precisely how much to elevate the wing flaps to avoid stalling and still maintain maximum height . . . these things were not charted beforehand. But the bird instinct was within me, and I was able to pilot my glider successfully, qualifying for national competition the following year.

Approximately six hundred glider pilots throughout Japan, mainly high school students, had qualified for the big event at Mt. Ikoma near Nara and the great city of Osaka. The competition was divided into two phases: group and individual. Contenders could participate in either or both events and were judged on such points as time in the air, distance traveled at a specific altitude, ability to turn within a prescribed space, and angle of descent.

Perhaps it was our intensive training, perhaps destiny, that led six of us from Onomichi High School in western Honshu to the group championship. What glee and wild rejoicing! In addition, two of us were selected from that number for individual competition against about fifty others. I was one of them.

Every contestant was to fly four times, and points accumulated during each flight would be totaled to determine the winner. At the onset I was exceptionally tense and nervous, but such feelings soon faded, and to my immense delight my first three flights seemed almost perfect. Victory was actually in sight!

Sunlight was warming the mountain summit when my final flight commenced. A hundred yards below on the spacious glider field, I steadied myself in the cockpit, feeling a tremor in the fragile structure that held me—delicate wood framework, curved and fastened with light aluminum and covered with silk the color of butter cups. The tow rope had been attached to a car ahead, a hook in the other end fastened to a metal ring just beneath the glider's nose. Opening and closing my hand on the control stick, I breathed deeply and concentrated on victory. "You can do it, Kuwahara," I told myself, "you can do it. You're invincible—you're going to win."

Simultaneously my veins, even the tiniest capillaries in my skin, began to tingle. This was the biggest test of my life, a chance to be crowned the greatest high school glider pilot in the *Nippon* Empire.

My craft lurched and began sliding irresistibly across the turf, and my heart rate increased along with the acceleration. Then I was lifting, confronting the air mass which suddenly seemed immensely heavy and resistant, almost like water. Lifting, lifting . . . straining with the controls, feeling disconcerting vibrations. Almost as suddenly, the pressure relaxed, and the bright day itself was bearing me upward. I was above Ikoma's calm, green summit, angled sunlight turning the leaves along its western perimeter the colors of polished brass and chrome.

I continued to climb, confident with the controls, now buoyed skyward on a powerful updraft. Soon I was beginning my first circle, working the flaps carefully to maximize my advantage, and now the glider was responding to my touch with great empathy, with a life of its own. Simultaneously, the two of us were becoming one, soaring exultantly, carried ever higher upon the mounting currents.

Then we were making our first, broad gyration. I gazed over my shoulder at the landing strip, the upturned faces and waving hands. Three times I circled, lofting and descending, sweeping far out beyond expectation on the final one as the glider field and its throng faded. Then I became one with a flight of gulls, entranced by their whiteness against the blue of the sky. It was a good omen. Kobe Bay rejoiced in the sunlight a short distance to the east, Lake Biwa a bit farther, to the north. Thirty-eight minutes after take-off I settled to the patient earth amid a chorus of cheers.

It took nearly half an hour for the judges to finish tallying our point totals and compare scores—one of the longest waits of my life, and my ears hummed with increasing volume as I listened for the results. I knew that I had done well, that my chances for the prize were good, but at that point nothing seemed real. Then . . . then, suddenly! My name was being announced, blaring stridently over the loud speaker: "Kuwahara-

Yasuo, 340 points—first place, individual competition!" Vaguely I heard the next name being announced for second place as friends slapped my back, shouted my name and cheered. I saw the faces of my family, beaming and radiant as they pushed through the throng. I was glider champion of the *Nippon* Empire.

At that moment I had no idea how such a distinction would drastically alter my entire existence.

Chapter Two

A Predestined Decision

Upon my return there was much festivity at the Onomichi Train Station. Teachers, students, close friends—all were there to congratulate the new champion. In addition, my family held a celebration and sumptuous dinner in my honor.

A few days later, however, my achievement was almost forgotten. Glider training continued, but for the first time in many months life had lost its vitality. I drifted rudderless upon aimless waters, steadily growing more restless.

In the evenings after training I wandered home with my friends, watching the sun settle beyond the mountains, a red cauldron turning the ocean westward to molten steel. Sunset was a special time—a time to have finished the hot bath, to have donned the *yukata*, a light-weight, casual *kimono*, to slide the windows open and gaze meditatively, or to sit in one's garden contemplating the filigreed silhouette of a mulberry tree against the horizon, to savor introspection in the steam rising from a cup of *ocha*.

Such traditions afforded a tentative kind of relaxation and comfort, but they did not relieve my lethargy. Nor did they assuage our growing uneasiness regarding the war. By now Guadalcanal had been lost to the

Americans, and doubts had begun to form. Very subtly at first like early winter mists among the pines on our hillside, but gradually they swirled and swelled till even the rising sun could not dispel them.

We who were young spoke of the war more enthusiastically than many of our elders. My friend Tatsuno's brother in the Navy Air Force had shot down an American plane, and many evenings such matters dominated our conversation as we strolled the road from school.

Young though he was, small and almost frail, Tatsuno Uchida reflected a special intensity in the way he observed the sky and spoke of his brother. At times, when planes passed over, he shook his head saying, fervently, "I know Kenji will become an ace. He will bring honor to our country and to the Emperor." And of course, I always agreed. It was comforting to realize that our pilots were innately superior to the enemy, more courageous, bearers of a proud tradition, that they flew better aircraft. Did not our teachers and parents, our radios and newspapers assure us of these facts each day?

One of those evenings shortly after my return from school, a stranger appeared at our front door, and I heard his introduction clearly: "I am Captain Hiroyoshi Mikami of the Imperial Army Air Force." Moments later he had removed his shoes and crossed our threshold. Having escorted him to our western-style reception room, our maid Reiko padded quickly off to inform my father.

My father, a well-known contractor and most affluent man in Onomichi, continued his leisurely bath and directed my mother to entertain our new visitor. Later he emerged to extend the formalities of introduction while mother retired to supervise the maid's preparation of *ban no shokuji*, our evening meal.

Meanwhile, I hovered furtively outside the guest room, certain that the visit signalled something highly portentous, listening nervously while my father and the captain exchanged the customary pleasantries, politely discussing the irrelevant, punctuating their sentences with a soft and courteous sibilance.

"Winter is at last upon us," the captain observed.

"Indeed, that is so," my father replied and slurped his ocha in a well bred manner.

After they had conversed at length on matters of little significance, it was time for our meal. Mother had planned *sukiyaki*, and the captain had, of course, been invited to dine with us.

As we sat upon our cushions surrounding the low, circular dinner table, the maid bustled attentively back and forth while Tomika, my sister, probed at the glowing coals with a slender pair of prongs. Mother, arranging and sugaring the beef slices with great care, half whispered, "Where is the *shoyu*" and Reiko hastened to the kitchen conveying much humility and murmuring plaintive, little apologies for her dereliction.

At times I peered at Captain Mikami, very covertly, always averting my gaze whenever his eyes fell upon me, eyes that reminded me of chipped obsidian. Penetrating, unnerving.

Throughout our meal only the two men conversed, the rest of us merely conveying our existence by faint, careful smiles and slight, courteous head bows whenever their remarks drifted our direction. In addition, however, I sensed an unusual atmosphere of restraint, of apprehension—especially on the part of my mother and sister Tomika. All of which only magnified my own.

Father and the captain spoke tediously about many things, and little of what was said held my attention excepting their comments upon the war, especially regarding the condition of Iwo Jima, Okinawa, and other key islands. Speaking of Guadalcanal. My father reiterated the firmly entrenched conviction of many others at the time: that the departure of our troops from that area had not been a retreat but rather a "strategic withdrawal." Most assuredly, it was not an enemy triumph!

Mikami strongly confirmed this view, discussing the great valor of our military men and their leaders at some length. As for the increased bombing of our homeland, he emphasized another common belief: our noble militarists had actually known from the onset that this would happen. Consequently, there was no need for dismay. Such an eventuality had been taken into account long before our assault on Pearl Harbor. Inevitable, yes, but we were prepared materially, in mind and spirit as well, for any form of retaliation to which the enemy might resort. Ultimately, unquestionably, our divinely ordained empire would triumph. The only alternative was unthinkable.

At last our dinner was over and I was invited to join the two men in our guest room. There, at last, our visitor's courteous evasion yielded to military directness. For a moment his dark eyes searched mine. Then, turning to my father, he said, "Kuwahara-*san*, you have an honorable son." I felt a sudden surge of pride. "Your son has already gained acclaim that few people his age, if any, have ever achieved."

Father bowed slightly in humility and assent. "*Domo arigato.*"

"He is one of whom his esteemed father and our noble empire can be proud." Again, I received his glance. "Indeed, he can bring great honor to the family of Kuwahara." Something began to ferment inside me, a sensation much like that which I had felt at the onset of my national glider competition. I gazed at the *tatami* in great humility.

"*So desu ka,*" my father replied, attenuating the first word gutturally, feigning profound wonderment and modesty. Again the bow, one more pronounced than the first. "*Domo arigato gozai mashita*" he added quietly, expressing his thanks and acknowledgement in the fullest, most formal fashion.

"Our gracious and esteemed Emperor and our honorable leaders at the *Daihonei,*" Captain Mikami continued, referring to the Imperial Military Headquarters in Tokyo, "are seeking such young men, as you must know, young men with allegiance to His Imperial Majesty, with talent and devotion to their country . . . men who will fly like avenging eagles against the enemy."

For an instant my glance flicked from the straw *tatami* at my feet to my father. His eyes contained a gleam I had never seen before, and he nodded. "Indeed that is so. It is good that we have such men, and the time has arrived for us to strike with our might—with great power like the winds from heaven."

"*Hai!*" The captain concurred with marked force and abruptness then paused solemnly. "As you may have supposed, I am here at your most gracious and hospitable domicile as a special representative of The Imperial Army Air Force."

Beaming once more with carefully calculated surprise, my father again replied, "*Ah so desu ka!*"

Throughout the conversation, Captain Mikami directed very few remarks at me personally, but I felt my insides begin to burn as he spoke of enlistment requirements for the Air Force and the various schools available depending upon one's performance and qualifications.

During those moments, it was impossible to assess my own feelings. Ever since the war's onset I had contemplated joining the Air Force. How many hours, days and nights, had I dreamed of becoming a fighter pilot, one of consummate skill and daring who knew no equal! How often had I envisioned myself plummeting from a golden sky to destroy and demoralize our hated American enemies! How many heroic air battles had Tatsuno and I conjured up together, battles wherein we inevitably sent our adversaries to a fiery death in the ocean! The sky, the water, the land—all waiting beneficently to help assure triumph.

But here now was reality, and in its abruptness my heart faltered. I had sensed my mother's growing uneasiness all during our dinner, Tomika's as well, and now I felt a great foreboding. It flowed over me like an icy wind.

Suddenly I realized that the captain was addressing me personally. My heart jolted. "So now, what are your feelings regarding this matter?" He waited, and I struggled to speak, faltered . . . and failed. For a moment I nearly gagged. Both men watched me intently, but I could not force out a single word.

"Take a few minutes to consider" Captain Mikami said at last. "I will wait." His tone was stern.

A few minutes! Suddenly I felt ill. Running my hands over my face and hair, I felt the sweat on my palms, felt more strongly my father's vexation and humiliation. The room had become stifling. Smiling wanly, I mumbled, "Please excuse me. I will go get a drink of water." It was a feeble response, and my face was burning as I left the room. A part of me had wanted to assure the captain that I needed no time to consider such a request. No real man would waver, feel his throat freeze and experience such coldness of soul. In the tradition of *bushido*, the *samurai* code of valor and chivalry, he would celebrate the glory of death, saying, "I rejoice in the opportunity to die for my country. It fills me with intense humility to have been so honored by my Emperor." But I was more boy than man. I wanted my mother.

Swiftly I went to her room only to find it empty. Softly I called her name but received no answer. Thinking that perhaps she was sitting outside in the cold by our garden, I slipped into the night and called again.

A full moon was rising above the bearded hillside, its light flooding over the top of our garden wall in a silvery glow. Beyond, through the trellised gateway, the road was still in shadow, stretching away in darkness and mystery, flecked by the distant orange glow of a lantern. The night was cold and expectant as though awaiting snow, utterly silent.

Glancing upward, I saw a light in an upstairs window and quickly entered the house, ascending the steep stairway. There in my room, seated cross-legged on the *futon*, was Tomika. My photo album was opened in her lap, and she was examining it with marked intensity. "Where is Mother?" I asked.

She glanced up, eyes glistening. "Mother has gone out," she replied, "for a walk."

Curiously I gazed at her, momentarily forgetting the urgency of my situation. "Tomika, what's the matter?" Gently I reached down and touched her lustrous, black hair. "Is something wrong?" Simultaneously I realized that she had opened my album to the photo taken when I won the glider championship—my own face warmed in a smile of triumph. Then a tiny tear drop spattered directly across that smile.

Whenever my sister cried, her round, rather moon-like countenance was transformed into something ethereal. "Tomika," I half whispered. "What's the matter? Why are you crying?" I sat down beside her, awkwardly placing my arm around her shoulders.

"Tomika?"

Thrusting the album aside, she seized my free hand, squeezing it almost painfully. Her gaze gradually lifted to meet my own, and she began shaking her head. "My little brother . . . my little brother."

Something in my throat pained sharply, becoming very dry and large. It was as if a thumb were pressing against my windpipe. "Tomika," I choked, "what can I do?" Suddenly I clapped my hands over my face, inhaling deeply. That way the tears wouldn't come so easily.

Then her arms were around me, *her* cheek against mine. "No, no, no," she repeated. "Not my little brother. They can't have you—you're only a baby!"

The final words jolted me, and I thought of my friends, especially Tatsuno. What would they think of me? Such a craven, maudlin display! Worse still, I thought of the captain and my father downstairs, waiting—most impatiently, my father suffering much loss of face. Both doubtless convinced by now that I was a sniveling coward.

"I'm hardly a baby Tomika" I replied angrily.

She sought to pull me closer, but I thrust myself free. A baby! For an instant I hated her. "I'm not a baby, Tomika—I'm a man! I'm fifteen years old! How can you call me a baby when I am the greatest glider pilot in Japan?"

"I . . . I didn't mean it that way," she murmured.

"Don't you realize, Tomika, that tonight I am being greatly honored—by the Emperor himself?"

"Yes," she replied softly, "I know that very well. You will even die for the Emperor." Then we were weeping together.

Moments later I broke free, totally demoralized. Scarcely realizing what I was doing, I stumbled downstairs to the bathroom sink and began dousing my face and neck in cold water. When I looked at my eyes in the mirror they were bloodshot, my entire countenance weak and distressed. Horrified, I doused my face again, then gently patted it dry with a towel.

In a near agony of embarrassment, I returned to my father and the captain. As I entered the room, their gazes seemed to combine, appraising me sternly, fixedly, in utter silence. I forced a frozen smile, struggling to speak. Captain Mikami's stare was unwavering.

Again, I struggled, faltering. It was as if I were on the brink of an abyss, hemmed in by countless enemies, knowing that there was no alternative but to jump or be hurled head-long.

"Well, my son?" Father said.

Bowing to the captain, I stammered. "I must apologize for . . . for such extreme inconvenience. I wanted to inform my mother of this extraordinary honor." I groped for the words. "But, apparently she has gone somewhere." No response from either of them, merely their combined, unrelenting stare.

"Please forgive me for this extreme inconvenience . . ." I struggled onward, ashamed that I was repeating myself, but finally the words came with more fluency and conviction. "I am greatly honored to accept your splendid and generous offer in behalf of our glorious Emperor."

A muscle to one side of my father's mouth twitched slightly, but I could see the relief in his eyes, in the very expansion and coloration of his pupils.

The captain gave a quick nod, face still expressionless. "That is good," he said.

Immediately I felt a profound sense of relief. I had not betrayed my father, after all. Nor had I betrayed my country. Without further comment, Captain Mikami opened a leather case, producing the enlistment forms. "Please read these," he said and laid them before us on the table.

"*Hai!*" Father spoke quietly, expelling the word in an abrupt little explosion, and began to scrutinize the document with great care. I tried to do so as well, but for some reason the words would not focus.

At length Father glanced up. "Do you find the terms satisfactory?" the captain inquired.

"*Hai,*" Father nodded.

"Very good," the captain said. "So you will kindly sign here." He pointed with a slender, tan finger. "Your son will sign there." Father arose to obtain his personal, wooden stamp, returned and pressed it against his ink pad, then firmly in the spot designated, an indelible, orange oval with its special markings against the stark white of the document: "Kuwahara, Zenji." Then I signed my own beneath it: Kuwahara, Yasuo. And there they were—our signatures—indelible and irrevocable. The formalities were over, and there was no turning back, nor in reality had there been from the moment Captain Mikami appeared some two hours earlier.

"Hiro Air Base—*desu ka?*" Father noted.

Captain Mikami gave a single downward nod. "Hiro, yes." For an instant he actually smiled. "He will be close to home—only fifty miles away. He will enjoy his days at Hiro immensely and receive a splendid education." I had not even comprehended enough of the document to note my place of assignment, but it was comforting to realize that throughout my training I would be close to my family.

Now, however, it was time for the Captain to leave. "You have made a wise decision," he said as we accompanied him to the door. Seconds later we were bowing, exchanging *sayonara*, and he vanished into the night.

For some time afterward my father and I sat together, gazing out our window at the surrounding hills and moon-washed sky. Father had been a lieutenant in the army years before and related some experiences from his days in China that I had never heard before.

Shigeru, one of my older brothers, was with the Army Counter Intelligence in Java, while the other, Toshifumi, was a dentist in Tokyo and had not yet been inducted. "It is very good to have worthy sons in the service of their nation and family," Father told me. "And you, Yasuo, will bring the greatest honor of all."

"*Domo arigato,*" I replied, feeling very humble and surprised. A transport plane was crossing the sky, lights blinking from its wing tips, the alternations of red and green making it appear to move strangely along its course in immense skating motions. We continued to watch, listening, as its light and sound gradually faded into the distance. "A few months from now you will undoubtedly be flying a plane of your own," my father observed and actually placed his hand on my shoulder.

"I hope so," I replied.

"But not one like that." His tone was commanding.

"No, not one like that. I have always wanted to become a fighter pilot."

Father nodded vigorously. His hand gripped my shoulder. "Most definitely!" He squinted one eye as though sighting in on a star and continued to nod his affirmation. "Yes, a fighter pilot. . . ." he mused at length. "I always wanted to be one myself, even though that form of warfare was very primitive back then. "There is something unique about a fighter pilot. Even the pilots of our fine new bombers—like the *Suesei*—cannot compare. A fighter pilot is the *samurai* of modern times. His aircraft is his sword; it ultimately becomes his soul." The very thought made my scalp tingle.

"The fighter pilot must work with others as part of a team," Father continued, "but he also has the best chance of becoming an individualist. He can do more for our Emperor than a thousand foot soldiers. With courage he can gain great honor, perhaps more than anyone in the military. And you do have courage, Yasuo, my son." Again his hand gripped my shoulder.

"I hope so," I replied.

"You do have courage! You have courage!" This time his hand literally hurt. "The family of Kuwahara has always had courage. No one has more noble ancestors!"

"That is so," I acknowledged, and glanced at his profile from the corner of my eye: a strong chin tilting slightly upward, a nose a bit like the beak of a falcon, eyes that seemed to glow from the moon.

"You will defend your home and country," he assured me, "and you will see the day when the Western Powers are driven back in great ignominy across the Pacific. In time The Imperial Way will sweep like a mighty tide across that land. They will suffer a resounding defeat, and you will play your part in that defeat." An inspiring thought, but one that also taxed my faith. I was, after all, only fifteen, a boy who an hour earlier had wept like a girl in the arms of his sister. The thought made me cringe.

"It may take many months," I said hesitantly. "The West has large armies and navies, many aircraft."

"That is true," Father admitted a bit irritably. It will not be accomplished overnight, but you must always remember, Yasuo, that physical size and material might are secondary. It is the great determination and valor of *Yamato damashii*, the spirit of the *samurai*, that will prevail in the end." I nodded, buoyed up by the power of his conviction.

"Consider, for example, the thousands of Americans we have already taken prisoner," he persisted. "Thousands of them!" Turning, he stared directly into my eyes. "But how many of our men have surrendered to the Americans?"

How proud I was to have my father converse with me in this manner. How honored! Almost as though we were equals. "Very few," I replied.

"That is correct. A mere handful! You see?" His chin jutted imperiously, lips forming a sneer. "The Americans lose a few men and they become terrified, utterly demoralized and surrender. Our prison camps are fairly bursting with cowardly, pitiful Americans." He shrugged. "Of course, a few of them are brave. It is foolish to underestimate the enemy." I nodded, attending to his every word, the slightest nuance. "But look at it this way. Suppose for a moment that one hundred American infantry men were pitted against a much larger force of our own men on a small island. How many of those Americans would have to be killed before the rest would surrender?"

"Not more than ten, I would guess."

Father shook his head reluctantly. "Well, it would probably take more than that in most cases—possibly twenty-five or even thirty." He paused, squinted, angling a reflective glance at the moon. It had risen considerably, changing from celestial white to a faint yellow. "On the other hand, supposing the situation were reversed. . . . How many of our own men would have to die before the rest surrendered?"

"They would never surrender!" I exclaimed, surprised at my on certitude.

"So you see?" Father replied triumphantly. Our only men ever taken captive are those who have been wounded so severely they cannot defend themselves—or those unconscious from loss of blood. Therefore, as I have explained, it is not merely a matter of physical and material strength. It is a matter of courage, determination, of spiritual strength! It is for this reason that Japan will prevail, that Japan will triumph." Again the pause. Again, his gaze absorbed my own. "Do you understand, my son?"

In response, I nodded, half bowed. "Yes, my father, I understand."

Chapter Three

Winter and the Waning Days

At school the following day I informed my friends of the honor that had come to me, and the news spread rapidly. Once again I was someone important, the center of attention. During lunch period I barely had time to eat my *sushi* cakes because so many people were clustered about, pressing me with questions.

"Did the captain come right to your home?" someone asked.

"Yes," I replied. "In fact, he stayed for two hours and had dinner with us."

"*Uso!*" someone exclaimed. "*Honto?*"

"Yes, honestly!" I said. "I'm not lying."

Kenji Furuno, one of the better glider students, plied me with question after question: "Did he just come right out and ask you? I mean, what did he do? Did he tell you that you had to join?"

"He asked me, of course," I said. "Naturally, we discussed the matter at some length with my father."

"What did the captain say, though?" Kenji persisted. "Did he just come right out and say, "Will you please be so kind as to honor the Imperial Army Air Force with your presence?"" Several students laughed excitedly.

I failed to join them, however. Kenji had suddenly become rather inferior, along with the rest of them. "Captain Mikami told me that I had been chosen to serve his Imperial Majesty and our great country."

"Yes, but didn't he even give you any time to decide?" another student asked, "Not even an hour or two?"

Almost unconsciously, I eyed him as the Captain eyed me the night before. His smile wavered. "Would you need time to decide something like that?" I challenged.

"Well . . . I guess not," he answered lamely.

Tatsuno had been listening quietly without comment until now, merely eating his lunch. "I don't think anyone would turn down an honor like that," he mused at last. "I doubt if anyone would even dare to." Often his reactions seemed those of someone almost elderly, his tone and expression perhaps as much as the words themselves. "Myself, I want to be a pilot like my brother, more than anything else in the world. Even so, when you think about it. . . . He paused for some time. I mean, after all . . . he might never come back."

"That is true," I admitted. "To die for one's country is the greatest of privileges." The words of my father. I wasn't sure I fully believed them, but they sounded impressive and certainly enhanced my prestige in the eyes of my friends. Everyone was silent now, either staring at the floor or out the windows. Then the bell rang. It was time for afternoon classes.

I went through the remainder of my school day in a kind of trance, as if I had somehow been set apart from the world. Old Tanaka *sensei*, our instructor, the students—even the desks, books, and the drab walls . . . everything seemed a bit strange and remote. I was seeing and listening as though from a different sphere. Somewhere out in the pale afternoon a plane was droning, the sound barely perceptible yet persistent. Incessant. At times it seemed only a vibration, an echo in the memory, but it made me tingle.

When it was time for glider training, I participated with renewed determination, performing every act with perfect confidence and precision. Abruptly, I decided that from then on I would make no mistakes during glider flying—not a single mistake, however, insignificant. This habit of perfection would become so well established that within a few months I would fly propeller driven aircraft just as perfectly.

Yes, I would become the ultimate pilot of pilots. I would shoot down a hundred enemy planes, and the time would come when the name Kuwahara would resound throughout Japan. On the Emperor's birthday I would be chosen to perform remarkable aerobatics in the skies over Tokyo while millions of people far below cheered exultantly. Later I would be escorted amid great fanfare across the green moat and arching wooden bridge. I would gaze down at the lily pads, the elegant, snowy swan and huge listless carp the color of gold and lime. Then I would enter the palace of the Emperor—the Grand Imperial Place where the Emperor himself would present me with the *Kinshi Kunsho*, the coveted medal of honor after the Order of The Golden Kite.

Such fantasies were fading as Tatsuno and I returned home in the evening, enjoying the sound of our wooden *geta* as we scuffed and shuffled up the winding road among the pines. Eventually, perhaps guessing my thoughts, Tatsuno remarked, "You know, Yasuo, if you weren't my best friend I would be very envious right now."

After a moment's silence I replied, "I'd give anything if we were going in together; that would truly make it perfect." I rested my hand upon his narrow shoulder, and we clopped along together. "But it wouldn't surprise me at all if you should get the same chance before long."

Tatsuno shook his head. "Oh, I don't really think so," he said. "After all, look who you are! You're the national glider champion!"

"Yes, but what kind of an air force would we have if they only chose glider champions?" I asked. "Besides, you really did well. You went to the finals, didn't you?" He merely shrugged. "Didn't you?" I prodded and began shaking him back and forth, trying to pull him off balance. "Didn't you?"

Suddenly I pushed the long visor of his school cap over his eyes. "Didn't you?" Laughing, he grabbed for my own and I ducked. Then we were cavorting along, laughing and grabbing, shoving each other, our wooden *geta* clattering loudly along the paved street near home. "And you've got the best grades of almost anybody in our school—right? Right?"

"Yes," he laughed, "except you!"

It was almost dark by then, and we parted at the gateway to our yard. I entered my home to find Mother hunched over a large book at the dining table. Food was cooking on the *hibachi*, and it smelled very good, but she did not seem happy. Her reply to my hello was subdued.

I looked at her curiously. "Is Father home yet?"

"No." I could barely hear her.

"Is he still at work?"

She shook her head. "He will not be home tonight."

Then I understood. It was never easy for her, even after all the years. Her veined hands closed the book, and she gazed silently at the cover— *Tale of Genji*. "My mother gave me this book when I was a young girl," she said. "I still remember almost all of it."

Sitting beside her, I spoke with great hesitancy: "No one could ever take your place, Mother. You know how much Father cares for you."

"Oh yes," she replied, unable to conceal the note of bitterness. But I am not so young any more—not like his darlings, his Kimiko and his Toshiko, and all the others. She laughed even more bitterly. "There was a time when your father never looked at another woman, nor was he the only man who thought I was beautiful."

"You are still beautiful!" I exclaimed. "I think you are the most beautiful woman in the world!"

"Reddening faintly, Mother replied, "I must think my Yasuo-*chan* is a full-grown man now, talking such foolishness." Then she kissed my cheek. "It's really nothing to worry about. Nothing has changed, and your father will return as usual tomorrow or the next day. Besides. . . ." She arose, attending to her meal. "I will always have my children. They are my greatest joy."

There was nothing more to say. It was a Japanese male's prerogative to have his mistresses, as long as he could afford them, and my father was the richest man in Onomichi. Although true *geisha* are not prostitutes, some are available as mistresses to men of sufficient means, and my father kept one of his own in nearby Hiroshima, an alleged ravishing beauty of marked talent in the dance and such stringed instruments as the *koto* and *samisen*. This I had learned from my older brothers long ago, the "unspoken secret" of which everyone was well aware.

So it was that whenever my father went away, except for legitimate business trips, which were almost always quite lengthy, my mother continued meekly about her responsibilities in the home as was befitting a wife in such circumstances. Her comments in that connection, in fact, were highly atypical and probably stemmed from her anxiety over my impending departure and realization that I would soon be caught up in a great war, the most devastating conflict in history.

In any event, I actually enjoyed my father's absences most of the time. Not that I didn't love him, but rather because I felt less restrained when he was away. They afforded me an opportunity to be with my mother and sister, to be the center of attention. As the weeks faded, and the time approached for my departure, in fact, I took ever-increasing comfort from being alone with them.

It was Tomika above all, though, who made the prospect of leaving poignant. She had been the ideal sister, even defending me against the occasional teasing and bullying of my older brothers when they were still in the home. Tomika, as well as my mother, washed and ironed my clothes, cooked my favorite meals, and fondly indulged my every whim.

Often, as the time drew nigh, we wandered by the ocean, along the cold sands that smelled of salt and fish and seaweed. On those rare days in January when the sun parted the clouds we gathered shells and listened to the quiet puttering of junks in the harbor. Even when the weather was cold, men and women bustled about in long dingy shacks along the shore, smoking fish and preparing them for the market. Aged people in the main, crinkled and brown, in tattered clothing, hunched there on the beach, at work with their nets.

I had never known their privation or gone shoeless and half clad like their children and grandchildren, but there seemed to be something pleasant about that life, about its utter simplicity that suddenly was exceptionally appealing. At times we would watch as those fisher people spread catches of tiny, shimmering fish to dry on woven mats, later collecting them in baskets. When sunlight warmed the beach they occasionally rested long enough to dig their bare toes in the sand and visit. Their voices and laughter were always mild—at one with the cries of the gulls and surging of the waves.

There was a timelessness and serenity about those ocean people that made the war seem rather remote. True, the enemy was bombing our homeland, but the immediate area had thus far gone unscathed, and occasionally even now, war was something that happened only in books and movies.

This same peace prevailed as we strolled the mountainside, viewing the terraced farmlands. Now, in mid winter, the terraces and paddy's were bleak and lifeless, but with the coming of spring they would explode a brilliant green. The rice would quest higher and higher from the muck that gave it birth, never losing its brightness until the time of harvest. Meanwhile, the mountains, cloaked in their own dense foliage, would brood ever darker as the summer moved on.

Now, however, all of nature was drab and gray, and my three months had fled with disturbing abruptness. Suddenly I realized that the time with my family and friends was nearly over, perhaps forever. Within only a few days I would depart from Onomichi and very possibly never return.

On an afternoon near the end of January Tomika and I sat in my upstairs room gazing outward upon the wintry landscape. The pines of the hillside were patched with slowly wreathing mists. I would be leaving the next morning, and the sense of finality simmered in my stomach with a mild burning sensation. My hands were slightly tremulous. Tomorrow! Excitement and anxiety roiled steadily throughout my entire system, even the capillaries of my skin.

Our back yard itself was blurred in mist, the rough-hewn gray stone of our family shrine invisible, the heavy wooden *torii* forming the gateway to the road barely discernible, its bright orange surface dull and muted like the waning of hope.

"I wish it were summer," I sighed. "Then we could go hiking, even take one more swim in the lake."

"*Hai,*" Tomika said and nodded. "I wish it were always summer." After a long silence she spoke again. "How can this be?" I glanced at her puzzled. "Why must people fight and hate each other?" Her words and expression had never been more imploring or distressed. "Is this really possible? People endlessly killing each other? People who actually hate us? Want to destroy us?"

"Why not?" I answered sadly. "We hate them. Don't we want to destroy and conquer them?"

"I don't want to destroy and conquer anyone." Her voice was sorrowful, almost ancient. "I just want people to live in peace. I want them to be kind to each other."

"But how can we live at peace when the western powers are strangling us?" I asked. It was a doctrine we had been taught in school, the conviction of our father and countless others. The West had long dominated so much of the world that Japan had no opportunity to expand and was gradually being stifled.

The Americans themselves were, in general, an objectionable people. Mongrels in reality, large, ungainly people, many of them obese, with pallid skins and strange hair. Red hair, some of them! I had never seen a red-haired American, very few at all, for that matter, but I had seen photographs of them in magazines. A greater number, in fact, had yellow hair. *Hana ga takoi,* big noses, on top of that! Worse still, some of them were almost black, having originated in dark and forbidding places such as Africa and South America.

The whole situation seemed highly unnatural, indeed, downright sinister. Furthermore, most Americans were greedy, prodigal and lazy, wallowing in undeserved luxury. Their soldiers were savage and guttural-voiced, yet also cowardly when their lives were in jeopardy as my father had assured me." Do you believe what they're saying about American Marines?" I inquired. Tomika eyed me quizzically. "That they have to kill and eat their own grandmothers even to become a Marine," I said. "That's the main qualification."

"No," Tomika replied firmly, "that's ridiculous! No one, not even an American, would ever do a thing like that."

"Well," I said dubiously, "that's what some of them are saying at school—even old Tanaka-*sensei* in our history class."

No doubt the average Caucasian view of Orientals was just as extreme in some ways. In the American view we were yellow-skinned, slant-eyed monkeys, dwelling in paper houses. We possessed no *spark* of originality and could only copy what others had the ingenuity to invent. Our soldiers—indeed every Japanese, Japanese Americans included—were considered sneaky, treacherous and fanatical. "Dirty Jap," was one of the more popular epithets.

At times I still wonder how much such forms of ignorance and prejudice among virtually all peoples have contributed to war throughout the ages.

In January of 1944, however, I did not ponder such matters very deeply. I had been reared to believe that the Imperial Way of Righteousness and Truth was the best way—the only way—and that ultimately, despite great obstacles, it would envelop the world. For indeed, it was divinely ordained to do so. In time all nations of the earth would be united in a vast hierarchy with Japan at the helm, but unfortunately such a condition could not obtain without war. The greatest blessings sometimes demanded the greatest sacrifice.

Furthermore, the population of our country was rapidly increasing with scant room to expand, and we were in desperate need of more territory. Drastic conditions required drastic solutions, and consequently our assault on Pearl Harbor three years earlier had been a solemn obligation, action requiring immense courage and foresight.

Such was the prevailing doctrine, yet in reality I often felt much as Tomika did. Now especially, I only wanted to live and let live in the most literal sense. Increasingly, in fact, I was becoming a split personality. Fear on the one hand, a desire for peace and sanctuary. Excitement on the other from my growing awareness that within a few months I could be flying, not a mere glider but rather an actual, bona-fide aircraft. Indeed, if I were good enough and very fortunate, if the gods were with me, a fighter plane. Already I was a hero in the eyes of my friends, but as fighter pilot I would experience even greater, more lasting, recognition.

Through with my studies now, I had bid goodbye to my teachers and classmates, having learned only a day earlier, that two more students from our school had been selected for training at Hiro. Better still, Tatsuno was one of them. He would not be entering the service for another two months, but both of us were delighted over what had happened. During my final days at home we were together frequently.

Our common bond with the Air Force had brought us even closer, closer in some ways than I was to my own brothers. When Tatsuno first gave me the good news I had clapped him on the back, exclaiming, "See, what did I tell you!" Tatsuno had only smiled shyly, the wise older man in the boy's body, but it was impossible to disguise his excitement.

On my final day at home I went with him to visit some of our other friends then returned to spend the remaining hours with my family. Father was obviously proud and in good spirits, talking with me more intimately than ever before while Mother and Tomika prepared a special farewell dinner from the best rice and *sashimi*, sliced, raw fish fresh from the sea—along with a variety of other delicacies.

Before midnight I bade my family a good rest and crawled beneath my *futon*. For many hours, however, sleep failed to come. My thoughts were an ever-unfolding panorama of memories, visions of the future, and ongoing apprehensions. Above all, I feared that I would not be able to compete with the others in basic training. Most of them were older than I, at that critical stage of rapid growth when even a year or two could make a marked difference. Would I actually be able to keep up with them? Captain Mikami had said basic training would be "very enjoyable" yet more and more I wondered if he had been speaking ironically. Stories were steadily mounting regarding the rigorous routine ahead, the harshness of the punishment for even the most trivial mistakes.

Half asleep, half awake, I tossed and squirmed for more than an hour, fearful that I would be exhausted with the arrival of morning. At last I began to drift off, aware that several aircraft had just passed over, purring steadily off, diminishing into the mysterious realms of night. Sitting there beside me, softly stroking my brow was my mother. Extending my hand, I felt the warmth of her own. In the darkness nearby came a faint murmur, and I knew that Tomika was beside her. Gradually my thoughts settled and sleep came.

PART TWO

Chapter Four

Instilling the Spirit

Hiro Air Force Base was only an hour's train ride from my home, but it was an entirely different world. Yes, I had been warned what to expect, and I had tried in some measure to prepare myself. I had also tried to hide from the truth. One way or another, however, it made little difference, because no man could possibly condition himself psychologically for what lay in store.

Sixty of us, all new recruits, were assigned to four of the base's forty-eight barracks. Hiro was some three miles in circumference, enclosing a long, narrow airstrip which ran the length of the base. In addition to the barracks, it also contained a large training field, airplane hangars, school buildings, dispensary, and storage houses along with various other structures and offices.

On one side of the airstrip were assembly plants, and a fighter-plane testing area. At that stage of the war Japan was in dire need of money and materials—especially aluminum. By then the assembly lines were being run by schoolboys, and about one of every six planes constructed eventually fell apart, sometimes in mid-air.

Shortly after our arrival we received an orientation lecture from one of the *hancho*, all of whom were NCO's, sergeants in our own case. We were instructed with great exactitude how to make our beds, arrange and display our clothes, and the importance of having our shoes and boots polished to a glossy finish at all times. Perfect orderliness and cleanliness were rigidly demanded. Further, we were informed that *Shoto Rappa* (Taps) would sound at nine p.m.

Obligations and procedures in such matters were essentially the same as those in any country. Military men, regardless of nationality, generally follow the same basic rules. The great difference in our case lay in how such rules were enforced. An American, for example, who failed to be clean shaven or to have his shoes properly shined might have his weekend pass revoked or be given extra guard duty.

For those at Hiro, however, as for almost all of *Nippon's* basic trainees, the slightest infraction, the most infinitesimal error, brought excruciating punishment. A siege of ruthless discipline and relentless castigation began, in fact, the first hours of our arrival, and it rarely ceased throughout the days of our training—a siege so terrible that many did not survive it.

American prisoners of war, "victims of Japanese atrocities", generally fared no worse than we did. Some, in fact, received milder treatment. Allied prisoners, such as those incarcerated at Umeda and Osaka, in fact, operated their own makeshift dispensaries and received better medical care as a result than most of our own men. Many of those Americans, forced to unload ships and trains, managed to smuggle large quantities of food not only for themselves, but also for their guards in return for their cooperation and silence.

Of course, there were others who suffered far more, and by virtually any standard imaginable they were terribly victimized, but so were Japanese trainees. No matter how perfectly we performed each task, the *hancho* found excuses to make us suffer. Punishment was an integral part of our education and served two basic purposes: to create unwavering discipline and to develop an invincible fighting spirit. For all of us, therefore, it was a matter of not only acquiring the necessary skills but of learning how to survive great hardship and brutality. Anyone who could withstand the *hancho* could withstand the enemy and would unquestionably prefer death to surrender.

Such training, combined with a form of nationalism that accentuated the preeminence of country and expendability of the individual, produced remarkable commitment, in any event. As my father had said, very few of our men were taken captive initially. Until the latter stages of the war and our defeat in Okinawa, in fact, only one man was taken captive for every hundred killed, usually individuals who had been wounded to a state of incapacity, sometimes having fainted from loss of blood.

During my first days at Hiro, however, I felt little desire to rush out and die gloriously for some great cause. Like all the others, I was overwhelmingly demoralized and intimidated. As though watching a movie, I can still see the frightened, homesick boy I was that first night in the air force. I lay on my bunk, assuming the day was over, but feeling like a rabbit surrounded by wild dogs, trying to imagine what the training would be like, wondering what the next day held in store. Anxiety had left me exhausted yet too nervous for sleep.

Suddenly our door burst open, and my heart lurched. The *shuban kashikan,* our NCO's in charge of quarters, were making their first inspection. Tense, breathless, I watched the white shafts from their flashlights play about the room and listened to their mutterings with little comprehension. Their tone did not bode well, however. I also realized that all the other recruits were lying in an agony of suspense just as I was. We all must have prayed that the *shuban kashikan* would leave quickly without incident, but our prayers were not answered.

Within only a minute or two the overhead lights flashed on, and we were driven from our bunks with slaps, kicks and commands: "Outside, idiots! Outside, Mamma's little boys—fast!"

Dazed and blinking, I leapt to my feet but not soon enough to avoid a vigorous cuff. "Hey, baldy," my assailant snapped, referring to my shorn head, "move out!" A violent shove and someone else delivered a kick to my rear, literally booting me out the door.

Clad in nothing but our *fundoshi* (loin cloths), we were lined up along the barracks and a fat *hancho* with an puffy, pock-marked face began cursing us—our first encounter with Master Sergeant Noguchi, "The Pig "

"Did you all live like animals at home?" he railed. "Or have you just decided to now that you're away from your parents?" He paused. "You were warned today about keeping your quarters neat. But apparently you thought we were only talking to hear ourselves—*soka?*" For a moment he eyed us thoughtfully. "*Ah so desu ka!*" To my amazement he was actually grinning, a sly grin like the spawning of an eel. "Don't even know how to stand at attention, do they?" For an instant he looked almost like a reproving father. "Green kids," he chuckled and shook his head. I exhaled with relief. Maybe training wouldn't be so terrible after all. Maybe they had a different policy now.

A foolish delusion born of desperation. The Pig motioned to one of the *hancho* and winked. The *hancho* darted to one side of the barracks and promptly returned, handing him a large baseball bat. "*Domo arigato gozai mashita,*" The Pig said, thanking him most politely. For a moment he examined it thoughtfully. "So now . . ." He held it up for our inspection. "Do you know what this says?" Silence. "It says '*Yamato damashii seishinbo.*" We knew the meaning well enough—a ball bat for instilling the Japanese fighting spirit, the spirit of *Yamato.* Yet none of us were eager to respond.

"Do you know what this is for?" The Pig demanded.

"Yes sir," a few of us mumbled.

"Oh, come now!" He clucked his tongue, feigning great distress. I was swiftly coming to realize that here was a man who had become the perfect master at handling recruits, that he knew all the procedures and relished his job. "Why, boys! Didn't you have enough to eat? I could hardly hear you. Now, seriously—don't you actually comprehend the significance of this magnificent bat?" Most of us answered that time, but still very timidly.

"Oh my!" He rolled his eyes, glancing mischievously at the other *hancho.* "That was no louder than someone farting in the bath. How long has it been since you stopped sucking your mother's tits?" A high-pitched giggle burst from him, and he shook his head at the grinning *hancho* who had handed him the bat. "Green kids! Tell me the truth, Sakigawa—have you ever seen such pitiful little bastards?" The *hancho* leered, and a few of us smiled very faintly. "Wipe off those idiot smiles!" The Pig roared. "Go on! Wipe them off!"

Halfheartedly, we passed our hands over our mouths, staring at him bug-eyed. At this he cackled almost uncontrollably. For some time he shook with helpless laughter, then wiped his eyes with a pudgy hand and moaned, "Oh God, I've been in this business too long!"

Still stifling little sobs of hilarity, he continued. "Obviously, it is high time to begin your training." Then, suddenly, he became very harsh and serious. "About face!" We turned at his command, awkwardly, facing the barracks. A metal bar, waist high, ran the entire length of the building.

"There now . . . see that metal bar? Very eye-catching and attractive, *na*?" He waited. "Oh? You don't think so? Practical, anyway, as you are about to discover. Each of you will now kindly bend forward and grasp the bar with both hands." Again the pause. "Yes, that's it—everybody! Very good—excellent!"

Again the almost maniacal laughter, culminating in a series of impulsive little chortles. "Look at those asses!" The other *hancho* were also laughing, but it was a harsh and cynical laughter devoid of humanity. "Have you ever seen such pitiful looking asses?" His laughter mounted to a kind of satanic glee. "All right boys. . . ." He struggled to gain control. "We shall now put some spirit into you!"

Those words filled me with terror, and I battled the desire to break and run. Simultaneously, I heard a loud whack, and the first man in line groaned in pain and astonishment, clasping his rear. Two *hancho* had closed in with bats. "Keep hold of the bar!" a voice shrilled and the victim grasped it again with trembling hands, writhing as the bat fell a second time. "Stand still!" The bat fell a third time with a wallop. The *hancho* were proceeding with great vigor, as the whacking and accompanying gasps rapidly increased. I was near the middle of the line, and sounds of wood striking flesh rapidly drew closer, the grunts and groans more immediate. Those who uttered the slightest protest were receiving additional blows.

Grinding my teeth, I gripped the bar with all my strength, staring desperately at the wall before me. The man on my left was getting the treatment, and for one frightening moment I waited, my heart beating wildly. Then—my whole body jolted—a tremendous wallop and flash of white fire shooting through my buttocks and up my back. Never in my life had I felt such pain. Yet somehow I managed to remain silent, almost motionless. Perhaps it was because I'd been given more time than most of the others to prepare myself.

The man with the bat paused, his eyes upon my quivering back muscles, waited endlessly while my heart pounded. Then he moved on.

At last the treatment was over and we were herded back into the barracks. As we tossed and moaned upon our cots, the door opened once more. Every one fell silent, a virtual explosion of silence. "Not again, not again!" The words roared in my head, unitedly in each of us, without question. Our friend The Pig was lounging in the open doorway, the outside light cutting across his face, leaving the eye sockets cratered in shadow. For some time he remained that way, dragging on a cigarette, expelling the smoke through his nostrils. I lay on my stomach, hugging the mattress, watching the smoke spiral upward past the porch light.

At last he flicked the butt into a trash can and called out, almost kindly, almost conspiratorially, "Hey, my dear little friends! Now do you know what the bats are for?"

"Yes, sir!" Every man in the barracks bellowed the words. Chuckling, he quietly closed the door.

Chapter Five

Taiko Binta–A Splendid Game

The following day the sixty new recruits from all four barracks were assembled for our first morning formation, and The Pig delivered a lecture. Gravely he intoned, "We are now entering the first day of your training. And henceforth, I want you men to regard me as your older brother. If you have any questions, requests, or problems I sincerely hope that you will bring them to me. That is why I am here."

I could literally feel the sense of wonderment. Was this actually the same man we had encountered the night before? Was it possible that our punishment had merely been some kind of initiation, and that now we would be treated humanely, with kindness and respect? There was an undeniable dignity about the man now, an understanding that engendered hope and relief. Somehow, he even looked better. At the moment, I only wanted to like The Pig and even felt ashamed that he had been dubbed with such a name. I wanted devoutly to deserve his respect.

"Now I know," he continued, "you have all heard that air force training is an unpleasant experience, and at times that may be the case. Nevertheless . . ." He raised an admonitory finger. "It need not be so—not if you simply do as you are told. Not if you learn obedience which, next to courage, is the most important of all virtues." He paused lengthily, strolling back and forth before us, hands clasped behind his back. "And why is obedience so essential?" Still pacing, consulting the sky, one eye squinted. "Because successful followership is indispensable to leadership, and because both are indispensable to victory." For a moment he regarded us speculatively. "Do you understand?"

"Yes honorable *hancho dono!*" we shouted. All sixty of us had learned quickly that it was vital to respond to such questions instantly and with great enthusiasm. That it was indeed impossible to respond too loudly or swiftly.

"Good." The Pig nodded to himself. "And that is why we begin with the little things. If men cannot learn obedience in small matters, how can they learn them in big ones? In The Grand Way of Heaven and Earth?"

Yes, I thought, that makes good sense. Completely logical. Shortly thereafter, he concluded his lecture, "The time has now come for you to put aside childish things. The time has come for you to become men." Almost providentially, it seemed, a dozen bombers were passing over in V formations of three planes each, and for a few seconds their roar was all-consuming. "And as men . . ." his words came in their aftermath, "you will soon carry the weight of your country, the weight of the world, upon your shoulders. Far sooner than you can possibly realize at this stage. That is why, among other things, you must learn to follow instructions implicitly! Instantaneously! Without faltering! Do not worry about the reasons for any instruction, no matter how strange it may seem. All instructions are given because they are correct! We are the head of the body; you are the arms and legs, the hands and the feet. Do you grasp my meaning?"

"Yes, honorable *hancho dono!*"

His eyes narrowed, searching each man's countenance knowingly. "As for last night—"

We held our breath. "You were given clear and careful instructions regarding neatness in the barracks, correct?"

"Yes, honorable *hancho dono!*" A rhetorical question, perhaps, that last, but we were taking no chances.

"However . . . not one barracks complied properly." Thankfully, we were not alone in our dereliction. "In one barracks a shoe was missing. In another, a locker was not tightly closed. In still another, there was dust on a window ledge, and so forth. If further infractions of this sort occur, we shall be compelled to give you some real punishment!"

The Pig glanced knowingly at the other two *hancho*, his assistants. "What you received last night was nothing at all. You were not harmed in the least, merely educated. However, by the time you have completed your training under *Hancho* Noguchi, you will be able to withstand anything. You will be able to enjoy having an insignificant ball bat laid across your rears; you will have joy and laughter in your hearts. *Hancho* Noguchi will make men of you!"

Thus ended our first inspirational lecture in the military, one of many more to come.

That morning and each one thenceforth we arose at six for the formation ten minutes later. Then came thirty minutes of calisthenics and running before chow. Our diet was healthy though hardly fancy, consisting mainly of rice, and bean soup, brought from the base kitchen to our quarters in large wooden buckets. Our utensils were limited to bowls and chopsticks.

Following chow we were briefed by the Officer of the Day, a tall, cadaverous individual whose face was patched with scar tissue, apparently the result of third-degree burns. Then we were given further instructions from The Pig. Except for our noon meal, the remaining time was spent in class instruction, more calisthenics, combat training, and glider practice.

From four until six p. m. we cleaned and scrubbed our barracks and shaped up our clothing and combat gear for the dreaded and inevitable nightly inspection. We were also required to clean the quarters of our *hancho*, and each day three men were selected to wash and iron their clothes. Perfection of performance in all these areas was, of course, critical.

At nine p.m. came final formation and roll call. Shortly thereafter we were in our cots, all lights out. Yes, lights out at nine, but it was then that the *Shuban Kashikan* made their appearance, and it was a rare night that they didn't find something amiss regardless of our most assiduous efforts to keep the barracks in a state of perfection. A few nights after our first acquaintance with the ball bats, for example, we learned another fascinating game called *taiko binta*, all, allegedly, because one trainee had removed another's shoe brush from its proper place.

Again, we were herded out into the cold with cuffs, kicks, and considerable ranting, clad in only our *fundoshi*. For some time the Pig merely leered at us, clearly a master of the suspenseful pause and dramatic effect.

"So. . . ." he said at length, attenuating the word with immense profundity. "So, my little darlings, you failed to heed our warnings." Then, abruptly: "You there!" He pointed an accusing finger. "Stand at attention!" He struck an idiotic pose, slumping, belly distended, arms dangling ape-like. A few of us grinned uncertainly as our friend adopted other weird poses. Pointing at various recruits, he would caricature their expressions, tilting his nose upward, gawking as though struck dumb with amazement, bulging his eyeballs and staring fixedly ahead in mock terror.

Under happier circumstances, The Pig would have been quite a comedian. Indeed, by now I was incessantly astonished at his versatility—a man of multiple personalities, each of which he apparently relished to the full. Only minutes after such preliminaries, in fact, he introduced us to our next experience in sadistic punishment.

"So now, tonight!" The Pig held up his forefinger. "Tonight we shall all participate in a game which may be a bit new for some of you." Again, the pause as his glance somehow took in our own, all sixty men, in a single, knowing sweep. "But consider how dull life would become without new experiences. So . . . yes, a pleasant little game, really—*Taiko Binta*. A new experience." His assistants grinned knowingly, almost simpering. Then the climate changed dramatically. "First rank, about face!" he bellowed, and we promptly did as commanded. "Third rank, about face!" Now ranks one and two were facing each other as were ranks three and four.

Then, approaching the recruit in rank one, The Pig ordered the man facing him to step aside, taking his place. "Now. . . ." he purred, staring his hapless opponent in the face. "We are adversaries, correct?" No reply. "Correct!" The recruit gulped, offering a dazed, convulsive nod. His face was ashen. "Very good. He's not deaf, he's only dumb. So, now . . . the object of our little game is simply—this!" Swift as a ferret, The Pig struck, and the boy fell to the ground with a moan, clutching his face.

A murmur flowed through the ranks. "Silence!" The Pig bellowed.

"Now, as you can readily see, the game is very simple. The object is merely to alternate blows—give and take. Unfortunately my teammate is a poor player. Look!" He pointed as though dumbfounded. "He has collapsed like a puny girl. So, much as I hate to do so, I must withdraw from the game. His so-called opponent was still lying on the ground in a fetal position, and The Pig leaned down solicitously, helping him to his feet. Then he turned to the man he had replaced. "You will kindly assist our fallen hero to the sidelines." The man responded very promptly.

"As you can see," The Pig intoned, "*taiko binta* is a wonderfully simple game" Even a hopeless imbecile can participate. It is also highly reciprocal. We simply alternate blows to the face. Ranks one and three will have the honor of being first. Then ranks two and four may repay the compliment." A shrill, little giggle, much like a sob, escaped his lips. "Now . . . on the count of three, first and third ranks strike on cadence. *Ichi . . . ni . . . san . . .* strike!"

The response was feeble and uncoordinated. I was in the fourth rank, and the punches from my opponent were quite soft and painless. "On cadence! The Pig shouted. "And much harder! Left, right, left right, left right! Harder, harder! Hah—you hit like dying butterflies! Put some energy into it, or I will have to give you a better demonstration." Gradually the force of the blows increased. One caught me on the lower lip, mashing it against my teeth, another in my eye. It throbbed, blurring, and began to water profusely. As the pain increased, those on the receiving end began shifting slightly, ducking at times instinctively.

This gave the *hancho* an excuse, however, to move in with the bats, striking their victims across the back. Unfortunately, rank four was the most accessible and took the brunt of it, but The Pig was not satisfied. "Hah! You *hancho* hit like butterflies yourselves, butterflies that someone has pissed on! Give me that bat, Kakuda." Chuckling, but still counting out cadence, he scuttled along behind us, delivering short, chopping blows to our calves.

Knocked off balance, I lurched forward, causing my opponent's punch to land much harder than he intended. It caught me solidly in the nose, and my whole face went numb, nostrils gushing blood. My eyes were blinded with tears, and I could feel the blood trickling down my throat.

Then, at last, it was time to alternate, and I began with only light blows, partly because I could scarcely see, partly because I didn't wish to harm my opponent. Immediately, though, a sharp-eyed *hancho* began whacking my thighs. Instinctively, I threw one hand back and received a numbing blow on the elbow. A hand grabbed my neck, finger nails nearly penetrating the skin. "Now, smart ass," he snarled, "let me see you draw some blood." Despite my heightened emotions, I was struck by the irony of that statement since my own blood was still flowing copiously, dripping off my chin onto my chest.

I stared at the face across from me, blinking. It was a strong, handsome face, but the eyes were furtive, even a little dangerous, like those of a trapped animal. "I . . . I can't," I stammered. The words were unexpected, completely involuntary.

"What? What did you say?" My taskmaster sounded incredulous. "We'll see about that!" I felt a searing pain across my rear, and then he began to kick me directly in the anus. I whirled, consumed in pain and rage, wanting nothing more in all of existence than to kill him, to insure his utter annihilation. My fighting spirit was short-lived, however, and he drubbed me right and left with the bat until I fell, groveling. "Next time, you little piece of shit. . . ." he puffed. "Next time I'll knock your putrid head off." Then he yanked me to my feet and delivered another kick. "Now, do you still want to fight?" I shook my head, vocal cords nearly paralyzed. "Then get back in line and start punching."

My body was burning, racked with pain, as the boy across from me urged, "Come on, hit me! Hit me, I can take it!" My knuckles struck his cheek solidly.

"Harder!" the *hancho* growled, striking me across the back, and I continued to punch with increasing force.

At last The Pig called it to a halt. "So, now! Now, you recruits you are becoming acquainted with *taiko binta*. A splendid game—correct?" What? you don't think so?" He sounded distressed.

"*Hai*, honorable *honcho dono!*"

"What was that?" He cupped one ear with his hand, and we repeated the words more loudly though obviously without sufficient enthusiasm.

"Well, you probably just need a little more practice." he replied, feigning much empathy and kindness. "Then you can write home and tell your families what great fun you are having in basic training."

Chapter Six

The Grand Way of Heaven and Earth

Afterward all of us lay in our barracks, sick in body and heart, trying to smother our groans. Two or three men staggered out the door to vomit. My head throbbed, my nose and sinus area still numb. The floor seemed to rock like that of a ship in mild swells as I lay there face down trying to comprehend what had happened. My entire body was bruised and aching. Life was a mass of misery and confusion.

Suddenly, I started. Someone had touched me. "Don't be afraid," a voice whispered.

"What?" I blurted.

"Quiet! It's only me—Nakamura." He was standing there beside my cot, a faint shaft of light from outside revealing his face and bare shoulders. Taller than I and well built with a rather bad complexion.

"*Ah so*" I responded. "The one who. . . ." I turned on my side, massaging my battered elbow," not knowing what to say. "Well . . ." I mumbled uncertainly, "please sit down." The pain shot through my legs even though I had barely shifted them.

"No thanks," he replied, "rubbing his hip gingerly with one hand. "My ass still hurts from that first night." He was actually grinning a little. "I just wanted to tell you, I'm sorry about hitting you so hard, especially that one time, right in the nose."

"It wasn't your fault," I said. "It was mine. I mean it was that stinking *hancho.*" I almost whispered the last two words. "He hit me on the back of my legs and knocked me off balance."

"Yes," Nakamura said, "and you got beaten up more than anybody else." Oddly enough, I felt a little surge of pride but made no reply. "Those rotten bastards," he added. "You know, somebody's going to kill those bastards some day—every last one of them . . . kill them all, smash their stinking heads in."

"I hope so," I said but wanted him to leave. The pain was coming in waves, and it took all my strength to suppress the groaning. Eventually the tension became unbearable, and I struggled to sit up. "Well," I grunted, "I'm sorry that I had to hit you so hard. I hit you pretty hard, and I hope you'll forgive me because I really hated to. I definitely didn't want. . . ." At that point, I actually didn't care much what I said, or what I had done. Anything simply to ease the pain, and the words fell out in a meaningless jumble.

But Nakamura just stood there, and inwardly I began to berate him. I closed my eyes, bit my lips, clenched and unclenched my hands. Why didn't the idiot leave? Couldn't he see what hell I was undergoing? He hadn't been hurt half as badly as I. Nor had anyone else. "You'd better not let the *shuban kashikan* find you up," I said and hated myself. We both knew they probably wouldn't be back again until morning.

"*Hai*" he nodded, "I guess you're right." Yet still, he remained there. Maybe, I decided, he felt sorry for me, wanted to lend some kind of moral support. Gradually, however, I discovered that by tightening all the muscles in my body then relaxing them I could ease the pain. Tighten muscles and inhale . . . relax muscles and exhale . . . steadily, rhythmically, over and over. Yes, a good system, and it actually worked. I was beginning to feel better. I glanced at Nakamura, suddenly sensing his loneliness. That was why he wouldn't leave.

"So where are you from? I asked.

"Kure," he answered. "You know," he confided, "I always knew this would be rough, but I never thought anybody could be as rotten as these dirty. . . . They're all sadists, you know that?"

"Definitely," I said. "How do you think they pick them? They go out and look all around the country. Whenever they see someone whipping his mother or kicking his little sister in the belly, they say, 'Come on, come on; we've got a great job for you—*hancho* at Hiro Air Base."

"Right, and that's not all," Nakamura said. "Every one of them is queer as fish in the desert."

I laughed despite myself then became serious. "Really?" I was very naive in such matters but ready to believe almost anything by now.

"Just wait," Nakamura warned, "you'll find out soon enough. My brother's in the army. He told me all about it. And that stinking Pig! You can tell he's a pervert just looking at him. He's also a complete maniac."

"Absolutely," I said. "Do you think they have it as tough in the army as we do?" I could still barely force out the words. "My brother's in the army too."

"I doubt it," Nakamura replied. "Maybe, though. Some of those forced marches they go on probably take a lot of guts—a lot of endurance. They take their beatings too, so maybe there's not much difference in the end."

The pain had eased now that I was concentrating on something else, supplanted by the need for sleep. I wondered how Nakamura could remain standing there so long. "On the other hand," he continued, "we probably don't have it as rough as those navy pilots do. The ones that make it through basic training in the navy air force—they're real tigers, believe me. Nothing can stop them."

How could anybody have it worse than we do? I wondered and drifted into a death-like sleep while Nakamura was still talking.

When I awakened it was six in the morning. I groaned, feeling, remembering, as the awfulness of our situation asserted itself. Momentarily it was impossible to believe that I was away from home, that Hiro was now my reality. The others were stirring, and reveille had just sounded. The groans became general as the badly-cropped heads emerged from the blankets. Yes, it was all real enough, and for an instant I closed my eyes, praying, striving with all my power to will it otherwise. For a flickering instant I was home, there in my own special room, warm and secure, Mother and Tomika preparing breakfast.

The vision shattered as Kakuda and Sakigawa, "The Snake", clumped into the barracks, shouting and slamming doors, cuffing and kicking the slow risers, even dumping some of them from their cots onto the floor. One recruit landed with a thud in a tangle of blankets. It was Nakamura.

I had to rise—fast, but suddenly could not move. My legs were like wood, refusing to bend, and I felt a wild spasm of terror. My right arm throbbed at the elbow and seemed completely paralyzed. With a violent wrench I rolled from my cot, the pain coming like splinters of glass as I struck the floor. But the shock brought life to my limbs, and somehow I made it to my feet. Hobbling and limping into my pants and shirt, I vaguely realized that my face and chest were still caked with dried blood. Frantically, I laced my boots, fully expecting more punishment as The Snake approached, but he passed by, apparently distracted by someone else, shouting, "Get a move on!"

Beds made in record time, we rushed to the first formation grunting and grimacing at every step. We fell into our ranks, staring rigidly ahead, but every man had welts and sores. Glancing about once or twice, I saw swollen faces, black and blue marks.

"Eyes straight ahead!" Kakuda bellowed, but The Pig was smiling with great beneficence as he surveyed us.

"Stiff?" he inquired "Sore?" His eyebrows vaulted toward his hairline in mock disbelief. "Ah, what a pity!" He shook his head, staring at the earth, then glanced up. Now his expression was stern, solemn, even noble like that of a *samurai*.

"You have. . . . no—stamina!" Japan's valiant sons! How disappointing! How distressing! Well. . . ." He stroked his jaw. "Perhaps twenty or thirty minutes of running will at least limber you up a little."

He glanced at the other *hancho*. "Naturally, we would enjoy running along with you, but as you know, we *hancho* are sadly discriminated against. Casting his eyes downward long-sufferingly, he added. "We are forced to ride bicycles."

Then, having us form single file, he commanded, "Forward march!" Every step was torture. We moved like crippled old men. "Terrible, terrible!" our *hancho* shouted. "Since you don't know how to walk we must try running. Double time, march!" Something cracked, and the rear man blundered forward, crashing into the one ahead. Slowly, achingly, our column moved out, like a row of lame ducks.

As we hobbled down the airstrip, our glorious friend and mentor, circled on his bicycle, alternately screeching, cursing, cackling, and cracking jokes, periodically flailing us with a length of bamboo.

Within a mile some of the men were straggling badly. One of them had fallen to the rear some distance. Glancing behind, The Pig caught sight of him and circled back full speed. As we reached the far end of the strip and headed the opposite direction, the man was down, and The Pig was flailing him with his rod. His efforts were fruitless, however, for his victim had fainted.

As the grind continued, others dropped out. One stumbled, pitching to the concrete. Two comrades helped him to his feet, but his legs collapsed, feet dragging as they bore him forward. It was impossible, of course, for them to keep up, and shortly The Pig returned to flog all three of them. Having finished, he sped down the entire line thrashing at us wildly. "This is how a fighter plane attacks!" he yelped. "Fast . . . unexpected . . . deadly!" Synchronizing his blows with each word, he powered forward steadily, striking at each man's head with his rod. "One . . . two . . . three . . . four . . . five . . . six!" Fortunately his aim wasn't always accurate.

I felt the stick glanced off my shoulder, and an instant later, intent on his role as fighter pilot, The Pig ran into one man and pitched over with a magnificent crash. "You clumsy idiot!" he squawked.

How I rejoiced! Our vainglorious and intrepid fighter pilot had just been shot down.

As the run became more grueling, men began collapsing one after another until there were only a few of us left, but The Pig had disappeared, apparently having sustained a few, well-deserved bruises of his own. It was our friend The Snake who eventually brought the ordeal to a halt. All of us were panting and gasping, in great distress, but I had to admit a lot of my stiffness was gone. Our formation was badly decimated, pitifully sagging. The Snake, however, apparently decided to exercise compassion. "Nothing like a brisk walk before breakfast, right?" His smile was almost kindly. "Fall out for chow!"

It was the beginning of an eventful day. Following our noon meal Kakuda introduced us to more games, the last of which involved squirming along on our bellies beneath our cots, around and around the barracks. This, because the floor was allegedly "dirtier than a pig pen." I squirmed my way forward in abject misery, eyes upon the man's boots just ahead. Contact with the floor had drugged me, and I was overwhelmed with the urge to sleep. The desire welled in a great, languorous whirl, and a voice shouted, "Move it, move it!" I flinched, blinking and nearly rammed my face into the flailing heels of the man ahead.

Afterward, Kakuda departed and the KP's brought our chow in the usual wooden buckets. Ravenously I attacked my bowl of rice, feeling my face throb and ache with each chew. "Hello Kuwahara, old friend," a voice said.

I glanced up, startled. It was Nakamura. "Hello," I replied. "Please sit down." Nothing but a stereotypical greeting, and we were too hungry to converse much, but it was good to have a comrade. Nakamura had been among those who had not succumbed out during our "brisk walk" that morning.

"That rotten son of a bitch," he said quietly. "He really looks like a pig. Got some of his own medicine this morning, though, didn't he?"

"*Hai*," I agreed, "came down right on his stupid head."

"He really did," Nakamura said. "Maybe it will knock some sense into him."

"Not likely," I laughed. Neither of us had actually witnessed The Pig's great downfall, merely heard it, but it was gratifying to imagine that he had landed on his head. Before long, in fact, several men were gleefully repeating our assertion that it had occurred in that manner.

"You wait," Nakamura assured me, "that fat-faced idiot will really get it one of these times. Some dark night. . . ."

"He'll be getting it, all right," I concurred. Again, only wishful thinking but it was enjoyable. Merely reflecting upon such possibilities and knowing that others were doing the same provided a sense of camaraderie and lifted our spirits. Initially we had been alone and highly reticent, but as brothers in suffering we rapidly became friendly. Having someone to commiserate with, someone to hate with, was very therapeutic.

Following our brief noon hour respite, however, we were back at it, learning more games. Upon failing to perform our calisthenics acceptably, we were forced to lie on our sides, then raise ourselves off the ground, balancing on one hand and foot with the opposite limbs extended upward at forty-five-degrees. An interesting experiment and rather easily performed at first, but with each passing second it became more difficult. Time after time we strove to balance ourselves in that absurd position, forming X's with our bodies, feeling our arms quiver and shake, more every second, then losing our balance and collapsing. All this, of course, accompanied by threats, commands, cuffs, kicks, and raucous laughter from our task masters. Within half an hour we were lying on the floor almost paralyzed.

By now The Snake and Kakuda had introduced a new element—whips, and once I felt the lash across my quivering back, a flick along my neck that burned like acid, but I merely cringed, huddled there helplessly trying to protect my face with my hand.

Other, equally innovative forms of punishment followed, and that night at final formation The Pig was back at the helm, bringing the day's activities to a fitting climax. I noted with satisfaction a bruise on one side of his forehead and the fact that his left arm appeared rather stiff, but my pleasure was short lived, for we had failed to recite the five main points of the "Imperial Rescript to Soldiers and Sailors." This rescript was issued by the Emperor Meiji in 1882 and was regarded as sacred—a document several pages long which every military man had to learn verbatim. All were required to absorb its complex rules and philosophy through continual study and meditation, to memorize, also recite it completely or in part at a moment's notice.

Sometimes Japanese fighting men had to recite The Rescript in full at each night's formation, the chanting going on for about fifteen minutes. Fortunately, we at Hiro were only held accountable for the five main points or precepts as follows:

1. The soldier and sailor should consider loyalty the essential duty. . . . A soldier or a sailor in whom the spirit is not strong, however, skilled in art or proficient in science, is a mere puppet; and a body of soldiers or sailors wanting in loyalty, however well-ordered and disciplined it may be, is in an emergency no better than a rabble. . . . With single heart fulfill your essential duty of loyalty, and bear in mind that duty is weightier than a mountain, while death is lighter than a feather.

2. Inferiors should regard the orders of their superiors as issuing directly from the Emperor. Always pay due respect not only to your superiors but also to your seniors, even though not serving under them. On

the other hand, superiors should never treat their inferiors with contempt or arrogance. Except when official duty requires them to be strict and severe, superiors should treat their inferiors with consideration, making kindness their chief aim, so that all grades may unite in their service to the Emperor. . . .

3. The soldier and sailor should esteem valor. Ever since the ancient times valor has in our country been held in high esteem, and without it our subjects would be unworthy of their name. How then may the soldier and the sailor, whose profession it is to confront the enemy in battle, forget even for an instant to be valiant? . . .

4. Faithfulness and righteousness are ordinary duties of a man, but the soldier and sailor, in particular, cannot be without them and remain in the ranks even for a day. Faithfulness implies the keeping of one's word and righteousness the fulfillment of one's duty. If then you wish to be faithful and righteous in anything, you must carefully consider at the onset whether you can accomplish it or not. If you thoughtlessly agree to do something that is vague in its nature, bind yourself to unwise obligations and then try to prove yourself faithful and righteous, you may find yourself in dire straits from which there is no escape. . . .

5. The soldier and the sailor should make simplicity their aim. If you do not make simplicity your aim, you will become effeminate and frivolous and acquire fondness for luxurious and extravagant ways; you will grow selfish and sordid and sink to the last degree of baseness, so that neither loyalty nor valor will avail to save you from the contempt of the world. . . . Never do you, soldiers and sailors, make light of this injunction.

These precepts were termed "The Grand Way of Heaven and Earth, The Universal Law of Humanity," and men who made a single mistake in their recitation have sometimes killed themselves.

Thus it was understandable that The Pig laid such stress upon this aspect of our training, for it was supposedly that very "soul of soldiers and sailors" and, of course, of our airmen. Simultaneously, it seemed a bit ironic that he and his cohorts should have such a curious way of complying with the injunction about treating inferiors with kindness and consideration.

That night because of our inability to memorize the requisite precepts with sufficient speed, we were lined up facing the barracks, and
this time there were no ball bats. One by one, our faces were slammed
against the wall, resulting in several bloody, broken noses, split lips, and
loose teeth.

"Recruits," The Pig later informed us jovially, "this has been a most
eventful day. A few more like it and you will start to become men!"

Chapter Seven

A Time to Cry

Within **a single** week my entire life had been transformed beyond comprehension—my entire concept of man, of good and bad, of right and wrong. Yet ironically, I could no more evaluate my feelings rationally than a wounded man might evaluate pain.

The initial trauma had produced a numbness, a kind of psychological paralysis, but emerging from it was an ever-increasing dread. It was utterly impossible to obey the Rescript's injunction not to fear a superior when our superiors failed to observe the related injunction regarding respect and consideration. We had become as furtive as rats frequently subjected to electric shock. We were constantly tensed and waiting for the next one.

Within only one week I had come to believe that life with my family, the days with my friends at school, were nothing but a childish illusion. How far off it all seemed now—how vague and insubstantial. Onomichi was only some fifty miles away, but it might as well have been thousands, at the most remote corner of the world. Time also was a relative thing. My youth was being purged away. A single week had made me old.

"*Shinpei, shinpei, kutsu migaki. Mata nete naku noka yo*" These words have long been sung by Japanese recruits at *Shoto Rappa* after the long, hard day. "Recruit, recruit, polish your shoes. Later you may cry in bed." The night has always been a time of sorrow for the trainee, a time when he could reminisce, take a deep breath, then under cover of darkness, release his pent-up emotions, the pain and the fear.

Once the *shuban kashikan* had completed their inspection and the disciplinary action that usually followed, we lay in our cots thinking of home, especially of our mothers. After all, some of us were only fifteen. Possibly we even took a kind of perverse satisfaction in our very sorrow as people sometimes do. Lacking others to sympathize with us, we sympathized with ourselves, and it was then that we shed tears, there in the darkness where no one could see and few could hear.

Some of the recruits, like myself, had barely entered puberty, and our voices were still changing. In our dreams we sometimes called aloud for our mothers, but I never heard a single recruit call the name of his father, Later, in fact, I learned that dying men also asked for their mothers. The father is master of the family, and it is partly his stern and remote love that helps instill a son with the fighting spirit. Yet when comfort is needed, or when a man has little time left, he wants his mother.

To one unfamiliar with the Japanese mind, some of our actions, our weeping and sentimentality, may appear strange. To the outsider we are an inscrutable people who rarely exhibit emotion. And it is true, in fact, that we often maintain a facade. Ours is a philosophy of stoicism and resignation in many ways, and frequently we display no feeling, even when filled with joy or hate.

Often we may even smile or laugh at adversity, but all people share the same passions. They are merely manifest differently according to one's culture and conditioning.

Westerners, especially Americans in my view, may be compared emotionally speaking to boiling pots with loose lids from which steam escapes fairly regularly and with relative ease. Orientals, certainly the Japanese, on the other hand, are more like pressure cookers. The same heat is applied and the same steam exists, but in the latter instance the steam often builds for some time without any outward manifestation. When at last it breaks forth, however, it may do so with remarkable violence.

The analogy has its limitations, of course. In many cases, for example, Japanese can minimize or eliminate much of the emotional steam because of religious and philosophical conditioning that fosters acceptance and resignation, a proclivity for bending with the wind like resilient bamboo which can withstand great storm without being uprooted.

Nevertheless, it is no exaggeration to say that Japanese people in general can be the epitome of serenity, of politeness to the point of toadishness in their deference to others on many occasions, that in others they can respond to great emotional duress with hysteria. It is not uncommon, for instance, for Japanese women who have lost a loved one to fling themselves upon the floor in a spirit of inconsolable wailing. Moreover, it certainly common for Japanese military men to assault the enemy with implacable determination, indeed, utter fanaticism.

Such considerations aside, every effort was made by our *hancho* to stifle all emotionalism, except as it pertained to country and Emperor. Constantly, inexorably, all emotion was funneled into the great crucible of patriotism. Ideally, every fear, anxiety, hope, and joy was to be subdued, transformed, and channeled into the fighting spirit—the spirit of the Yamato Race, of the *samurai*.

Consequently, whimpering because of pain or crying for one's mother were not only evidence of degrading weakness, they were indications that our lives had not been consecrated. We had yet to comprehend fully the doctrine of individual expendability. To acquire that unwavering testimony called for in the Imperial Rescript—that duty was indeed weightier than the mountains, that death was lighter than a feather.

If a single recruit was overheard moaning in his sleep we were all punished. At night we were constantly rousted from bed, for our audience with The Pig. Sometimes he was the ultimate comedian, sometimes quite the opposite. The smirk would be gone, the flaccid face contorted or, in some cases, extremely glum and weary.

Frequently, he would pace back and forth before us, hands clasped behind his back, head bowed, lips pursed, studiously perusing the earth beneath his feet, or unpredictably casting a glance at the night sky. Then, at length, he would deign to acknowledge our presence. "Can it be . . . can it truly be?" he would mutter with immense solemnity and incredulity. "That such pitiful specimens of humanity, such helpless and hopeless boobs . . . such miserable excuses of manhood, are soon to be honored sons of the great *Nippon* Empire, privileged to defend the glory of our most esteemed Emperor?" Shaking his head grievously: "The very thought fills our souls with untold trepidation!"

Nakamura was standing next to me at the time. "It fills his fat ass with trepidation." The faintest whisper. "With a ton of shit." His lips were barely parted and scarcely moved. I was actually shocked at such sacrilege, but I also struggled to keep from smiling.

"Nevertheless . . ." our mentor continued, "the grand designs of heaven and earth shall never be frustrated—never, never—never, even in the most infinitesimal manner, even within the mind of a wretched flea."

The Pig paused for at least a full minute, scrutinizing our faces with much severity. "So now, *shinpei*. . . ." His tone clearly signaled that the oration was over. "I am going to give you some fatherly advice, especially those who bawl their lungs out every night like snot-nosed babies. You are here at Hiro Air Base for only one reason." Another lengthy pause. "Do you know what that reason is?"

"*Hai* honorable *hancho dono*!" We chorused the words loudly.

"Do you?"

"*Hai*, honorable *hancho dono*!" This time we all bellowed from the depths of our bellies.

The Pig shook his head, slowly, emphatically, in a spirit of resignation. "No, you do not. But you will learn. Before the end of your training under Sergeant Noguchi there will be no question." The pacing increased. "At present, however, you must learn one thing." For a time, he frowned at his feet as if they were melting, waiting so long I decided that he had lost his trend of thought. Maybe there was something wrong with his brain. Then, with a great surge of energy: "There is no past!" His words were so loud, so unexpected, so formidable, that many of us literally quaked. At that point he actually turned his back upon us, surveying the stars. "There is no past." More subdued now but equally irrefutable. "Only the present and the future."

Eventually, he turned to face us again, and now almost gently, as though confronted with some cosmic sorrow: "You must forget about everything except those concepts we are authorized to teach you. Forget about civilian life, forget about your mothers, forget about your families. Live instead for the Emperor—for Emperor and country without the slightest equivocation. If you do so, all fear will distill like frost in the morning sun. And you will attain liberation. You will attain joy, and strength, and freedom—like that of the eagles!"

Even more softly: "So now . . . the *binta*, the ball bats and other things . . . they are nothing, nothing at all in and of themselves. They exist only to the extent that they help us to make men of you." His glance was fierce and probing, utterly uncompromising. "Do you understand?"

"*Hai*, honorable *hancho dono!*" we roared.

For a moment The Pig almost smiled. "That is good, and now comes the proof." He motioned to the ever-vigilant Sakigawa and Kakuda. "Bring forth the bats!"

That night many of us were beaten unconscious but no one uttered a sound.

Strangely, although the majority of us were very young, there were a few recruits at Hiro anywhere from forty-five to sixty years old. Stranger still, those individuals were treated with no more consideration than anyone else. Basic training was an enormous melting pot, wherein each man was deprived of his identity as fully as possible. Every man's head was barbarously cropped. Every man wore the same ugly, swamp colored uniform. The elderly, even people of wealth and prestige in a few cases . . . were all treated just like the rest of us. The *hancho* who would have bowed in obeisance to some of the trainees in civilian life, or who might never have been able to associate with them, was tyrant and ruler over all. He could kick, strike, bully, and humiliate any recruit with impunity. Even murder in some instances.

Despite our anxiety, however, after the first few days at Hiro we slept as though drugged. Our bodies had not yet become conditioned to the arduous training and the punishment. During the night we lay in a near coma, and at times The Snake and Kakuda would enter the barracks with some of their cohorts to perform their clever tricks. On one occasion they stealthily tied our hands and feet, then flashed on the lights, awakening us with wild shouts. Aroused from our stupor, we struggled from our beds unaware of what had happened, and tumbled to the floor groping about frantically to untie ourselves. This to the uproarious laughter of our tormentors.

When Nakamura had first declared that many of our *hancho* were perverted, I was startled and incredulous. By now, however, my outlook had changed radically. The Snake, especially, enjoyed humiliating the younger recruits in various degrading ways, and those of us who had barely entered puberty suffered most. During a formation he would leer at some unfortunate who had made a mistake and say, "Hey, *shinpei*, you still act like a kid—*na*!"

There was no helpful answer to such questions, because he would merely persist to the conclusion. "Hey, *shinpei*—aren't you a man yet? Didn't you hear right? I asked if you are a man!"

"Yes, honorable *hancho dono*!"

To this The Snake would feign great amazement. "*Ah so*! Then prove it-take down your pants!. Now your *fundoshi*—quick!"

Then the hapless trainee would stand shamefaced while The Snake, sometimes Kakuda and The Pig as well, poked fun and made snide comments regarding his meager endowments. Such things I actually dreaded more than the physical punishment.

Late one night three of us were rousted from bed to clean the *hanchos'* quarters because our work there during the day had allegedly been unsatisfactory. Afterward we were forced to strip down and leap into icy showers. The Snake then herded us out naked into the cold demanding that we run around the barracks ten times before consigning us to the shower room for the remainder of the night.

There for the first hour we huddled on a wooden bench, cramped and shivering in total darkness. As the time dragged on, we decided to exercise. It was the only way we could keep from growing numb, perhaps freezing. Periodically, however, we succumbed to exhaustion, and once I awoke from a half-sleep to begin doing push-ups. In the midst of these exertions, feeling the cold knife upward through my feet and hands, I thought about the showers. A flash of optimism which died as quickly. So far as I knew, the hot water was turned on for only a short period each evening following our training.

Eventually, however, having nothing else to do, I groped my way over to the showers and barely twisted one of the handles. A slight whoosh of cold water, and I jerked back. Then, as I reached out to turn it off, the water actually felt tepid, steadily growing warmer.

Seconds later it was coming hot, steaming hot. Quickly I turned it off, glancing about furtively. Had our *hancho* heard the noise, the sound of water running in the pipes, from their rooms? I waited for some time, and decided that by now they were snoring deeply, the sleep of the unjust. I peered through the dark at my companions. Vague outlines, squatting back to back on the bench, dozing fitfully.

For a moment I battled with myself. Possibly the hot water was a mere residue, a bit remaining from the evening before. If I alone were to shower, though, it might last for some time. If the three of us used the showers. . . .

After a moment I whispered, "*Yai*—Oka! Yamamoto! Come over to the showers."

"Hot water?" Oka blurted.

"Quiet!"

Instantly they were next to me, rubbing their arms and bellies, hunching over, treading up and down. "Turn them on quick!" Yamamoto groaned through chattering teeth.

"No, just one," I insisted. "We won't turn it on too high, or all the water will be gone before we can even get warm." Obediently, they stood aside while I regulated the shower. Then we crowded beneath it, back to back, exclaiming our delight in muted tones.

"Ah, this is great," I murmured tilting my head back, "this is fantastic!" Then another idea struck. "I wonder if . . . Where's something to stop the drain?"

"Sit on it," Oka replied gleefully. "Your rear is big enough."

It might be possible, I decided to fill the small shower room three or four inches deep without flooding the rest of the floor. Suddenly I knew what to use—toilet paper! And the plan worked perfectly. I covered the drain with a layer about half an inch thick, and the water expanded across the floor around us, soaking through the paper just fast enough to prevent the outer room from flooding and to maintain a steady warmth.

"Why don't you both admit I'm a genius? I said and settled back in the gurgling liquid. Eventually the shower created enough steam to also warm the surrounding atmosphere. I stretched supine in the deepening liquid. There in the midst of all that cold, dark, cruelty, we had found our secret place, and in that warm, beneficent seclusion we fell asleep.

Chapter Eight

The Cost of Sushi Cakes

Despite the constant behests to forget our past, after two weeks our families were permitted to pay us a brief visit. Only fourteen days since I had said goodbye, and it seemed ages. As the visiting hour approached I began to tremble. So much had happened, home seemed years into the past, a thousand miles away.

At four p.m. I was waiting in the visiting room where a counter separated the trainees as if they were convicts from their families. I watched people enter, observed how each trainee's eyes lit in recognition. Some of them seemed almost embarrassed, strangely hesitant. The bar hampered them from the intimacies of a normal greeting, and the best they could do was clasp hands.

Twenty minutes passed . . . thirty, and no sign of my own family. I was beginning to fret and fidget. Where were they? What could have possibly happened to them? Didn't they realize that we had only this one fleeting hour together? Maybe they wouldn't arrive until too late—if they arrived at all. Soon I was growing angry. If they never got to see me it would serve them right.

On the other hand, maybe they had misunderstood the visiting date. Maybe I had somehow written it down wrong in my letter. Yes, that was probably it. What a hopeless idiot! I cracked my knuckles and stared bleakly at the floor.

Then, furtively, even superstitiously, I glanced toward the door. There, miraculously, was my father in his gray business suit, its conservative shade blending with the two drab, wartime *kimono* behind him. Mother and Tomika. "Oh, my Yasuo, my Yasuo!" Mother murmured. "We were caught in a terrible traffic jam!" Simultaneously, Tomika was saying something about a bomb crater, but it barely registered. They were here. That was all that mattered.

Now we were clasping hands, looking into each other's eyes. Mother and Tomika made no effort to disguise their feelings, and their tears glistened conspicuously despite the smiles. For a moment I couldn't speak because I was struggling to restrain tears of my own, actually biting my lower lip to avoid displaying any weakness, especially before my father.

Father was even wearing one of his rare smiles. In fact, I had never seen it so warm: "How is your new life, my son?" he inquired.

"Oh . . ." I faltered. "it is fine, Father. Very. . . ." I groped for the right words. "Very educational." But something writhed inside me, and the real words in my mind pounded: "Why do you lie? Tell the truth! Tell of the unbelievable brutality, the awful injustice! Tell him that you can't stand this place a day longer! Maybe he can do something!"

I knew full well, however, that my father had received similar treatment in the army. Surely he realized what I was going through. The thought spawned feelings of incredulity. How had he managed to survive so well? Survive at all? Father squinted one eye, raising the opposite brow as though reading each thought. "Do your *hancho* love you? Are they kind and gentle like your mother and sister?" I groped for an appropriate reply, but he continued. "You look very well. Your face has even filled out a little from all the delicious food—right?"

Truly my face had "filled out"—swollen from being slammed against the barracks and the previous night's *binta*. "It's not from—" I began and caught myself. Father's eyes held mine, and his head gave an abrupt, little shake of warning. "Are they treating you well, Yasuo?" he demanded.

I forced a pallid smile. "Yes, thank you, Father, quite well." His expression remained stern, uncompromising. "I mean very well."

"Good," he replied. "There is nothing like military discipline to bring out the best in a man."

For a few seconds none of us spoke. Then Tomika bent forward, her brow wrinkled, gazing into my face as though it were a mirror. "How did you get all those cuts?" she asked, looking highly distressed.

"*Yasuo-chan*, your eyes are black!" Mother exclaimed. "You've been injured!" It was that appealing tone of concern with which I had become so familiar, and again I battled inwardly. The childish part of me took comfort, wanted to be coddled, yet I also felt irritation. "They've been cruel to you, absolutely brutal!" She spoke so loudly I flushed and glanced in chagrin at the people nearest us. But they were all absorbed in their own conversations. "And your nose is swollen!"

"Yasuo is all right," Father said.

"But his eyes" Mother persisted. "His poor, dear——"

"He is perfectly all right!" Father said. This time his tone allowed no opposition.

"It's nothing, Mother, nothing at all!" My voice cracked embarrassingly, partly because it was still changing. "I just . . . I just ran into . . . a tree branch." I held my hand over my eyes as though shading them from the sun, breathing jerkily in the silence. All the while my mother's hand pressed mine so warmly I could actually feel her pulse. At that moment I loved her more than at any time in my life, more than anything else in the world.

Quietly Father was saying, "My son can take care of himself. A few little bruises are inevitable. They are helping to make a man of him. A *samurai*!"

I looked up, massaging the lower half of my face with one hand to keep the muscles from twitching. Then I smiled, nodding. "*Hai.*" That was all I could say.

"Your sister and I have made some *sushi* cakes," Mother said. "Will they permit you to have them?" Both Mother and Tomika had concealed food under the cloth *obi* about their waists. Their *sushi* cakes had long been a favorite with me.

"Well, we're not supposed to," I answered reluctantly, "but they'll never know anything about it—if you can just hand it to me without anyone seeing." Mother and Tomika both looked worried. "Did you bring the shirts and towels?" I asked. Mother nodded and placed a bundle tied in a red *furoshiki* on the counter. "Just put the cakes inside," I urged. "No one will ever find out."

Reluctantly, very surreptitiously, Mother complied, but ironically, only moments later, there was a commotion. We glanced about startled to see a *hancho* cuffing one of the trainees. "Beat me! Beat me!" his mother wailed. "It wasn't my son's fault! He didn't ask us to bring him anything——it's my fault!" The cuffing wasn't severe, but it was mortifying to all of us, especially the trainee's family.

Sunday was the one day in the week when we were supposed to receive decent treatment. This was to have been our brief interlude, this visitors' day in particular. A fleeting, precious moment in time when all could be serene. The *hancho* himself was only eighteen or nineteen with a long neck and shiny, arrogant face. He could easily have punished the recruit later. How I hated him, literally would have rejoiced to kill him.

Mother and Tomika, of course, were now greatly alarmed, imploring me in hushed, urgent tones to return my contraband the instant it appeared safe to do so. For an instant I wavered. Then my fear gave way to rebellion. "No! Those . . . you and Tomika made them for me, and I'm going to keep them."

Both Mother and Tomika were still murmuring anxiously, their eyes haunted. "Let him have his *sushi*," Father muttered. "They cannot hurt a Kuwahara. Let him keep them."

The matter was settled, and soon the visiting hour was over, our women again becoming tearful. "Stop that!" Father ordered. Reaching across the counter, he clasped my arm. "We shall see you in a short while, once your training is over, *hai*?"

I nodded. "We get two day's leave."

"So, you see?" Father said. "He gets two day's leave. We will all have a splendid celebration and hear of his experiences. Meanwhile, Yasuo will make the most of his opportunity. He will make us all proud of him." His gaze coalesced with my own. "Make us proud of you, my son."

I merely nodded, fearing that my voice might betray me. Seconds later they were leaving. Father strode out of the door without a backward glance. Mother followed, covering her mouth with one hand, but Tomika turned briefly, eyes large and limpid like those of a fawn. She waved and tried to smile, but the smile collapsed piteously. Then they were gone.

Later in the barracks, most of us relaxed on our cots, a privilege accorded only on Sunday, and stared at the ceiling. The visit hadn't elevated our spirits greatly. Nakamura was hunched on the edge of his cot, chin in his hands. Strolling over, I stood eyeing him, but he failed to notice. Reluctant to intrude, I paced slowly about the room, then stopped by his cot once more. "*Yai*, Nakamura!" I whispered. "You like *sushi* cakes?"

Grinning faintly, he glanced up. "You have some too?"

I nodded. "Yes, I've hidden them under my blankets."

Still grinning, he patted a spot next to him by the foot of his cot. "Me too."

Soon we discovered that nearly everyone had received food of one kind or another—cake, candy, or cookies. Oka and Yamamoto had secreted items in their shirts and were becoming a bit boisterous. "We'll all have a party!" Oka exclaimed. "Tonight after *Shoto Rappa*!" The thought filled us all with glee, and there was much hearty laughter for the first time in two weeks.

Unfortunately, our happy interlude was short lived. Upon returning from our evening meal, one held in the chow hall on Sundays, we found our beds ransacked. Several of us were whispering nervously when The Pig made an abrupt entrance.

"Oh!" Oka exclaimed. The word had escaped his lips of its own accord.

"Oh?" The Pig raised his eyebrows. "What do you mean, 'Oh'?" Gently, very disarmingly, he laid a hand on Oka's shoulder. "Is something wrong? Something missing?"

Oka stiffened. "No, honorable *hancho dono*."

"Hmmm . . . well then, I'm afraid I don't understand." As usual, he was relishing the situation. "Why, did you say, 'Oh'?"

Oka stammered incoherently. "Hmmm, very strange—most mysterious." The Pig stroked his jowl, and began his usual pacing back and forth. "I simply don't understand this at all. Could it be that I'm not welcome here? Come now, gentlemen—I sense a strange restraint. What, oh what, is wrong?"

"Nothing is wrong, honorable *hancho dono*," Nakamura bravely volunteered.

"Ah so!" Suddenly The Pig whirled, jabbing his finger at the tip of Yamamoto's nose. "Why, then, is your bed all torn up?" Yamamoto gagged. "Very curious indeed," The Pig muttered and struck a melodramatic stance, one hand on his hip, the other massaging his brow. "I come here . . ." he said slowly, "hoping for a little courtesy and friendship, but instead, what do I get? Not one kind word, only coldness. I merely ask a simple, decent question, yet people barely speak to me."

He flounced down on my cot, nearly collapsing it, gazing at me with a stricken expression. Then he buried his face in his hands, faking ridiculous sobs. "Kuwahara, what can this all mean?"

I . . . I don't know, honorable—"

"I'm a stranger in my own family! Children! My children, don't you even recognize your mother?" Then he reverted to his weeping. An incredible performance, and several of us laughed nervously but knew that it presaged something unpleasant.

And indeed it did. Eventually, tiring of such antics, The Pig informed us in a rather bored manner that we would have to be chastised for attempting to fool him. We were herded outside, and our faces were slammed against the barracks. By now most of us had learned to take much of the force with upper rounded area of our foreheads acquiring some fine bumps and bruises in the process, but it helped minimize the number of broken noses and split lips. That particular treatment, however, was only a preliminary.

Afterward, we were forced to crawl around the barracks with our combat boots tied together by the laces and dangling from our necks. In this manner we traveled down the halls to visit the *hancho* in their various rooms. It was much like certain college initiation ceremonies, I suppose, though a bit more harsh than most. Each man was required to knock on one of the closed doors, entering—still upon his hands and knees, to apologize.

I was one of those to have an audience with The Pig himself. As I entered he was seated under a bright light, no doubt for theatrical effect, legs crossed and an arm hooked over the back of his chair. He was also smoking a large cigar. Sighing and blowing a jet of smoke toward the light bulb above, he inquired, "Aren't you well enough fed here, Kuwahara?"

"Yes, honorable—"

"Then why did you bring food into your quarters, unhealthy food, in fact, when you knew perfectly well that it was forbidden?"

I had never considered *sushi* cakes unhealthy, but perhaps he was referring to our group in general. It was scarcely a point for argument under the circumstances, however. "I am sorry, honorable *hancho dono*." Rarely had I felt more contrite. It was abundantly clear now that I had committed a grievous sin.

"Well, Kuwahara—look at me, not at the floor. I am afraid that 'sorry' is not adequate." Meanwhile he kept blowing billows of rancid cigar smoke into my face. When I began to gag from the effects, he asked, "What in the world's the matter with you? Are you ill? Do I disgust you?"

I fumbled hopelessly for a reply, but he continued. "As I was saying, Kuwahara, we wouldn't accomplish much at this base—as a matter of fact, we'd actually lose the entire war if every man in the military could break the rules then simply say, 'I'm sorry.' Do you understand what I'm getting at? Or have you already forgotten my inspirational lecture last week on the virtues of obedience?"

"Yes, honorable . . . I mean no, honorable *hancho dono*—I have not forgotten."

"I devoutly hope so," he replied, rolling his eyes melodramatically. Under less threatening circumstances, in fact, his response would have seemed ludicrous. "But in view of your temporary lapse of memory, I trust that you will appreciate my need to underscore the problem in this manner." He studied me thoughtfully, exhaling more cigar smoke. "Besides," he added wearily, "I resent not being invited to the party you were planning after *Shoto Rappa*. I was a recruit once myself, you know."

He then kicked me in the face nearly breaking my cheekbone and called out pleasantly, "Next, please!"

"Thank you very much, honorable *hancho dono*" I mumbled and crawled blindly for the door, face numb, boots swinging.

Chapter Nine

The Parting of Miyagame

S evere though it had been, the punishment of the first two weeks was negligible compared to what came later. As our conditioning improved, the daily running regimen increased from two or three to five miles. Eventually we were running over eight miles, and those who fell behind were bludgeoned with rifle butts.

During *taiko binta*, instead of exchanging fist blows in the face, we now used shoes with hob nails, and the face of every trainee bore lacerations and rips, especially around the comers of the mouth. One man in the adjoining barracks nearly lost an eye. Except for Sundays, the torment was almost incessant.

By the first month's end many in our group were breaking emotionally, beyond remedy. Continual pain, continual humiliation, continual pressure. Endless stress! It could not be endured forever. The two remaining months of basic training loomed like centuries. I did not believe it possible that all of us could survive. And I was right.

Early in the second month six men from our original group deserted. They scaled the barbed wire enclosure and fled only to be captured a short while later. One of them remained free for several days, hiding in the mountains, stealing vegetables from the farms by night. Then he was apprehended by the civilian police near his home in Hongo City. In order to verify his identity, they delivered him to his family. What igno-miny! "We are sorry," the police explained, "but this man has betrayed his country, and we have no recourse but to return him to Hiro." He was then led away in handcuffs.

Deserters from all branches of the military were sent to army stock-ades where they were at the mercy of the vicious MP's. Reports had reached us, in fact, that prisoners were often tortured to death with no recourse whatever to justice and a fair trial. Stockade authorities simply lied with impunity fabricating reasons for the demise of those they killed. They were rarely questioned.

For all of us, time squirmed by with the speed of an earthworm, but those who didn't collapse under the ordeal were gradually becoming tougher, hardened in both mind and body. Somehow we made it through the gristmill of the second month. Two thirds of our basic training was behind us now, and that imparted encouragement.

During my weeks at Hiro I had grown a bit and was grimly satisfied, even proud, that I had withstood some of the worst they had to offer. I was one of the best in calisthenics and endurance running, and I con-tinued to excel at glider practice along with my other training classes. I had now acquired several friends who seemed impressed with my former accomplishments as national glider champion, and the news was being spread. No denying, I enjoyed the recognition, and my general outlook was rapidly improving. Then came a shock that left me demoralized for days. One evening, having just polished my boots, I strolled to the latrine. As I approached the door, however, a recruit informed me that it was locked. "Out of order, I guess," he said and wandered off.

Feeling an urgent need to enter, I seized the door knob, turning it and giving a vigorous shove. "Anybody in there?" I called. No answer. Maybe, I decided, The Snake had locked it simply to create a little more confu-sion and discomfort. It was definitely the sort of trick he might pull.

I called again. No answer, but the lock was a flimsy one, and my need for relief was quickly increasing. Glancing about to insure that no one was watching, I reared back on one leg and crashed my boot heel against the lock. It creaked and the door shuddered. Once again, I glanced about, then assaulted the lock even harder. This time it gave, and the door fell open.

I entered hastily, leaving the light off, Almost simultaneously, I collided with someone . . . something. "Pardon me," I mumbled. No answer. Something, a presence, seemed to loom before me in the dark. Backing toward the door, I blurted, "Who is it? What's wrong?" Someone was there. I had touched someone, felt human flesh. Yet he simply remained there in frozen silence like a madman. Roiling darkness, the stench, the silence . . . all mingled ominously.

Groping for the wall switch, I flipped it on. The light exploded revealing a limp figure, dangling from the rafter by a rope. The rope was knotted around his neck, and he was still swinging slightly from our contact.

This was my first direct encounter with death. The face was purple and bloated, the eyes bulging slightly and egg white with no sign at all of the irises. In my shock I failed to recognize him. Then the realization enveloped me. Miyagame, a recruit I had talked to more than once. Yes, I remembered now . . . always quiet and withdrawn, rather frail. Yes, Miyagame! The one that idiot *hancho* had cuffed before his family on visitors' day.

He was still swinging, and I stared in horrified fascination. Stupefied, mesmerized . . . paralyzed in the clutches of a nightmare.

Back and forth . . . back and forth. . . . Then came the panic. Maybe, maybe, by some remote possibility he was still alive. Somewhere in that graying flesh there might be a tiny pulse of life. I was wasting precious time! Stumbling backward, I whirled and rushed into the nearest barracks. "Quick, give me your trench knife!" I commanded a startled recruit.

"*Nani?*" He blinked at me stupidly. "What is it?"

Seizing the knife in its sheath on the pack atop his locker, I shouted, "There's somebody in the latrine—a dead man! Hanged himself!" The recruit arose from his seat on the cot, looking as though he had accidentally swallowed arsenic. "Come on," I ordered. "Help me for god's sake!" Dumbly he followed, and I had the quick impression that he thought I'd gone mad.

Then he saw Miyagame and began to exclaim and mumble incoherently. "Cut the rope," I said, and he complied as I hefted the limp body. An instant later the rope was severed, and Miyagame collapsed over my shoulder, staggering me. "Help me lay him down." The recruit complied.

Feverishly, I turned the body on its stomach, straddled it, and began artificial respiration pressing rhythmically on his back as we had been trained to do. Minutes passed, how long I didn't know. "You're wasting your time, Kuwahara—he's dead and gone," a voice said. It was The Snake, and a dozen men were clustered about us.

Almost inaudibly someone murmured, "Anyway, he is happy now."

Swiftly the news spread, and the following day I learned through Nakamura that Miyagame had left a letter addressed to his family, an apology for having dishonored them and begging their forgiveness for "dying ahead of you before my rightful time." His final words read, "I await you in the next world."

This was another breaking point for several in our group. Now only the fittest would survive. Miyagame's suicide had evoked a terrible psychological effect. My own special glow of hope, pride, and strength vanished. What good would it do to grow strong, anyway? After basic there would simply be more punishment, more harassment, more humiliation. More and more and more. Then what, provided it ever ended? I would probably die for an Emperor who had never even heard the name Kuwahara, who would never have the faintest inkling of my existence.

My naive conception of heroism soured, putrefied. In its place was the bloated face of Miyagame with its blind, egg-white eyeballs . . . always swinging. Visions began to assert themselves, flashbacks of Miyagama being cuffed before his family, all of them burning with fear and shame. And always, after that, the dark, stinking latrine and the lifeless body. After *Shoto Rappa*, the inspections and ongoing punishment, I would lie face down on my cot, gripping my mattress, trying to exclude the visions I knew would come.

At times, I would jolt to wakefulness in the night as though falling. At times I would cry out, bolting upright, staring wildly into the dark. Always the corpse that had once been Miyagame—swinging, swinging . . . always swinging. Tossing, moaning, clutching my mattress as though it were a raft on the waves, I would clamp my eyes desperately, only to embrace the vision more fiercely.

Eventually it began to fade, enshrouded in the mist of time, partly because others had decided to follow our friend. Watanabe, a recruit from my own quarters, went next in the same way. Then others, not only with ropes but also bayonets. One leaped off the water tower, crushing out his life on the asphalt assembly area below. Nine men from our original group of sixty took their own lives during my basic training.

Suicide! It was a way out, perhaps the only answer. Could it hurt any more to hang than to be bludgeoned with a rifle butt? Could it hurt more to impale one's self on a bayonet than to hug a tree naked, clinging to the cold, rough bark while your back was lashed? Surely the bayonet, used properly, would be far more swift. Irresistibly, I began to toy with different possibilities, then to plan more seriously. Slashed wrists, I decided, would probably be the best way. Or maybe the jugular vein. Hone my trench knife to a fine razor edge. Then. . . . My obsession with Miyagame was being replaced by an obsession with Kuwahara.

Yet each day I could feel my body toughening, feel the swelling in my biceps, triceps, and deltoids as I performed my push-ups. I could now do one hundred push-ups perfectly. Perfectly, because anything less laid us vulnerable to the whip. I could do twenty perfect pull-ups—sit-ups indefinitely. Each day I felt the growing strength in my legs as we ran. Ten miles a day now, and always I heard my father's voice calmly commanding me to return a man, a *samurai*.

No, I could not dishonor my father by taking the easy way out. Not my family, not the illustrious name of Kuwahara. Only two more weeks now, and spring was coming. The sunlight increased, daily, dazzling our eyes as we ran, transforming the distances into tantalizing patches of blue. Tiny lakes and ponds as blue as the sky that evaporated enchantingly as we drew near. Frustratingly . . . yet I felt that I could run forever. I could keep right on through life, the life that fate or the gods had decreed. Nothing could stop me now until my appointed time.

One week left. The punishment had reached its zenith, but the fittest had survived. We could not be vanquished, and The Pig had attained his grand objective. The end was nigh at hand, and we who had prevailed felt a powerful camaraderie. Nakamura was like a brother—frank, sometimes outspoken, courageous, yet also highly empathic. How I admired him. Oka and Yamamoto invariably lifted our spirits. Irrepressible, they always rallied, seeming to take strength from each other, then imparting it to the rest of us, even in the face of disaster. *Gokudo*—great pranksters, both of them—the ultimate extroverts.

By now, strangely enough, some of the punishment itself had become humorous. Occasionally, when our *hancho* were in their more mischievous moods, they would put us through routines that were far more ludicrous than painful. One of Sakigawa's favorites was to have a recruit climb atop his wall locker where he would squat, legs crossed, arms folded like a meditative Buddah. He was then expected to maintain that position while one, sometimes two, *hancho* shook the locker violently, jarring and teetering it erratically with greater and greater energy. All this to the accompaniment of loud, almost deafening, metallic clanging and raucous laughter from everyone present. Sooner or later the hapless recruit would tumble to the floor, and anyone not agile enough by now to light on his feet was offered no pity and spared no scorn.

Occasionally also we were ordered to climb a tree near our barracks. We then had to roost there for ten or fifteen minutes, making high-pitched humming sounds like those of a cicada. This undertaking, like the preceding one was not only amusing to our *hancho* but also to the rest of us. I remember especially Oka laughing hysterically and slapping his leg while Yamamoto hummed piercingly away in the branches above.

"*Ah so!*" The Snake growled, unable to stifle his own laughter, and the cuff was half hearted. "If you like it that much, you'd better try it yourself." Oka promptly went up the tree like a squirrel, then perched near Yamamoto, wildly trying to out-hum him. It was indeed hilarious, and those unable to contain their laughter were also ordered up the tree. Soon the branches were clustered with recruits, myself included, all emitting the weirdest sound I have ever heard.

And now, as the end drew nigh our punishment diminished. Our initial trial by fire was over, and it was also rumored that the base commander wanted us to look hearty and healthy during our coming leave.

Remarkably, The Pig—*Hancho* Noguchi—whom many of us had sworn to kill, invited the men from the most outstanding barracks to his home in Kure for a *sukiyaki* dinner! Remarkably also, that barracks was my own! What a weird reversal! The man we had most dreaded, the man who had been largely responsible for our constant fear and misery, for the suicide of nine of our comrades, was now honoring us in his very home. We were respected guests!

Noguchi's wife was surprisingly young and very lovely—a perfect hostess—and his two children, a boy and girl, ages five and seven, were charming. For nearly two hours we sat there on the *tatami* around a large, oval table while his wife filled our bowls again and again with her cuisine or replenished our *sake* cups.

Throughout it all, The Pig chatted pleasantly, occasionally cracking jokes at which we laughed most dutifully. Vainly I strove to comprehend this strange turn of events, the man's new persona. For once he seemed perfectly genuine, and in none of his conversation could I detect the faintest sarcasm or sinister nuance.

When The Pig spoke of punishment, he addressed us as if we were confidantes who not only empathized but fully concurred. Wiping his mouth politely and sipping his *sake*, he confided "In one respect it is unfortunate that our trainees must undergo such duress. However—" His sigh seemed one of honest regret. "I myself have no recourse but to obey our commanding officer, while he, in turn, must obey those above him. And so it goes all the way to our Imperial Military Headquarters, to the *Daihonei*. The very foundation of a successful military operation is obedience, all along the chain of command."

Pausing, he glanced down obliquely across his cheek bones, thrusting his chin out truculently. "Loyalty! Performance of one's duty! No matter how formidable the requirement may appear. Even to the forfeiting of life itself. Indeed, the forfeiting of life becomes our grand and ultimate privilege."

All of us nodded sagely. Then, in a somewhat lighter tone, he recurred to his earlier reflections regarding chain of command: "The *Diahonei* becomes unhappy with their commanding officers and reprimands them, the commanding officers become unhappy with those under them and do the same. And so it goes, on down to the *hancho* and non-coms. The *hancho* take it out on their trainees . . . and what do the poor trainees do, Kuwahara?" Firing an unexpected glance my way, he actually winked! I grinned bemusedly, shaking my head. "The trainee goes home on leave and kicks his dog!" he explained.

The Pig slapped his thigh, laughing uproariously, and the rest of us joined in. His beautiful wife tittered, a sound of enchantment, and glanced down shyly, placing a tiny, exquisite hand to her mouth. "So. . . ." he continued chewing a mouthful of *sukiyaki* rigorously and swilling in half a cup of *sake* to wash it down. "So, my friends, obviously punishment is indispensable. Indispensable! It is the oil that makes the machinery work." Another great mouthful with the chop sticks, another draught of *sake*. I was beginning to understand, in more ways than one, how The Pig had acquired his name.

"Sad to say, very few are born with the true spirit of *Yamato*. His eyebrows leapt, eyeballs swelling in mock amazement. "Ah hah! Does that disturb you?" Noguchi continued to devour his food for some time without further comment, and it appeared that he had lost his trend of thought. But not so. "You acquire that spirit! You earn the *samurai* spirit through much hardship! By responding to that hardship with grand and glorious fortitude, until ultimately you attain. . . ." The dramatic pause this time was most marvelous to behold, extraordinarily impressive.

"Invincibility!"

The word was like a thunder clap, a revelation, and suddenly the blood in my veins had turned to liquid fire. "So now," he continued very quietly. "Have I been cruel to my *shinpei*!" Or have I rendered them an inestimable service?" For a long time he stared into the dark, lacquered surface of the table, lips pursed in profound introspection. What he sought there, what he might descry, I did not know.

Then to my utter and ultimate astonishment, I detected a tiny drop of moisture coursing down his cheek. A tear? Could that possibly be so? Or merely a drop of sweat? The night was exceptionally warm and humid. "You must be the judge." His voice was scarcely audible. "The manner in which you answer that question will determine your future . . . your destiny."

Noguchi discussed the matter no further that evening. Instead, he spoke of philosophy, poetry, of music. His home was filled with books, also what appeared to be costly paintings, and he expatiated upon a wide variety of subjects with impressive ease and insight. His wife then graciously played the *koto*, singing in a quivering, haunting, at times exquisitely lyrical, voice that caused my skin to tingle. First, the popular *Kojo-no-tsuki* then an ancient song I had never heard before.

There in that dimly lit room, the flowers on her *kimono* seemed to glow with enchantment and mystery, and the shadows on her face and hands had turned to quiet green. Half closing my lids, I watched the curve of her cheek, the delicate nostrils, how her brow vanished in the ebon flow of her hair. By squinting, I could make her hair blend with the darkness, leaving only the face, the moving lips, and line of her neck.

Glancing at the others, I realized that they too were spellbound. I watched the woman's graceful fingers moving along the *koto* strings as it lay on the table before her like the coffin of a young child. And by wishing very hard, I could obliterate everyone else in the room. Noguchi, my comrades . . . all gone. Now we were alone together, and soon, I would draw close, looking into those liquid eyes. And when the songs had faded, she would slowly gaze at me, her face full of sorrow and immense longing, of tender inquiry. Then . . . then, her lips would flow and arch in welcome, barely exposing the white of her teeth. Her hand, her heavenly hand, would reach out across the still-vibrant strings of the *koto* to touch my own, and the intonations would blend within us.

But now, the music had ended. It was time to go, and we were bowing to The Pig, our gracious host, thanking him profusely . . . bowing, bowing. His wife, in turn, was bowing to us, laughing with the shrill, tinkling notes of a little girl, notes that were also ripe and womanly. Her laughter was not of amusement but rather the laughter of graciousness. Again, she acknowledged each of us with a bow as we filed out—each of us exactly the same.

She was unaware of how close I had sat beside her, how she had reached out to me when no one else was there.

Chapter Ten

A Brief Reunion

S o now, at last, my basic training was over. On the one hand it seemed that time had evaporated, as though I had only arrived a few days ago. On the other, in light of all that had happened, it seemed that I had been at Hiro for a great while, an entire year at least.

More importantly, one way or another, I had done it. They had not broken me. At times they had come close, admittedly, but somehow I had clung on through worse trials than I could have previously imagined. I had prevailed.

On the morning our leave commenced, Hiro's Commanding Officer assembled us on the parade ground for a brief graduation address. He spoke quite generously of our accomplishments, what we had learned and why. We had been drilled daily in the basics of combat, and we were no longer the timid, whimpering juveniles of the first few weeks. We could withstand pain, and now we could not be defeated in battle without great difficulty. It was, he admitted, unfortunate that some had died, but those deaths had served a good purpose, all been part of the grand design to toughen the rest of us. Those deaths had also helped us to realize that the weakest were always the most expendable.

A light mist was lacing the base that morning, but as our commander spoke, it dispersed, revealing the rising sun. The rising sun! Surely it was an omen. Our commander was a small man, but vigilant and intense, like a finely honed razor, and his entire bearing reflected confidence and power. Each gesture was unique, memorable, emphatic.

We watched as the sun gathered about him, gleaming from the eagle insignias upon the visor of his cap and upon his lapels. When he had finished, fifty basic trainees chanted the main precepts of the Imperial Rescript without error. As our words poured forth I could hear the throb of planes in the distance—the two sounds merging and expanding, a symbol of our new-found strength. Suddenly I was part of something grand, something of immense and indescribable significance. There in the rising sun, I knew that the Imperial Way would not fail. I knew that it was destined to encompass the earth.

So now, it was over. I was returning to Onomichi on my two-day leave before flying school. My family and several friends were gathered at the train station for the long-awaited welcome. "Toshifumi will be here this evening to see you!" Tomika babbled joyfully.

"Toshifumi? All the way from Tokyo, just to see me?" I exclaimed.

"Well, perhaps your brother will at least say hello to the rest of us," Father said. That was the closest he ever came to levity, and we all laughed heartily. Life at that moment was too good to be real. Two whole days, blessed days, with my family, my relatives, my friends. And upon my return to Hiro, it would not be as a green and helpless *shinpei*. I would be prepared.

Our home had never looked so beautiful. It was nearing the end of April, and the cherry trees in our back yard were blossoming—everywhere throughout the entire area, tiny celestial explosions of white blossoms. The garden walls were wreathed in multi-colored azaleas, and the fields were turning bright green. It was difficult to believe that we were at war, under attack, and that soon I would be a participant.

Upon entering the house, I visited briefly with my family, talked in general, rather evasively, about life at Hiro. Then I headed for the bath. Minutes later I was seated on a short-legged stool in the *yudono* vigorously soaping myself when Tomika called to me outside the door. "Brother," her voice chimed, "Do you want to have your back washed?"

"Yes!" I called. It seemed more fitting than ever that a woman should wash my back now. After all, I had become a man. I hunched over, hugging my knees as she entered, exposing only my rounded back. What occurred next was totally unexpected.

Tomika gasped, crying out. "Yasuo, what have they done to your back?" I had momentarily forgotten about the lash marks, but it was good to have her make something of the matter.

"Oh, that's nothing at all. Those are merely reminders of a little game we learned," I replied.

Unfortunately, my words were not to be passed off so lightly, and I had not anticipated their full effect. Concern, certainly, but my sister softly traced her fingers over the wounds then burst into tears. "My brother, my own little brother!" she wept.

"Tomika, I'm all right," I insisted. "Stop crying, it's all right!" The weeping continued. "Stop, I can barely even feel them. I hardly even flinched when they——" The wrong words, and I had cut them off too late. Tears flowing down her cheeks, Tomika stumbled into the adjoining alcove and cast herself onto the *tatami* wailing.

Hearing the commotion, Mother rushed into the room with an expression of great alarm. "What's wrong?" she exclaimed.

"It's nothing Mother," I replied, almost angrily. "Just a few sores on my back." Mother cautioned Tomika to be silent, peered in at me in shocked silence. Upon entering, she began soaping my back very gently. Then she scooped a little water from the steaming bath with the wooden dipper and cautiously poured a small amount on one shoulder.

"*Atsui?*" she asked.

"*Hai*" I admitted, "a little hot," and caught my breath as the water trickled down my back into the drain. The scars were still very new and tender, a blend of pink and gray-blue, the color of earthworms.

Gently mother laid a scented towel over my back, pouring the water through it with even greater care. "All right? Better?"

"*Hai!*" I nodded, "much better. It was a procedure she had followed many times before when I was a child, and it brought me great comfort.

By now Tomika had regained her composure, but her cheeks still glistened. "I'm sorry," she murmured. "It was just that——"

"I understand," Mother intoned. "Everything's going to be all right. Just be very careful, getting into the bath, Yasuo. It may be too much for those tender, sore areas." A tear sparkled in her own eye. Shortly thereafter they left me to my bath. "Just be very careful getting in," Mother repeated.

Cleansed and rinsed, restored to complete privacy for the first time since I had departed that winter, I eased into the waiting cauldron. I gasped as the water accosted my first lash mark. The scar seemed to writhe and cry out with a life of its own, almost renewing the pain of its origin. But, after all, I told myself, I had learned to withstand much worse trials, and I refused to be denied my bath. It was something I had dreamed of almost every night after our punishment was over.

Grimacing, and gritting my teeth, I lowered myself with utmost care, inch by inch, lash by lash, feeling the pain renew itself then dissipate. Eventually, after several minutes, I was in up to my neck, the pain ebbing, replaced by pleasure . . . bliss, euphoria. Langorous . . . exhausted beyond measure, I entered my own little nirvana.

Half an hour later, I emerged, barely able to drag myself from the water, lying there for a time, half in half out, as the cold floor restored reality. Weakly, I dried myself, donned my *yukata* and slippers and shuffled up the stairs to my room. For a moment I gazed from my window at the mountains. My eyelids closed as I kneeled there, clinging to the window ledge. I blinked, seeing a great gyrating flight of starlings, light glittering along their wings. Or was it merely dancing spots, a visual aberration, or hallucination?

No matter. My family and friends were gathering, and there was so much to say and do. So little time. But not now, for I was barely able to crawl beneath the *futon*, barely able to feel its caressing warmth, its infinite softness and lightness. Sleep was a dark and slowly whirling vortex that carried me irresistibly downward.

When I revived, the sun was beginning its descent, infusing my room with gold For a while I lay there blinking, yawned and stretched. The gold welled, achingly beautiful, and unexpectedly, without the slightest forewarning, I began to sob.

An instant later I heard my door glide partly open on its rollers. No mistaking Tomika's excited whispers, but who was with her? Someone. Wiping my eyes against the *futon*, I bolted upright. And there he was, handsome and smiling, his hand on Tomika's shoulder, a mischievous glint in his eye. "Toshifumi!" I cried. "You came! All the way from Tokyo!" I greatly hoped that he could not detect the moisture in my eyes.

Grinning more broadly, he squatted beside me and roughed my head. "Hello, *hage channu,*" he said, referring to my ragged, close-cropped hair. "So now . . ." He was eyeing me quizzically, "You've changed. You're almost a man."

The word "almost" hurt, even made me a trifle angry, but I beamed back. "I hope so," I said. Toshifumi again, after two whole years. He was not the same person who had so often grappled and cavorted with our brother Shigeru before the war. Now, dignified and handsome with a hawk-like profile, he looked more like father than ever. There was even a faint white streak in his hair—rare for a Japanese his age.

Following a brief visit, he went downstairs, leaving me to dress. An hour or so later my uncle and aunt arrived from Innoshima. My return was becoming quite an event, and despite the scarcity of food, Mother and Tomika had prepared a feast with all my favorite delicacies.

How touched I was by their devotion. Again, I struggled to restrain the tears. Never before had I felt such emotional fragility. In 1944, food was heavily rationed, and Mother and Tomika had walked two or three miles into the country the day before my return to obtain whole, polished rice from a farmer—a precious commodity which he refused to relinquish for mere money. Instead, Tomika had given him one of the beautiful and costly *kimono* which was to have been a part of her dowry. Then they had trudged all the way home, carrying the bags of rice on their backs.

An exceptional act of devotion, and I thanked them most earnestly. When I mentioned Tomika's sacrifice she smiled and replied. "It is nothing, nothing at all. Anyway, by the time a man takes me for his wife I will have accumulated dozens of *kimono*"

"Oh come now!" Toshifumi chuckled, trapping a small pickle with his chop sticks and popping it into his mouth. 'There are plenty of men who would be elated to have you. Just wait!"

Tomika smiled wistfully, and her gaze fled to her lap. "I am waiting," she said, "and I am already twenty-six years old."

"Tomika shall have a husband in due course," Father declared and proceeded with his food. "When we find one worthy—one of proper station." He chewed methodically, sipped his tea. "But I refuse to consider that fawning . . . ah, what's his name? For one thing, his gestures are effeminate in the extreme. I find them highly exasperating. Furthermore, his voice—"

"Must you humiliate your daughter before our relatives?" Mother chided. Her words reflected much courage, but before Father could reply, Tomika arose, hiding her burning face, making swift little steps toward the door.

"Tomika, come back here!" Father commanded. "I merely speak the truth—don't be so touchy."

After a moment Tomika returned and sat staring at her plate.

This was hardly the mood I had hoped for, and for the first time I actually felt vexed with my father. It was not my place to speak out, however, so I changed the subject. "By the way, where is Reiko?" I inquired.

"Oh, we had to let her go," Mother answered quietly. She smiled at my aunt and uncle a bit ruefully. "Well, I mean it just seemed an extravagance with the war going on and on like this . . . and only the three of us at home now."

"Yasuo," my uncle said, "why don't you share some of your experiences at Hiro with us? How did you like your training?"

I hesitated. "My training. . . ." I groped for words.

"My training was . . . challenging—highly educational." Something of an understatement, of course, and everyone laughed as though we all shared an amusing secret.

Afterward, while our women attended to work in the kitchen and their own private concerns, the rest of us talked further of my training, of the war, the military experiences of my father and uncle, of Toshifumi's dental practice in Tokyo.

That evening when my relatives had departed I received a visit from Tatsuno. During our separation he had sent me two letters, neither of which I had answered. Obviously, there had been little opportunity for such things, but I certainly could have sent him a brief note. Somehow, though, each time I considered doing so something had stopped me. Probably it stemmed from my feeling that Tatsuno, despite his courage, was too sensitive for such an environment. He seemed too much like poor Miyagame, the recruit who had hanged himself in the latrine.

Nevertheless, he would soon be there and would have already arrived had he not torn the ligaments in his arm during a glider training mishap at school. Consequently, I felt obliged to offer him some advice. "It will be very hard," I confessed, but remember that the first two months are the toughest, so start getting in condition right now. The stronger you are the easier it will be."

"*Hai!*" he exclaimed and nodded vigorously.

"Seriously," I said, "it will make a big difference. As soon as your arm's better, start doing push-ups. Do them about five times a day and build up to at least fifty each set. And how's your endurance? If you can double-time three or four miles when you go in, that will help a lot too." I then stressed the importance of being respectful to his *hancho* and avoiding actions that would attract unnecessary attention.

"Remember not to make any noise no matter what when they hit you in the rear with a ball bat, or you'll just get more. And don't move. Just cling onto the rail and grit your teeth. And when they start to slam your face against the wall, just tilt your head forward a little. Not so it's noticeable, though, or they'll do it again twice as hard. "Just do it a little," I persisted. That way you'll get a bump on your forehead, but it won't mangle your nose and mouth very much. And another thing . . . tell everybody in your barracks to write home and warn their families not to bring them special treats when they come to visit. If even one recruit gets something and tries to hide it, believe me, your *hancho* will find out, and there will be serious trouble."

I decided to avoid the details, for suddenly Tatsuno's face was gray. "I'm sorry," I said, and felt guilty. On the other hand, I'd have felt far more guilty had I failed to prepare him in some measure. "You'll get through it all right," I assured him, trying hard to believe my own words. "Just take it one day at a time." I shrugged. "After all, what about me? Don't I look all right?"

"You look terrific," he said. His tone sounded slightly envious. "But your face has quite a few sores and scars."

"A few," I admitted, "but I'm perfectly all right, and if I can make it through and come out this well, so can you. Besides, when we're flying those fighter planes we'll be tough as *sumo* wrestlers."

Tatsuno laughed. "But not as big and fat."

"Right—lean and hard, muscles from our toes to our nose! Seriously, we'll be ready for anything."

Tatsuno's smile became mournful, the expression in his eyes uncertain. "Yasuo," he said, "remember how we used to dream of flying together—fighter pilots, in the same squadron?"

"Of course," I said, "and we will."

Tatsuno shook his head. "I doubt it. You're already too far ahead of me."

"Well, we might not end up in the same squadron," I admitted, "but we'll both be flying—that's what matters most."

Again he shook his head. "Yasuo," he said, "I'm afraid. I really wonder whether I can make it through that first three months."

"You'll make it," I insisted. "Don't you think I was afraid at first. Everybody is; I don't care who. And three months seems like a long time in the beginning, but now I can't believe where it's gone. "You'll make it through as well or better than I did. Then before you know it, you'll be in fighter school."

"It sounds good," he said.

"It is good," I persisted. "Besides, we've always been a winning team, haven't we? We'll be flying together yet, Tatsu-*kun*, I can feel it."

"I hope so," he said. "Well, I'd better let you get back to your family."

He gave me a pat on the shoulder and I clasped his forearm. "Thanks for coming, *tomodachi*." I said. "You're my best friend ever."

"*Arigato,*" he said, "the same to you," and started down the stairs. "See you later."

"Right," I nodded. "In the morning. I'll be coming by the school."

The sudden attention of family, relatives and friends was most gratifying, and I was fast becoming a hero. During my first day at home I had uttered all the patriotic platitudes that were expected. I had felt a powerful surge of determination and courage, and I was viewing the hell of basic in a different light.

Later that night, having talked again at length with Father and Toshifumi, I went to my room tingling with pride and elation. From my open window, I gazed at the rising moon. It hung there in the sky as it had the night of my first departure—evanescent and faintly glowing like a thin, silver bracelet. As I lay back and drifted off to sleep, Hiro seemed very remote, strangely unreal. For the moment I was totally at peace.

The following morning my school friends greeted me as though I had already performed deeds of great valor. Daily before classes a general assembly was held in the auditorium. During my visit, however, the announcements were dispensed with, and I was asked to address the students. The thought of speaking extemporaneously was frightening, but several insistent teachers ushered me forward amid much loud cheering and laughter.

To my surprise, I spoke rather easily for about ten minutes. I never mentioned The Pig, *taiko binta*, the deserters, or suicides. One simply did not refer to such things in public. Instead, I described the rigors of combat training, of the great conditioning, and talked of the classwork. I spoke of our divine heritage as sons and daughters of *Nippon*, of our future, and of the obligation of all able-bodied young men to serve their country. Closing, I bowed to a rousing ovation.

Our weathered old principal Hori-*kacho* then addressed us briefly in his familiar, quavering voice as follows: "This school is honored and proud to have helped mold such outstanding citizens. We will follow Yasuo Kuwahara's future accomplishments with constant interest, and we will all rejoice as he continues to discharge his sacred obligation to our Emperor and to the glorious nation of *Nippon*. May all of you here today note with care his stellar example and follow in his path."

I left Onomichi High School unaware that my next and only return would be under very different circumstances.

The remainder of that day I visited a few friends, one of whom was soon to enter the marines. Then I spent the final hours with my family, and we spoke for some time about my brother Shigeru. No word from him for weeks, and our concern was increasing. As a captain in the counter-intelligence in Java, he could reveal little regarding his work. A few months earlier, however, one of his rare messages indicated that he was well but also concluded as follows: "If you should not hear from me again, I will await your visit to the *Yasukuni Jinja*"—the national shrine for Japan's military dead.

Shortly after supper we saw Toshifumi off on his train for Tokyo. My leave had vanished with inconceivable speed. I had barely found time to relax and breathe normally, and now it was over. Just before midnight I bid Tomika and Mother *sayonara*—for the third time in three months. Even though I was returning with greater confidence, the anxiety was mounting again, and I concluded that farewells never become much easier.

Father accompanied me to the station where, to my amazement, a crowd of some two hundred and fifty students were awaiting me, a brass band playing. Shouts arose at our approach, and a cordon of friends pressed in to clasp my hand and offer their best wishes. Father had never looked more proud.

I was also presented with gifts including the school pendant and several autographed flags of Japan. Some of those students had actually cut their own fingers and signed their names with blood in a token of eternal friendship. I was to wear these mementos as scarves into battle, and now only minutes remained.

"Well," I said and glanced at the train nervously. "Maybe I'd better. . . ."

"Yasuo!" someone called. It was Tatsuno, there on the crowd's fringe, wriggling toward me. In a moment we were clasping each other like brothers. "I'll be seeing you soon, Tatsuno-*kun*," I said. "Don't forget what I told you."

"Speech, Kuwahara, speech!" someone bellowed, and several others chimed in.

"I gave my speech already," I told them. "This morning!"

"Yes, but we need one now!" The band was playing "Light of The Firefly"—a bit blatantly and off key, but it brought back a tide of memories, and my eyes began to smart. Watching their smiling faces, I mumbled, "I hope many of you will follow me. Until then–*sayonara*."

The conductor's voice was a plaintive, nasal twang, sounding departure amid the flurry of good byes from my friends. Moments later the train was click-clacking toward Hiro, gaining momentum, and I was still hearing my father's parting admonition: "In all things be sure to conduct yourself with honor, my son. Remember now that your life is no longer your own. If you should ever fall into dishonor, do not return to bring unhappiness and shame upon us. Live proudly, fight gloriously. Should you die . . . I will have a grave prepared." Gripping my hand fiercely and gazing into my eyes, he inquired, "Do you know my heart?"

As the train tunneled onward into the night I watched my own reflection in the window— a transparent ghost of myself through which I could see the receding lights of town. Suddenly I felt a profound need to remember everything, to lodge somewhere in my mind and heart a picture of the past. Family, friends, places . . . the ocean on a wintry day, fishermen with their nets, the sunlight and lofting winds of Mt. Ikoma, greening rice fields, the moon balanced upon our trellis, and the smell of azaleas. All that and much more—a poignant need to store it all away in some special place, safe from the ravages of war and the erosion of time.

PART THREE

Chapter Eleven

The Praying Mantis

Flying school, as I had anticipated, was much better than basic training, although the punishment and arduous conditioning continued. We had formed friendships and were hardened both physically and mentally. I was elated to discover that all the survivors from our original group were assigned to another four-section barracks together. Each section housed fifteen men as before, but our quarters were somewhat better, and we lived on a separate part of the base near the pilots.

Although most of our airmen were not much older than the rest of us, we regarded them as a proud, audacious lot and with a certain awe. Daily we watched their flight performances with excitement and admiration. They were the ultimate warriors, the eagles who, above all others, would lead us to victory.

We were now designated the Fourth Squadron, and the first stage of our six-month course involved an intensive study of aeronautics. We also began learning to parachute. We did not begin flying, however, for three months, and then only in a small biplane called the *Akatombo* (Red Dragonfly) with cockpits for both the instructor and student.

Unfortunately our new *hancho* were just as harsh and cruel as The Pig and his cohorts had been. Rentaro Namoto, our first sergeant and flight instructor, was called The Praying Mantis because of his lean, insectivorous appearance and vicious nature. Unlike that of The Pig, his personality had few dimensions. He rarely joked or laughed and was by very nature, it seemed, unlikable. Nevertheless, he possessed remarkable skill and cunning. Nearly six feet tall, with a supple whip-like body, Sergeant Namoto was the coldest, most calculating man I had ever encountered. When he inflicted punishment it was devoid of all outward emotion, every movement methodical and precise like that of a robot.

During most of our basic training we had been utterly bewildered and terrified. The sudden insecurity of being wrenched from our families, the fear of the unknown, the softness of our minds and bodies, the constant pain, anxiety, and humiliation had made life an almost-incessant nightmare.

Now, however, we were undergoing a metamorphosis. Very surreptitiously at first, we began striking back at our tyrants. Few crimes are greater in the military, especially the Japanese military, than disobedience, or outright defiance in particular. Such things automatically incurred severe retribution if not destruction. Open disobedience or defiance, in fact, had terrible implications and not only meant that one was insulting his immediate superiors but also his commanding officer, the *Diahonei* in Tokyo—indeed, ultimately even the Emperor himself.

Subtle misdeeds, on the other hand, were viewed somewhat differently, perhaps because they were more consistent with the covert and cunning elements of our general makeup. Although never acknowledged openly, our chicanery with The Mantis developed into a kind of game which ultimately he always managed to win.

Our first efforts in that regard occurred one day before evening chow, just after we had been required to perform the "low crawl", wriggling along on our bellies, across three hundred yards of hot airstrip. As the KP was carrying Namoto's evening meal to his quarters, Oka called out softly, "*yai*, Furuhashi, wait up! We have some special seasoning for our leader's rice!"

"What?" Furuhashi glanced back nervously. "Hey, you'd better not do anything," he protested as we approached. "Look now, don't do that. Hey, don't—don't"! Do you want to get us all killed?"

"He'll never know a thing," Nakamura insisted, "if you'd just stop squealing like a stuck pig for a minute." By now, all of us were taking turns vigorously massaging and scratching our scalps over the steaming bowl of rice. Despite the KP's terrified protests we managed to deposit a large quantity of dandruff in the bowl. "Now," Nakamura patted his forlorn shoulder, "mix the seasoning in well. This is our special gift to The Mantis because we all love him so dearly." Reluctantly, the KP went on his way, shaking his head and muttering a few appropriate curses.

Secluding ourselves, we watched him enter The Mantis' room. A few seconds later he returned empty handed. "Is he eating his rice like a good boy?" I asked.

"Yes, yes, yes!" the KP muttered and stalked back toward the chow hall.

"Hey, does he really like it?" Oka called from the barracks doorway. "Did he kiss your lovely little hand?"

"Go screw yourself!" the KP growled.

Truly, this was a splendid way of retaliating. It didn't matter to us that The Mantis was unaware of his humiliation. The important fact existed that he was being humiliated. His ignorance of such indignity only made it better. That way also there would be no reprisal, or so we hoped.

Our first rice seasoning escapade had been so successful, in fact, that we determined to follow the same procedure regularly. Almost every evening we seasoned Namoto's supper in like manner, and before long Oka ingeniously suggested that we mix in a little of our excrement for variety. Yamamoto agreed but maintained that we try urine first since, presumably, it would be less detectable. We were seriously considering those recommendations when something unexpected happened.

Moriyama, another KP, became especially nervous one evening when nearly a dozen of us approached him for the standard dandruff application. "All of you can't put your dandruff in the rice," he moaned. "The Mantis will notice it. Why don't we forget about the whole thing for a while? This is really getting dangerous, and you're pressing your luck."

"Oh yes," Nakamura said, "since it's your turn at KP, why don't we just forget about it for a while. We'll all be taking our turn, so don't be a spineless jelly fish."

"I'm no more jelly fish than you are," Moriyama countered angrily. "I'm just not as stupid." Eventually, however, after much cajolery, he capitulated. "But come on now," he whined, "not all of you—you'll flood the bowl over."

"No, no, we need everybody," Oka declared. "Some of us are running low on dandruff." This to the accompaniment of much half-smothered laughter, and the first man proceeded to make his offering. "Next!" he said briskly, and I stepped forward, each of the others following suit.

"Now mix it in, Moriyama," I advised, "if you don't our friend will know."

"Mix it with what?" he asked. "I've got to hurry or he'll be coming out here to see what's happening."

"Use your fingers, naturally," someone said.

Reluctantly, Moriyama began to probe with his fingers. "God, this is hot!" he complained.

"Brave *samurai*," Yamamoto said, "be a brave, brave *samurai*."

Again Moriyama complied. "Now, what do I wipe them with?"

"Just lick them off," Yamamoto said, "That's the quickest way."

Again, he complied, or at least began to. Suddenly, he stopped, fingers only an inch from his extended tongue as though frozen, and again we shook with strangled laughter. Moriyama appeared to be on the verge of vomiting. "*Bakayaro!*" he cursed then went his way like a man expecting the firing squad.

With the door to Namoto's room slightly ajar, we listened intently, pressing close to the wall just outside. Moriyama had apparently turned to leave when The Mantis spoke, his words resonating harshly. "Kindly wait one minute, my friend."

"Yes, honorable *honcho-dono*" Moriyama quavered.

A long silence then ensued, but finally the dreaded voice spoke again: "This rice—it stinks. What makes it so putrid and oily? It stinks like hell! Where did you get it, from the latrine?"

"Let's get out of here!" someone warned, "before it's too late." A moment later we heard a crash and then what sounded like a blow, perhaps a terrific boot in the rear.

"Quick, outside!" I hissed as Moriyama stumbled out the door, the remains of Namoto's feast plastering the back of his head, dribbling down his neck and face.

"We're in for it now!" Moriyama gasped. "He'll skin us all alive."

This time no one argued. Instead, we fled to our barracks and waited out the night in great anxiety. To our growing astonishment, however, nothing happened until the following morning. Namoto's response, in fact, was far less virulent than we had anticipated though certainly more ingenious.

It was reveille formation, and we stood stiffly at attention, perhaps even holding our breath, as The Mantis surveyed us all thoughtfully. A flight of fighter planes was circling overhead, coming in to land a short distance off. "It appears. . . ." He spoke in loud, high-pitched tones, penetrating the sound of their motors. "It appears. . . ." Again his words were obliterated as the first fighter arched by with a ferocious roar and began its final descent. "Eyes straight ahead!" The plane landed with a lurch and screech of rubber. "Doesn't know how to handle it very well, does he?"

For a moment it seemed as though he were simply talking to himself. "As I was saying," he continued, "it appears that some of you men have become concerned about my health." Another pause while the next plane headed in. "You have been supplementing my diet. Maybe you think I too skinny—na?" He paused, eyeing us calculatingly. "In any case, even though I am doing well, I want you to know that I appreciate your kindness. Of course, it is only natural to love your instructors. When I was a trainee, we loved our instructors. We were concerned about their health just as you are "

Oka made a strange little noise like a spurt of air from a valve. "Shhh!" I hissed.

The Mantis appeared to take no notice. "However, you may put your minds at ease. We instructors are well fed, and there is no need for concern. As a matter of fact last night, when our KP brought my dinner, I wasn't even hungry. I actually gave it all back to him." I glanced at Oka and Yamamoto from the corners of my eyes and realized that they were struggling desperately to avoid laughing. "Terribly sloppy eater, though." They both wheezed, and I began to pray that they would be able to contain themselves. "So!" He raised a rapier-like forefinger. To demonstrate my appreciation for your kindness, I wish to propose a toast, *Hancho* Kitamura! *Hancho* Mukai!" Two *hancho* hastened among us distributing *sake* cups, and we watched in growing amazement as they proceeded to fill them from a gigantic blue bottle. "Be at ease!" Namoto instructed. "Wonderful Awamore *sake* all the way from Okinawa!"

We were all dumbfounded. Could this possibly be an actual salute to our cleverness? Our ingenuity? "*Dozo*, fine," The Mantis observed. "So now I propose a toast to all of you, to the men of the Fourth Squadron. *Kampai!*"

"*Kampai*—bottoms up!" we cried in unison. "To the men of the Fourth Squadron!" We downed our drinks as one, and it took a few moments for us to realize what had happened. Each man's mouth had turned dark blue. The awful-tasting elixir was ink.

For a while we played no more tricks. Tatsuno had arrived at Hiro and was undergoing the hell of early basic, living in the same barracks that I had. Fortunately, he had known quite clearly what to expect and had prepared himself as well as possible, but on our rare encounters I continued to offer advice.

One night I was quietly conversing with Tatsuno outside his quarters when The Pig passed us carrying two of his beloved ball bats. For a moment I didn't think he had noticed me, but upon leaning his bats against the wall, he turned back and remarked, "*Ah so?*" The mighty Kuwahara has returned." Then he glanced at Tatsuno. "You see how attached these men become to their first home away from home? They can't stay away—right, Kuwahara?" He actually gave my shoulder a friendly pat as he entered the barracks.

"*Hai*, honorable *hancho-dono!*" I called. I no longer hated The Pig and even felt a minor thrill at being recognized and worthy of his attention.

"Looks as if we're going to get some more of the fighting spirit," Tatsuno observed wryly. "I'd better go in."

"No, stay outside a minute," I said. "If he herds them out now there won't even be a roll call. It's not even eight o'clock, and he won't notice whether you're missing." Tatsuno was understandably fearful, but I suggested that he follow me behind some shrubbery a short distance away.

"If they start calling the roll," I advised, "we can hear them. You can just walk up and get into the rear of the formation."

Still dubious, he relaxed a bit, and we strolled back to sit down behind the bushes. Moments later, to our surprise, The Pig emerged from the barracks and headed for his quarters. "There goes the strangest man I have ever known," I said. We remained there conversing until nearly time for *Shoto Rappa*, then parted. "Maybe they won't even harass you tonight," I added.

"I hope so," Tatsuno replied. "I hope The Mantas and his friends won't harass *you*." That was the last we saw of each other for some time.

My first three months of flight school raced by far more rapidly than basic training, largely because I was learning to fly. At last, at last, I was actually training in a power-driven aircraft. I will never forget those first days in the *Akatombo*, and I took to the new trainers as readily as I had to the gliders. I had studied aeronautics zealously, and at times The Mantis or one of the other instructors warned me against being too eager. So thoroughly had I familiarized myself with the instrument panel, the entire flight operation, I secretly felt that I could take off and land unassisted my first time in the cockpit.

During my hours in the air, watching the earth transform voluptuously beneath me, I felt an exhilaration and power that dispelled all the unpleasant and painful associations of the past. Fear, unhappiness, and frustration all receded earthward as I became at one with the sky. Nothing could harm me in that new and magic domain. It was mine, and I belonged there.

Our hours on the ground were a vivid contrast. Steadily, relentlessly, The Mantis and his cohorts poured on the punishment. Because it took more to break us, he gave more, and the anger and bitterness were mounting. Several men threatened to kill him, and someone even managed to procure poison, planning to place it in his food. Nakamura considered the idea quite amusing, insisting that since our dandruff had failed to kill him, nothing could. Fortunately for all of us, those in favor of it were finally dissuaded after much heated argument.

The Mantis had a large whip which he cracked at the slightest provocation. He handled it with admirable finesse, and with little exertion often inflicted excruciating pain. One day after several of us had received a lashing we gathered behind an empty warehouse to concoct more retaliation. Everyone knew by now that The Mantis went to town each night where he drank heavily and often caroused with prostitutes. It was said that he could consume alcohol endlessly and still only become mildly intoxicated. Furthermore, according to one of the fighter pilots, he was a satyr supreme who performed incredible sexual feats, whose fire was never quenched. All this, of course, seemed to contradict our image of that fish-cold, metal-eyed individual with whom we had to cope each day.

Every evening Namoto left for town at seven or eight o'clock. Then, about midnight he returned, weaving his way along the hall and crunching on down the short flight of stairs to his room at the end of the barracks.

Thus originated our plan, and we awaited its realization one night with much interest. As midnight approached we were poised tensely in our own quarters listening for the sound of his arrival. An hour passed, and we drifted in and out of sleep, assuming at last that he would not return until morning.

Eventually, though, the door banged, and footsteps echoed down the hall followed shortly by a resounding crash. Every man in the barracks was undoubtedly wide awake, tense and listening but also highly gratified. The taut rope we had stretched across the stairway only a few inches above the floor had done its job.

The next morning The Mantis appeared at formation with a bandage across his nose. Never cracking a smile as usual, he paced back and forth before us, hands clasped behind his back, trailing his whip like a great rat tail. At length he faced the formation and spoke. "I am pleased to note that some of you are such practical jokers. A good sense of humor is often very refreshing." All of the Fourth Squadron knew by then what had happened.

"So today," he continued, and the words were rather adenoidal because of his swollen nose, "I have prepared a little joke of my own—just to show you I am not thoughtless and unappreciative. This afternoon when the day is pleasant and warm you will wear your flying suits." He paused for a moment, allowing the prospect to register. "Quite humor-ous—wouldn't you agree?"

We awaited the afternoon with mounting apprehension, but during the morning Namoto and his assistants scarcely laid a hand on us. Clearly, it was the lull before the storm. Then, at last, the fated time arrived, and, true to his word, The Mantis had us don all of our flying accoutre-ments: our feather-lined suits, boots, leather helmets and scarves—even our parachute packs!

Heat waves were shimmering on the airstrip as we commenced our usual hour of calisthenics, the weather extremely hot and humid. For the first few minutes our flying suits served as protection from the sun. One or two of the men even suggested that we should always wear fly-ing suits, but I was highly skeptical. Already the first few drops of sweat had formed under my arms and begun trickling down my side. The heat was building from within and had no means of escape. "In about five minutes you'll find out how crazy you are," I informed one of the more optimistic.

"Oh come on now, Kuwahara," he retorted, "don't always be such a pessimist."

We were doing push ups side by side, and I grunted, "You'll be changing your mind before its over, my friend."

"No I won't!"

"Fool!"

"Boob!"

Never before had anyone intimated that I was a boob. Unreason-ably furious, I got to my feet. "Stand up, *shinpei!*" I said, "and we'll see who the boob is."

Obligingly, he arose, grinning impudently, and I struck with all my strength, staggering him, but also losing my balance. We fell in a tangle among the other men, grappling awkwardly. There were curses, our comrades grabbing and separating us. Nakamura had hold of my arms. "Ease up!" he urged. "Do you want to get killed?"

By then, however, The Mantis was lashing away at us, though with only moderate effect because of our thick flying suits. As we stood, pant-ing, I was still seething with anger, literally trembling, but I also realized my stupidity. Already burning inside, I continued to pant, my throat dust-dry. Sweat was seeping from my forehead into my eyes, blurring the backs of the men before me. I was quivering uncontrollably now and my legs felt hollow. I refused to look at Tanaka, the man I had fought.

At the conclusion of our calisthenics fifteen minutes later we were virtually broiling in our suits, and that was only the beginning. Now it was time for our daily running.

We moved out like elephants in our heavy clothing under a blazing sun, and once I removed one of my gloves to test the heat of my flying suit. Its hot leather almost scorched my hand, and we lumbered steadily forward down the vast concrete expanse of our air field. Meanwhile, The Mantis pedaled comfortably along beside us on his bicycle dressed in nothing but his light-weight fatigues. The land of concrete seemed to stretch interminably, and at length I began to reflect upon the declaration of our commanding officer at the end of basic training: "The Imperial Way is a long way, never-ending. The Imperial Way will never end."

"Long," the words came, "long . . . long. . . ." repeating themselves regularly with every other stride. Yet now I could see only a short distance through my sweat-filled eyes. The Japanese way of life was destined to fill the earth as we were often told. Perhaps that was why it had to be such a long, hard way. Minute after minute our boots clumped rhythmically forward. Long . . . long . . . long. . . .

Intermittently my vision cleared, but why had I ever imagined that there was an end to the air field? And what direction were we going? I had no idea. On and on we went, boots clumping steadily, and gradually it seemed that there were fewer men behind me. Ahead someone staggered and hit the concrete rolling. The runway was rocking now. Thirty seconds later another man grabbed his stomach, staggered and went down. As I passed his inert form, it seemed a bit as though he were sinking, sinking like a leaky boat into a flat gray sea.

Another man was going down now, tripping the one behind him. They too seemed to be vanishing, sinking inexorably into the concrete. Their bodies, I told myself, would become a part of it, and years hence when men broke up this strip to build a new one they would find the remnants, mere hollow statues. But even then I would still be running beneath the inferno of the sun, onward and onward into infinity.

On the other hand, perhaps I too would ultimately become a statue. If I were a statue with the rest I could be at peace. There in our family shrine I would know the inestimable bliss of nothingness. There in the cool of evening under the trees among the flowers, the cicadas singing, and Tomika would come quietly each day to cool the hard stone of my being with her tears. She would whisper, "My brother, my dearest brother."

I never felt the airstrip rising to meet me. Tepid liquid from a canteen sloshed against my face, and I saw the spokes of a bicycle wheel whirling by.

Chapter Twelve

A Full Reparation

We devised no further schemes for some time. Namoto's practical joke had left an impressive impact. Several men had been hospitalized afterward, in fact, from heat prostration. Nevertheless, his savagery continued almost unabated, and again someone managed to obtain poison. Again heated arguments. "I don't care what they do to me," the would-be assassin had muttered. "At least that rotten devil will get what's coming to him. And he'll never hurt anyone again."

"Yes, but what will happen then?" someone else challenged. "Not just to you but to all of us—the whole squadron?" After a day or two the poison was poured down the toilet.

Barely a week later I underwent my first unpleasant experience in the air because of a far less deadly alternative. Our rancor against The Mantis had reached another crest, and we were contemplating more games. Certainly our relationship with that strange person was bizarre, to say the least—indeed, even incredible. It is difficult, perhaps impossible, to explain the perverse spirit that enticed us to continue in the face of such retaliation. The term "sado-masochism" seems most appropriate here, however, for in striking back against Rentaro Namoto we inevitably emerged on the losing end.

That latter in mind, we decided our next attack should at least be more subtle than, say, tripping him down the stairs. "How about a good, strong laxative in his food?" Nakamura said, "enough to make him shit his pants, shit enough to fertilize a whole rice paddy?"

"He already does that with his mouth," Moriyama said.

"Sleeping pills!" Oka exclaimed. "Why not sleeping pills? He'd never make morning formation. Then he'd be in big trouble—they might even demote him to private, even throw him out."

Tanaka, the man with whom I had fought earlier, laughed boisterously. "Wouldn't that be wonderful? Rentaro Namoto a *shinpei*. We'd give him such a bad time he'd go over the fence the first week."

I shook my head. "No. No matter what else you say about him, The Mantis is tough. He would never break."

"Aaa," Tanaka sneered, "he'd bawl for his mother the first day. He'd go hang himself." I stared at him in disbelief, fighting down the anger. The feeling had been festering ever since our scrap on the airstrip. One thing I could always count on with Tanaka—we would rarely agree on anything. And always, that impudent grin. I could imagine smashing his stupid face in, changing it so that even his mother wouldn't recognize him—except for one thing. The grin would still be there.

"All right, *shinpei*" I said, "go ahead and get the sleeping pills. We'll see who's right."

"All right, *shinpei*" He gave an exaggerated bow. "I will since everybody knows you don't have the guts for it."

"Oh, really?" I snapped. "Well, at least I've got enough to take you on. That doesn't call for any guts at all, in fact." At that point we would have come to blows a second time if our friends had not prevailed upon us to calm down.

Despite our animosity, I found myself eagerly awaiting the results of Tanaka's efforts. Unfortunately, he was never able to procure the necessary pills. How anybody had managed to obtain poison, in fact, was a mystery most of us never unraveled.

Gradually another plan took form which everyone involved responded to with enthusiasm, and it also included the men from another barracks. "We'll fix your *hancho* if you'll help us fix ours," Nakamura advised them. "What we need right now are the needles from every man's sewing kit in your barracks. We'll trade you our own in a day or two." At first there was great reluctance, but eventually we prevailed because of the plan's uniqueness and apparently minimal risk.

Shortly after ten one night while The Mantis was enjoying himself in town, four of us sneaked into his room and turned down the covers on his bed. Next we inserted the needles heads downward into his mattress so that the points barely projected above the surface. Then we carefully re-made the bed, having stretched the undersheet so taut that nothing was visible beneath it, and returned to our quarters.

There we sat on our cots in the dark, whispering and laughing. "I hope he has sweet dreams," someone said.

"Their holy men sleep that way in India," Yamamoto said. "We can't have them outdoing us." We were all brimming with mirth and hilarity, partly, no doubt, because of our anxiety.

"Hey, hey, look at me," Oka called. "I'm Namoto—I'm lover boy!" Staggering down the dark aisle, he yawned and stretched blissfully. "Good night, my children. Pleasant dreams," he murmured and slowly lay back on his cot. We watched closely in the dim light as Oka's eyes closed then suddenly popped open, his mouth forming a silent, agonized scream. Legs and arms flailing, he catapulted to his feet and began leaping about wildly, yelping and clutching at his rear.

An amusing performance, one that nearly broke us into convulsions. Then Yamamoto and Nakamura launched their own versions, and by now everyone in our section was awake, listening. "What this time?" someone groaned.

"Oh, Oka and Kuwahara and those other *gokudo*," Moriyama replied. "More of their stupid tricks, getting the whole squadron into trouble again." It was now after eleven, and eventually we went to sleep.

Following morning chow all the men from our barracks were summoned to Namoto's office in the orderly room. For a moment he sat there, contemplating the ceiling, idly drumming his fingers on the chair arms and trying to decide, it appeared, whether we were actually worthy of his attention. Projecting from the top of the table in front of him in four neat, silver rows were sixty needles.

Eventually he plucked one of them up and sighted at a spot on the wall with it, closing one eye. "Well?" he said. No reply. "We never thought of this one when I was in pilot school. Very clever. Yes indeed—very clever!" Suddenly his chair slammed upright. Regarding us balefully and shaking his head, he said, "And, of course, you don't know a thing about these, do you?" Stiffening, he pointed at Nakamura. "You, pimple face!" Nakamura's acne had worsened considerably of late for some reason. "Let's have an answer!"

Nakamura swallowed, struggled to reply, and failed.

"Splendid! A nice, direct answer. It seems rather strange, though, my fine pimple face, that you manifest no surprise, no lack of understanding. Apparently you know what I'm referring to—correct?"

Nakamura swallowed again. "No," he managed at last. "I mean, no honorable *hancho-dono.*"

"Hmmm. . . ." The Mantis mused. "Not a very convincing liar, is he?" He plucked another needle from table. "So all right!" Rising abruptly, he commenced pacing the room. Once he paused before Moriyama, staring at him through cold, remorseless eyes. Even his eyes were mantis-like. "No, no . . . you wouldn't know, would you? Too stupid." Casually he flipped Moriyama's nose so hard his eyes watered. Then we were dismissed.

As we filed out, however, he called, "Just one minor detail, friends. Every single man in this squadron will bring his sewing kit to morning formation. See that the other sections are informed."

Upon discovering that all our kits contained the requisite needle, The Mantis appeared impassive. He merely complimented us upon our strategy, adding that he had prepared a special token of appreciation. Then we were dismissed.

The morning passed rather tranquilly. Even our physical training was uneventful. Then came our flying lessons, and The Mantis unveiled his plan. "A short time ago," he observed, "some of you apparently became rather warm while wearing your flying suits. Worked up a slight sweat. Even became a bit weary—correct?" He nodded slowly, steadily, confirming his own words. "Well, that may have been somewhat unkind, now that I think about it. So today, just to show you what a grand fellow

I am, we will forego the hot suits during flying practice. How does that strike you?"

Minutes later as I climbed into the rear cockpit of an *Akatombo*, the instructor before me turned, and I realized that it was our old nemesis from basic training. Sakigawa, alias The Snake. "Greetings, Kuwahara." His grin was both mischievous and empathic. As I began to fasten my safety belt, he shook his head. "No safety belts allowed, Kuwahara—Namoto's orders."

"No seat belt?" I was shocked.

"Afraid not," he replied, "sorry." Another surprise. The Snake actually sounded as if he meant it, as if perhaps he even liked me!

We took off, climbing rapidly. At about five thousand feet The Snake glanced back at me. The sunlight glinted on his goggles, and his eyes appeared to be mere slits. "Hang on tight!"

Already the chill air was buffeting me through the open cockpit.

"Don't let go!" Seizing the dead controls, I watched and felt the world turn upside down—felt it rushing toward us. We were forming a lazy loop, and I pulled my chin against my chest, thrusting my knees upward beneath the control panel. Black spots clotted my vision, and we began our first descent, pulling out, slicing into a cloud bank. I had almost tumbled from the cockpit!

The spots faded slightly, but already we were heading into another loop. Terrified, I grasped my seat straps, and felt the sky wrench at me like the hands of a giant, tearing at the corners of my mouth, at my clenched eyelids, roaring ferociously within my ears. Desperately, I tightened every muscle, grimacing, striving to resist the tearing, freezing wind.

For a time, I did not know whether we had leveled out or not, literally which side was up. As I struggled to regain my breath, we nosed over into sharp, downward spiral By now my forehead was freezing, my stomach churning savagely. I had never known such overwhelming nausea. The vomit erupted from my throat, even my nostrils, spraying about the cockpit, sheening off into the air.

My vision blurred, and I struggled desperately to keep from fainting. At last, though, we were preparing to land. The black spots were slowly fading, but I was so numb from the cold Sakigawa had to assist me from the cockpit.

All of the men in our squadron underwent the same experience that day, and for several minutes afterward most of us were unable to stand. Our facial muscles were so cold it was impossible to speak. We were so devastated, in fact, that The Mantis half apologized. "After all, men," he piously intoned, "this is the Imperial Army Air Force. You must accustom yourselves to things like this or end up as miserable failures. The mind and spirit must learn to prevail over the body!"

Unfortunately, that was not the only unpleasant occurrence in the *Akatombo*, not by any means. Only a week or so later, I underwent a far worse one, something so amazing that to this day I cannot fully explain it. Moreover, the consequences were far more traumatic than any I had yet encountered.

Six of us were flying formation at about ten thousand feet, The Mantis in the lead, when his voice buzzed over the intercom,

"Today we will find out just how well you have learned your maneuvers. We will now play follow the leader." Second in formation, I followed behind as he made a wide bank right, angled into a dive and began to loop up and back the opposite direction. I followed him all the way with relative ease, pulling out close on his tail. Then, for some strange reason, instead of slowing, I accelerated.

Sensing our proximity, The Mantis veered and began climbing, but I followed precariously near. It was an odd sensation, one wherein I seemed to be under the control of some perverse force beyond myself, as though suddenly I had been hypnotized. The Mantis performed a half loop, righting himself at the apex, and by now he was ranting into my ear phones. "Get off my tail, you madman! You stupid idiot! Drop back!"

Already the rest of our flight was trailing at some distance. The Mantis angled into a steep dive, and I followed as though attached by a cable. Had he been piloting a faster, more maneuverable craft I could not have stayed with him. But his attempts to escape in the trainer were futile. Twisting, rolling, climbing, circling . . . all to no avail. It was impossible to shake me, and with each passing second the thought of crashing into him, snuffing out his miserable life in mid-air, became more appealing—overwhelmingly. Simultaneously, I was terrified beyond measure.

Cutting in a tight left circle, The Mantis bawled, "Turn right! Turn right!" The order, meant nothing. It had no more meaning than the quacking of a duck or the braying of a jackass. Instead, I turned left, cutting inside his arc, and we missed colliding by only a few feet.

Desperately, The Mantis headed full throttle for the mountains above Fukugawa, and soon we were roaring between their shoulders, winnowing insanely down a long ragged valley. A bearded ridge loomed before us, and I pulled back on the stick as The Mantis climbed frantically— almost too late! His wing nicked off the tip of a pine. Still I followed, the victim of a terrifying yet relentless compulsion, and we continued to climb as one. Now we were ascending above the first peak, circling. Some extraordinary power beyond comprehension seemed to have virtually fused our two aircraft together.

Seconds later, something utterly unexpected happened, something incredible. Uttering a final, frantic oath, The Mantis bailed out! I watched in wonderment as his parachute billowed like a huge silken mushroom, snapping the plummeting figure beneath it into slow motion. Angling gently away on the morning breeze, it gradually grew smaller, and soon the figure beneath it was no larger than a doll. Then it was gone, vanishing into the folds of a distant valley. Moments after that, something flashed against the mountainside beyond. Namoto's *Akatombo* had come to rest.

By now my head was roaring, my body like a swarm of bees. Perhaps I would have simply crashed somewhere, resolving it all forever, except for the warning voice buzzing against my ear drums. "Kuwahara! Go back, go back! Remember your family, remember the Emperor! You have an obligation!" It was The Snake, circling just above.

The entire episode, like the fragments of a bad dream, had lasted only a few minutes. Somehow I joined the main formation as sanity returned along with feelings of terrible dread. Minutes later I was landing with the others at Hiro, and approximately two hours after that I was summoned before the Commanding Officer. By now our frolic over the mountains of Fukugawa had attracted much attention.

The Mantis was already there, having been retrieved by one of our military vehicles soon after his parachute landing. He appeared to be uninjured except for a two or three scratches on his face and neck, apparently the result of tree branches. His eyes stared through me, bleak and frozen with hatred as I entered the office of our commanding officer, Captain Yoshiro Tsubaki.

"Be seated, Kuwahara," the Captain said courteously. I sat, feeling a bit like someone on the electric chair, but our commander seemed completely unperturbed. "Now. . . ." he began, closing a large, black loose-leaf binder and pushing it to one side of his desk. "I wish to determine as precisely as possible what actually happened out there over Fukugawa this afternoon." He frowned slightly and pursed his lips. "And above all, why. We will hear from you first, Namoto."

The Mantis shot me an oblique glare. "Honorable Commanding Officer, I must tell you that this man is completely insane!" Tsubaki's eyebrows arched quizzically. "An absolute lunatic." The eyebrows arched still more. "During a routine flight practice, he disobeyed every order he was given and did everything in his power to ram me. Had I not bailed out, we would both be dead. He—"

"Exactly how long did he pursue you?" Tsubaki interjected. Did I detect I faint purr of irony? It was impossible to be certain.

"For several minutes, Honorable Commanding Officer. In fact, he—"

"An inexperienced trainee, and you were unable to elude him?"

Namoto's features constricted. "The *Akatombo* does not possess the requisite speed and maneuverability, Honorable—"

"Yes, but even so. . . ." Namoto glowered, anger and humiliation seeming to exude from his very pores. The Captain stroked his jaw, frowning thoughtfully. "Curious . . . very curious. Many strange things have occurred since I arrived at Hiro, but never, never anything like this."

Opening the drawer to his left, he extracted a pad of lined, yellow paper then plucked up a pencil as though to take some notes. Instead, however, he merely twirled it a time or two between his fingers and began tapping it on the desk top. "Of course, we have lost a *hancho* or two from time to time." The Mantis stiffened, staring into the wall.

Still tapping the pencil, Mikami shot me a searching glance. "So what do you have to say about this, Kuwahara?"

I struggled to speak yet hadn't the slightest idea how to reply. The words stuck in my throat, and after a moment the Captain merely gave a slight nod as though seeking to liberate them. "I do not know, Honorable

Commanding Officer," I stammered. My throat was painfully dry like that of someone languishing in a wasteland, my voice an embarrassing croak. "I . . . I, cannot explain."

"Was it your intention to kill this man?"

I swallowed. "No, Honorable Commanding Officer. I just—"

"So what possessed you?" Tsubaki leaned forward on his elbows exploring my eyes intently with his own as though, perhaps, that would permit him to examine my brain. "Were you trying to retaliate in that manner?"

"No, Honorable Commanding Officer." That was my second lie.

"*So desu ka!*" The words hissed softly between his teeth.

"Were you. . . ." He bobbed his head a little from side to side, casting a reflective glance about the ceiling. "Were you trying to show off for the others? Impress your fellow trainees?"

"No, I—"

"Honorable Commanding Officer!" The Mantis snapped, correcting me, but our inquisitor silenced him with an impatient wave of the hand.

"So . . . hmmm, and when did you decide to do this thing?"

I swallowed again. My throat was dryer than ever. "I didn't. I mean, I don't know, Honorable Commanding Officer. I just followed—as he instructed us to. I—I just followed him."

"*So des.* But weren't you following a little too close for comfort? Obviously Sergeant Namoto thought so. He was so uncomfortable that he promptly bailed out permitting one of our perfectly good training planes to crash and burn." Namoto's jaw muscles tightened. His nostrils narrowed.

"I am extremely sorry, Honorable Commanding Officer," I said and realized how foolish I sounded, how utterly senseless the entire absurd episode must seem to anyone of sound mind. Yet there was nothing more to say. The Mantis had commanded us to play follow the leader. I had followed.

For some time Tsubaki sat there, fingers locked, absorbed in thought. Once he massaged his brow. Once he shook his head and swore softly. Our commanding officer was a small man, one who would pass unnoticed even on the streets of Onomichi. But the military environment seemed to draw forth the largeness of his personality, his spirit. As on the day of his oration at the end of basic training, I could sense the big man dominating a smaller man's body.

"Do you know what I wanted to be back in my college days?" he said suddenly. We both glanced at him startled. "I wanted to be . . . as a matter of fact, I was determined to be . . . a psychiatrist. However. . . ." He reached in his shirt pocket for a cigarette, struck a match on the sole of his shoe, and lighted up. For a moment he puffed introspectively, squinting and expelling the smoke in rich blue swirls. "You know how these things go. Costs a lot of *okane* to become a doctor."

Another puff, exhaling and jetting the smoke through his nostrils. Squinting almost painfully now. "Perhaps, private, you are like I was. My mother was a widow, and she worked like a slave to buy me a bicycle." His expression was nostalgic. "I was—oh, not more than ten. Never even knew my father. But anyway, my older brother taught me how to ride." He smiled faintly. "At least, he tried. Let's put it that way."

He shifted, leaning back in his chair, arms folded. "My brother already had a bicycle; Stole it, as I recall." For some reason the thought struck us all as quite humorous, and Tsubaki even laughed a little. "Anyway, he was going to teach me the right way. 'Follow me!' That's what he kept saying. 'Just do what I do.' I hardly even knew how to balance the damn thing, but that didn't matter. I had to follow him."

Another puff. "So . . ." He pursed his lips, frowning pleasantly, absorbed in the distant past. "We were going along this narrow, little road out in the country, and I was beginning to get the hang of it. But every time I'd ask a question, my brother would just repeat himself. 'Follow me—do everything I do.' Before long, though, I started following too closely, and my front wheel must have hit a rock, because it rammed me into his rear wheel, and we both went down. Right into a newly dunged rice paddy!"

Suddenly all three of us were laughing—three comrades. That was the only time I ever heard The Mantis laugh, and it was like the cawing of a raven.

"Just do everything I do"! We were about ostracized from the community for a while after that." Our captain shook his head and wiped his eyes, but it was impossible to tell whether the tears were from laughter or cigarette smoke. Perhaps both. "Silly damned brother. 'Just do everything

I do!'" Then he grew more serious. "Dead and gone now. Killed a long time ago during the war in China."

There the conversation ended, and I was sent to the guardhouse to "reflect upon the consequences of your actions" or words to that effect. Certainly the commanding officer had treated me with astonishing consideration, but The Mantis wasted no time in seeking to balance the scales. Quietly he ushered me into my private prison, closing the door behind him.

"Maybe that stupid commander doesn't intend that you should pay for this," he muttered. For an instant my shock at his disrespect to Captain Tsubaki outweighed my fear regarding what lay ahead. Then I saw the club. "But believe me, you shall. For this indignity, you shall be repaid in full!" Reflexively, I ducked and flung up my arm to ward off the blow, but it came too fast, too hard. There was an explosion in my brain, and I seemed to hear the sound of wood against my skull—hear it with my entire body. Then I was swallowed into a great, swirling, black hole. No pain. Nothing.

Gradually I became aware of sensations, but for a time I was no particular person, merely a glimmer of something in an area of unfeeling. No sensation, except for the cold and dampness. Eventually words formed in my mind. "What am I doing in the ocean?" It occurred to me that I was dead. When you are dead they bury you beneath the earth, but somehow you keep sinking, sinking until you reach the ocean. You lie there quietly at the bottom of the ocean where it doesn't hurt, beneath all harm. None, if you lie quietly with serenity and acceptance. But, of course, it is dark there and cold, very cold.

Yet something puzzled me . . . the sense of hardness. I was lying face down, carefully working my hands and fingers outward across the surface maintaining me. A floor—concrete. A concrete floor. Then, vaguely I began to remember. For a time I could not recall who I was, but I had angered someone, humiliated someone, incurred his animosity. I could feel the mounting hatred, growing powerful and virulent like the stench of a rotting carcass.

Who or what was the source, and how did it happen? Slowly my brain began to clear, echoing the last words I had heard: "For this indignity you shall be repaid in full." The floor was not only cold and hard, it was also damp, and the taste of sea water lay on my tongue, sea water with a faint coppery flavor. Then I touched my face, feeling a sticky oozing sensation. It was beginning to throb, and the throbbing was expanding into my head. Above my left ear was a large swelling, half welt, half lump. My face was also very bruised and sore. It was impossible to determine how long I had lain there. Minutes or hours, I could not tell.

I touched my face again, felt the stickiness, and looked at my finger tips. They were smeared with blood, blood that looked as black as tar in the dim light. Now I remembered almost everything, but Namoto had struck me on the side of my head. Why the blood on my face? Perhaps I had scraped it as my body hit the concrete.

Painfully, I sat up, staring at an oblong square of light on the floor at my feet. The light was sectioned, and my gaze ascended slowly toward its source, the barred window. Struggling to arise, I hobbled to it and peered out.

Hiro was quiet, except for the remote, faintly strident voice of a *hancho* marching recruits in the distance. Evening now. Again, I explored my face and decided from its extreme tenderness and the extent of the bruising that The Mantis had also used his feet. The guardhouse was merely a small empty room—no table, no cot, no chair, not even a straw *tatami* to lie upon.

For several minutes I simply stood there, gripping the bars, and looking out as the shadows of night extended. Not much to see except for an expanse of hard, yellow clay and an unlighted barracks. Soon my legs began to sag, and I eased myself to the floor, back scraping down the wall to keep from falling. Then I worked my way into the corner, drawing my knees up to rest my head and arms on them.

A clicking at the door startled me. It opened slightly as a guard leaned inside to place something on the floor. "Here's your chow and a blanket," he said. The door clanged shut. Suddenly I was very hungry, ravenous. Only rice, pickles, and water, but I gulped it all down in seconds like an animal, smearing my nose and chin. My face throbbed savagely, yet it didn't matter. Some rice had fallen on the floor, but I pinched it up, devouring it to the last kernel. Then I licked the bowl and my fingers.

The light pattern was brightening on the floor now, extending. Spreading my thin blanket, I lay on its outer edge and slowly, in great pain, rolled up in it. By rolling tight I could have two layers over and under me. A cold fall night was filtering through the bars, and for a time I shivered helplessly. Gradually, though, I became warmer and lay there, feeling the breath ease in and out of my mouth and nostrils. Somehow, by concentrating on each soft inhalation and exhalation, I could ease my misery.

Anyway, I had humiliated The Mantis irreparably I told myself. I had not only stayed with him but out flown him. Ironically, although I had insisted earlier that it could never be done, I myself had broken his steel nerve and vindicated the entire squadron. In a way, I was glad that he had treated me so viciously. Maybe he would consider that enough, and possibly the morrow would set me free. Eventually, I fell asleep.

My hopes, however, were in vain. My sojourn in the guard house proved to be the worst experience of my entire training. All the next day I waited, longing for release, but only two incidents lessened the emptiness of those hours. Once I was permitted to visit the latrine in the building nearby, and that evening I received another bowl of rice and pickles. This time I ate more slowly, carefully savoring each morsel. I tried to remind myself that food was unimportant, that one's attitude was actually what counted. After all, hadn't the early *samurai* been able to forego any food for days? When food was unavailable, they would sit calmly, picking their teeth, pretending to have just completed a sumptuous repast.

Completing my own sumptuous repast, I rolled up once more in my blanket, hoping to sleep until the morning. Hoping, in fact, that perhaps I could sleep most of the remaining time away. After about two hours of fitful dozing, though, I arose and began pacing about my cell. The floor had not grown any softer, nor had my special rolling-up technique kept the cold from gradually penetrating.

My shoulder blades and hip bones were becoming sore. One can only relax on concrete for so long. The left side of my head continued to ache viciously from the club blow, and my eyes were still black from The Mantis' feet. Even though I could not see myself, I could tell from the painfully swollen tissue that he had kicked my face more than once. I decided that at least the punishment was probably over, that release would come soon.

The afternoon had vanished, and evening was thickening when someone called my name. "Kuwahara!" I awakened, startled, wondering if I had merely been dreaming. Several times during the day, words had sounded in my own mind. "Kuwahara! Hey, come over to the window!" No mistake this time. Undoubtedly, I decided, my friends were concerned about me. Maybe they had even brought some food.

"Gripping the bars, I peered out into the gathering darkness. A cricket was chanting faintly, muted by the cold. "I'm here—who is it?"

"Are you all right? Let's see your face. Is it getting any better?" The words filled me with hope.

Pressing my swollen visage part way through the bars, I whispered, "Nakamura? Who is it?"

"It is I!" a fiendish voice snarled, and something cracked, searing my face like a blow torch. Screaming, I staggered back against the wall. The Mantis had been crouching there with his whip. As I slumped to the floor, he hissed, "Why carry on so, young bastard? I was only checking to make sure that your face is all right."

The lash mark traveled from my mouth upward across my cheek and the lower corner of one eye. The eye was watering profusely, and after several long minutes of agony I worked my way back to my blanket and draped it about my shoulders. Awkwardly, I rolled back up in it once more, leaving one hand free to gently stroke and pat the injured area. Each time I stopped it began to smart and burn insanely.

Thus I continued, deep into the night, dozing fitfully, trying over and over to will away the pain. At about four a. m. it began to diminish a bit, and at last I slept more peacefully. Eventually I awakened to discover that the window had turned from gray to blue, and I arose to begin pacing about my cell. Off on the air strip motors were revving—a wonderful sound that made my skin tingle. Then a dismaying thought struck me. If I remained in the guardhouse much longer, my chances for making fighter school would be eliminated. My head began to teem with sickening possibilities, and at that moment the door grated open.

It was my friend, The Mantis. "Come over here!" he ordered. "Turn around!" So, another whipping. Well, I had received plenty of those before. Bitterly, I complied, telling myself that it was at least a break in the monotony, but I was no more prepared for what followed than I had been for my lash to the face that previous evening.

The first blow slammed me to my hands and knees. The second flattened me on the floor. The Mantis was using a length of wet rope about an inch and a half in diameter.

Time and again that day the same punishment was repeated. Heavy, braided rope with harsh, prickly strands, freshly soaked in water to increase its weight and solidity. One lash usually flung me down, and if it failed to knock me unconscious, I fainted from pain anyway. Again and again and again . . . waiting from one lashing to the next, quivering and moaning, swearing, pleading to the god who had forgotten me. When the guard opened the door for my daily trip to the latrine, I smothered a cry. When my supper came, I cowered in the corner, trembling. For several minutes after the guard's departure I continued to shake, gnawing on my knuckles. The rope treatment had been coming about every two hours.

Somehow the third day blurred into the fourth, and early that morning rational thought returned. I began to wonder how The Mantis would react if the tables were turned. Could I make him cringe, and grovel, plead for mercy? Well, I had accomplished the unimaginable only a short time earlier, forcing him to abandon his plane.

Nevertheless, his reaction seemed exceptionally atypical. To my knowledge that was the only time anyone had shattered his cold and calculating demeanor, his unyielding self control. Even my current punishment, though fraught with vengeance, was administered with machine-like aloofness.

Once I recalled our survival training in the mountains near Hiro. The Mantis had kept us without sleep for nearly four days, without food for two. I remembered the picture vividly: grim recruits surrounding him with loaded pistols, determined to take his life regardless of the cost. But the man had displayed no emotion whatsoever, not even the faintest trace of uneasiness. He had merely eyed them coldly and remarked, "Why do that? You'll only get into serious trouble—trouble that will make this seem like a school picnic." Gradually they had wavered and backed down. "After all," he had added, "you have been learning how to eat and sleep ever since you were born. Now you must learn how not to eat and sleep."

And this was the man I had managed to humiliate! Namoto not only hated me but, as I was beginning to realize, he felt morally obligated to "repay me in full." True, he was a sadist of the first order, but my punishment would have been severe regardless. It is the moral duty of a Japanese to repay an injustice as well as a favor.

Eventually my thoughts returned to fighter school. It was still my grandest goal. Indeed, it mattered more than ever now. For a while I could not recall how many days had passed. Maybe I could still qualify. That was all that mattered. I scarcely even thought of home.

Then the flash of optimism was gone. The door lurched open with an ominous clank, but by now I had lost all control. "Kill me!" I shouted. My voice was like the sound of a wood rasp. "Kill me and get it over with!"

Slowly he approached, rope in hand. "Get up, Kuwahara!"

"No!" I shouted, "No—you can't make me!"

"Get up!"

Instead, I cursed him: "*Konchikusyo*! *Bakayaro*! *Gaki*!"

He loomed over me, cobra-like, rope readied. "All right, if you want it on the floor—" I thrashed out, kicking his shins, and The Mantis staggered backward, cursing me with every foul word he could think of, and he knew more than I did.

So again! Again, I had shattered his calm, and he hated me more than ever for it. I tried to roll away as the rope lashed across my neck, nearly breaking it. Then it came again and again, like repeated strikes of lightning. I could even feel its livid yellow color. Again the black hole yawned, consuming me.

Some time later the door opened once more. I stared vacantly.

"Get up!"

"No," I barely croaked. The arm raised, the rope descending ravenously, and there it was once more—the black hole. The wonderful, blessed, great, dark hole. Oblivion.

By afternoon I lay thinking about the hole. It was very good, my only hope now, yet it could hold me only so long. Inevitably, I would drift to the surface. Occasionally, when the light began to expand I would swim back down toward the depths, but each time my stay was shorter. That hole and the dark corner of the cell shared a mutual relationship. Why did I always have to return? Why couldn't I stay down? Why? Why?

Then it came to me with exciting certainty: I could stay down forever!

A sense of triumph, near elation, filled my soul. Idly I began dragging myself about the room, feeble and crippled like an old man, but that didn't matter. I was looking for something that would work—my metal rice bowl perhaps. Possibly I could crush it to create a jagged edge. I bent down, groaning, and picked it up. Or grind it on the cement floor until the edge was knife sharp.

Propping the bowl sidewise against the wall, I tried several times to stomp on it without success. Plane motors were grumbling in the sky now, a continual crisscross of sound. Glancing at the barred window, I saw a dragonfly. Slowly, miserably, I limped my way toward it, toward the light. The insect's wings shimmered silver, making a strange brittle sound as it danced off into the day.

Gripping the bars, I peered out, hoping to trace its flight but to no avail. It had vanished. The window ledge was shoulder high, indented about six inches to the bars, and suddenly I had my answer. Yes, a perfect ledge! Men had done it that way before —a bench, table, a railing . . . a ledge" A ledge like this one would be ideal. Simply thrust my tongue out, clamp it between my teeth, lock my hands atop my head . . . then slam my chin against the ledge—hard, with all my strength. That way my tongue would be bitten off and I would bleed to death. Yes, more than one man had died that way at Hiro. How simple! How wonderful!

Fingers interlaced, I locked my hands upon my head, testing the idea carefully, very slowly, to determine the exact angle of impact between my chin and the ledge. It would be absolutely essential to do it correctly, not botch the job and simply mangle my tongue. Otherwise, I might survive to speak nothing but gibberish. Definitely not the time for a mistake. Thrusting my tongue out still further, I clamped it tighter attempting to assess the level of pain. No doubt it would be very painful, agonizingly so. That was the only problem. Nevertheless, I would bleed copiously, and it probably wouldn't last long.

Again, I performed my special test, chewing tentatively. A tongue was a strange thing, really, a highly incongruous organ. For some reason it didn't seem consistent in any way with the rest of my anatomy. Strangely, as well, I was not especially afraid, not nearly as much as I might have imagined. Instead, my body was slowly burning, simmering in a kind of sympathetic vibration to the fading drone of motors.

Then the dragonfly returned and balanced delicately upon the outer ledge as though bearing a message. What was it I had learned in school biology? Something about how a caged dragonfly, without food, would eventually begin eating its tail, never ceasing until it had devoured nearly half its own body. Surely, therefore, I could do a small thing like biting off the tip of my tongue.

What immense, almond-shaped eyes it had! I had never realized that eyes could look like that. I stared in fascination at the shimmering, blue body—at the transparent filament wings. Why did it have four instead of two? I pushed my finger toward it and the dragonfly flared upward and sidewise, balanced upon the air and vanished.

Blankly I stared into space. Then I glanced down at my hands, watched them open and close of their own accord. My hands were shaped like my mother's; that was what she had always said. The nails had those same half-moons. Once more, this time with a devout sense of finality, I locked my hands over my head, and felt my hair. It was dirty hair, matted with blood, sweat, and grime. But it was mine. It was important, my own special hair. I held a palm against my forehead and stroked my fingers down very carefully over my nose and mouth. They were battered and swollen, but they were mine, my own nose and mouth, and they were unique. The plane motors were suddenly growing louder, louder than I had ever heard them.

Well, I would wait for just a little while. Yes, I would kill myself, but I would wait for just a little while. Slowly, agonizingly, knees sagging, I slumped to the floor and began to cry.

Chapter Thirteen

Fighter Pilot

On the evening of the fourth day I was released and placed on latrine duty for an entire week. During that week I found that by simply groaning quietly to myself I could ease the pain considerably. There wasn't much work involved, but it was humiliating and intentionally so.

The Mantis had beaten me more times than I could remember, at least a dozen, and I hobbled and limped about, more bruised and sore than ever before. Nevertheless, I mopped the floor, cleaned the toilets and urinals frequently. I also kept the mirrors spotless, not wishing to provide my friend excuse for further penalties.

Indeed, my week of latrine duty was crucial. If I had succumbed to the pain, I would have been hospitalized and probably lost any chance for fighter school. Flight training was proceeding rapidly, and at graduation we would all be assigned according to our aptitudes and level of performance: fighter, bomber, signal, or mechanic school.

Most of us, of course, aspired to the first. In my own case, in fact, failure to qualify for fighter school would prove devastating. After all the pain, the struggle, the heartache—consignment to mechanic or signal school would be intolerable. Becoming a bomber pilot would certainly have been better, but still unacceptable.

Had it not been for my friends, I surely would have gone to the hospital. Each night Nakamura and Yamamoto massaged my wounds and bruises with oil. Several times they even helped me clean the latrine—true acts of devotion. I was something of a hero in the Fourth Squadron now, and twice during the week Tatsuno visited me because news regarding my whole experience with The Mantis had apparently spread throughout the entire air base. Fortunately, Tatsuno was faring well, considering his circumstances, and would soon be training in the *Akatombo*.

Eleven days after the fateful air chase I was again in the skies. During the interim my comrades had progressed considerably, but I was still numbered among the better fliers, and curiously enough, our esteemed mentor The Mantis no longer indulged in follow-the-leader games. Undoubtedly the training had progressed too far by then for such childish pursuits.

Each day I took to the sky more elated. I was a natural when it came to flying, and everyone knew it. The bird instinct I had felt over Mt. Ikoma was growing ever more powerful. By now, however, there were no further attempts—certainly not from me—to humiliate Namoto or the rest of our *hancho*. The reprisals would be too great, the price too high. Furthermore, the end of our training was near, and the punishment had abated. Even our worst task masters apparently wearied from time to time.

As graduation approached, I became increasingly excited and also more anxious. True, I was flying with the best in the squadron, making few mistakes. Nevertheless, doubt and fear constantly battled with my sense of confidence. Despite frequent rumors, none of us knew how many would be selected for fighter school. Some maintained that only two or three top flyers would qualify. Others estimated that there might be as many as twenty. No matter the time or the country, rumors run rampant in the military.

Added to these doubts was the possibility that my conduct toward The Mantis might be held against me. On the other hand, I reminded myself that the commanding officer himself hadn't seemed angry with me. He had merely displayed great curiosity. And wasn't it true that very few men, certainly none of my fellow trainees, could have followed a skilled instructor through his most desperate maneuvers as I had? Optimism and pessimism were constantly grappling inside me. With only a week remaining, the pressure became so great that I was in mental agony. If I failed . . . well, suicide would be the only possible way to atone. No backing out this time.

Some of the others may not have felt as strongly about it as I, but the tension was mounting throughout our entire squadron. Close friends often flared at each other, sometimes fighting with little provocation. Twice Oka and Yamamoto nearly came to blows, and it was all I could do to refrain from battling Tanaka each time we drew near. Always the sarcastic grin, always the belittling comments, and I promptly responded in kind. It was something, I suppose that neither of us could understand, for we both had the same circle of associates.

Somehow, despite all, we survived the tension of those final days, and suddenly graduation was upon us. The assignments had been posted! It was an autumn afternoon as I shouldered my way through a throng of nervous companions. They were clustered about the orderly room bulletin board, peering, jabbering, exclaiming. Upon reading their orders, many of them turned and walked away, countenances empty, shoulders slumped, entire bodies conveying dejection.

I strained forward, stood tip toe, craning my neck to read the words spelling life or death, but shoulders and heads kept getting in the way. My face was flushed, and I was becoming impatient beyond all reason. "Bomber school!" someone exclaimed upon reading his name. "Well, that's not so bad. I was afraid I'd be a mechanic." Steadily, men read their assignments then turned, wandering off silent and crestfallen, or noisy and jubilant.

"*Oi*—Kuwahara!" Oka bellowed, "I made it!" Someone got in his way as he hastened toward me, but Oka shoved him aside. "Kuwahara, I made it!"

"Good," I said, "that's wonderful," but my voice was hollow. I was ready to explode.

"I looked for your name," he explained, "but they wouldn't give me time—just kept shoving like a bunch of stupid goats. Hey, there's Sakamoto up there. Quick, ask him to check your name. Hey, Sakamoto—check Yasuo's name!"

Sakamoto turned back to the board reluctantly but was crowded away. "I think it's signal," he said dubiously, "same as me."

"What?" I gasped. Never, not even in the guardhouse, had I experienced such coldness. Nearly choking, I lunged forward, crashing into the back before me.

"Take it easy, Kuwahara. You made fighter pilot all right. Just don't knock everybody down." It was Tanaka, and for the first time his grin was gone. He turned away and wandered off.

For an instant I actually pitied him, yet I was too concerned with myself, still uncertain. Hadn't Sakamoto said . . . ? Then I was standing directly in front of the bulletin board. Feverishly I went down the list of names. Where was it? My name wasn't even. . . . No, wait. There it was! "Kuwahara–Fighter School!" I stared, turned to go, started back again to make absolutely certain. I was still in a state of joyous shock, disbelief. Yes, fighter school—Sakamoto, the idiot! He had been wrong. "Oka!" My voice was hoarse, and I held up my thumb.

"*Oi*, Kuwahara!" he beamed. "Good man! Yamamoto's in too!"

Moments later we spotted Nakamura, thrusting forward on the fringe of the crowd, neck extended, eyes full of worry. "Hey, fighter pilot!" Yamamoto yelled. "What are you doing over there with the foot soldiers?"

Nakamura turned, smiling uncertainly. "*Honto*? You read my name?"

"*Hai*—sure! Get over here. You're a fighter pilot along with the rest of us, you and Yasbei!"

Yasbei was the name of a famed and ancient *samurai*, and I beamed at the spontaneous compliment. We tendered our congratulations by slapping Nakamura so violently on the back that he staggered. None of us had ever been so elated—not in our entire lives. For me, this was even better than winning the national glider championship.

Approximately one fourth of the men from our squadron had been picked for fighter school—far more than we had anticipated. We four, however, were the only ones chosen from our section of the barracks, and our exuberance was dampened when we realized what a trying time most of the others were having.

That night, the night before graduation, many of them sat forlornly in the barracks, brooding and staring emptily, but strangely enough, I felt especially sorry for Tanaka. At last the insolent grin had been destroyed. A number of us had expected him to become a fighter pilot, and we were all mystified as to why he had failed. I honestly wanted to comfort him—at least some small word of consolation—but I feared that he might take offense. He had, at least, made bomber pilot which, I now assured myself, was no cause for shame.

Moriyama and Furuhashi sat together on Furuhashi's cot, and Moriyama was leaning on his knees, pondering the drab, unpainted floorboards. Clapping my hands on their shoulders, I said, "Don't feel sad, my friends. From what I've been hearing, mechanic school is not bad at all. As a matter of fact, it's supposed to be quite interesting. They made no reply, barely glanced at me. "Anyway," I continued, "you might have a chance for fighter school later on." I was amazed at the stupidity of my own words; they merely seemed to have exuded without the slightest rationality.

Moriyama shrugged and actually sneered. With each remark I was getting in deeper, growing more offensive. "Well. . . ." I mumbled, gave them both a feeble pat on the back, and wandered off feeling more foolish than ever.

For the rest of that evening I stayed away from them, and when Oka became boisterous I cautioned him to use restraint. The four of us assigned to fighter school left the barracks quietly and sat together staring at a distant red light on the control tower. Gradually, however, we forgot the plight of our comrades and began to discuss the future.

I remember well our commanding officer's graduation speech the following day. I had good reason to like the man and was prepared to feel another glow of patriotism and dedication similar to what I had experienced at the end of basic training. This time, however, his tone and demeanor were not the same, and I recall his speech for a very different reason, especially his conclusion. "Our future continually grows more serious," he informed us, adding solemnly, "In consequence, it is for you, *Nippon*'s valiant sons, to dedicate your lives—to die courageously for the great cause."

I felt the wave of concern, surprise. For the past half year we had all been so engrossed in our training, often in the mere process of survival, that we had lost touch with the world around us. It struck me personally like a bucket of cold water in the face, that we were not only at war, but that for the first time anyone in authority at Hiro had admitted the gravity of our situation.

It was October of 1944, and much had happened since I'd left home in February. Kwajalein, the first Japanese territory, had been invaded that same month, and the Marianas had fallen in June. By July, Tojo had openly admitted our loss in the "great disaster" of Saipan and had been relieved as chief of the general staff. His entire cabinet had resigned simultaneously. Still, at graduation time, most of our citizens were oblivious to the rapid turn of the war.

For some of us, however, it was taking on grave substance as was my prospective role as fighter pilot.

PART FOUR

Chapter Fourteen

The First Human Bombs

Again, life had changed abruptly. With fighter training before us, we were accorded far greater courtesy. The tremendous load of punishment had been lifted, and now our lives were dedicated to the air. During the first two months we flew training planes similar to regular fighters, though not nearly as powerful and maneuverable, with only one small-caliber gun on each wing. This was our preparation for the advanced *Hayabusa* the best army fighter then in production.

The course was stringent involving gunnery, formation flying, basic aerial maneuvers, and suicide practice. The latter entailed diving from specified heights at a large oval painted on the airstrip and about twenty feet in diameter. This was the most difficult part of flying because of the psychological effect—the idea that we were practicing to die. It was taken for granted that any pilot with a disabled plane would do his best to die in true *samurai* tradition provided he couldn't make it back to home territory. Given the opportunity, he would dive into an enemy ship or plane, taking as many of his adversaries with him as possible.

These thoughts were disturbingly in mind the day I made my first death-enhancing plunge toward the tower. From two thousand feet I gazed down at Hiro and the surrounding landscape—ridges and dales a darkening green—farm land stretching out to where the sea sparkled. Beneath me lay the airstrip, an ugly concrete scar on the earth's face, planes and hangars lining one end. Our trainers were droning above in a series of three-man V's, separated in tiers and slowly rising in a wide circle, the tower gradually diminishing below to our left.

Seconds later our instructor, in the lead, peeled off and began his dive. The man just behind him angled slightly, winging over in like manner, and the third followed, all three fast fading toward the earth. Then the next formation was descending, and now, as the lead pilot in our own, it was my turn.

Easing the stick over left, I saw and felt the earth tilt toward me. The first formation was already pulling out, then the second, and I was descending fast on their tail—the airstrip rushing toward me as though that part of the world were suddenly inflating. The buildings were growing magically. For an instant I was almost hypnotized. Larger and closer . . . larger and closer still— everything. There was the control tower, starkly looming, the deadly black circle only a short way off.

Terrifyingly near now, and I was astounded at my own daring. Now! Stick back, and my plane commenced its groaning pull out, the blood in my head straining, determined to continue its straight downward course.

Black splotches were surging at me through the cockpit, and I realized that I was suddenly on the level, still a good two hundred feet above my target. Dismayed and chagrined, I followed the formation ahead. Seconds earlier it had seemed that I was pulling out with only a few yards to spare. One does not pause in mid air, however, to contemplate his mistakes. Once again we were climbing, but I had apparently done no worse than most of the others. That was my only comfort, and with little chance for reflection, I was into my next dive. Thundering downward once more, and this time, this time, I would amaze everyone on the field. I would not allow the rising earth to hypnotize me—not this time.

Concentrating on the flight ahead, I watched it level and felt a slight disdain. They were pulling out far too high above the target, but for some reason also, I seemed to be seeing a second, duplicate wave, slightly transparent, continuing straight on to its destruction, fourth dimensional versions of the impact, the explosions, erupting smoke and flame.

Unnerved, I actually pulled out higher than before. Disillusionment! Vexation! Humiliation! All of that and more. For a brief instant, however, it was as if I had actually known what it would be like to see others die, and to be drawn relentlessly after them. To keep right on going to the devastating point of impact. Decimation! Annihilation!

Again and again we repeated our suicide runs, but that day no one except our instructor pulled out with less than one hundred feet to spare. Gradually as the days passed, however, our confidence increased, and we began diving at the outlines of ships and carriers, painted on one end of the strip. After a few weeks we were pulling out with only fifty or sixty feet remaining.

Steadily we became more confident, and after three weeks we were given an added challenge. We were to complete every dive with our eyes closed. Dropping from approximately six thousand feet initially, we would count to ten before pulling back on the stick. Later, from half that height, we would count to six, coming even closer to destruction.

The tendency initially, of course, was to count very rapidly, and also either to peek or merely squint hard, eyes only partially closed. In time, though, we conquered this challenge as well. Although no one else would ever actually know whether we cheated or not, it became a matter of personal pride for many of us. We became masters at "blind diving", and in time even dispensed with the counting entirely. We could actually feel our proximity to the earth, just as sightless people can sometimes sense the wall before them.

Daily now, also, we engaged in mock air battles with blank ammunition, perfecting our skill at cutting tight circles, barrel and aileron rolling, leaf-dropping, performing loops and other more complicated maneuvers. And each day my confidence increased, for at this point I was completing each practice session with precision, making few mistakes.

My three companions were also proving themselves very capable. While Oka and Yamamoto flew with bold abandon, Nakamura was more conservative and precise. Even so, there was no doubting his courage or determination. His suicide dives were executed to near perfection, and each time he pulled out at the same level with only slight variation.

By now, as well, our dives had become less disturbing because we were far more confident regarding our reflexes and ability to judge distance. In addition, they were now more of a game than preparation for death. Yes, I still understood their purpose, but their full significance was a growing abstraction, something that only happened to people in a novel or on the movie screen.

Consequently, we received a traumatic awakening a short while later in October. That month our first *Tokkotai* (special attack group) struck the enemy—Japan's first actual suicide pilots. Within the next ten months five thousand more pilots would follow in their wake.

"A *samurai* lives in such a way that he will always be prepared to die." Every Japanese fighting man knew these words. "We are expendable." "Be resolved that honor is heavier than the mountains and death lighter than a feather." This was all part of the timeless pattern, an ancient and revered religious philosophy, national Shintoism.

Its modern outgrowth involving the purposeful destruction of thousands of our pilots, however, originated in the mind of one Colonel Motoharu Okamura of Tateyama Air Base. His plan was covertly presented to Vice-Admiral Takijiro Onishi, Father of the *Tokkotai*, as he became known, and later approved by the *Daihonei*. Okamura believed that suicide pilots could fan the winds of battle in Japan's favor. "I have personally talked to the pilots under my command," he stated, "and I am convinced that there will be as many volunteers as are necessary." After some deliberation his proposal was accepted.

In the latter part of October, shortly after American troops had launched their assault to take back the Philippines, the *Daihonei* released the following memorable communique:

"The Shikishima Unit of the *Kamikaze* Special Attack Corps, at 1045 hours on 25 October 1944, succeeded in a surprise attack against the enemy task force, including four aircraft carriers, thirty nautical miles northeast of Sulan, Philippine Islands. Two Special Attack planes plunged together into an enemy carrier, causing great fires and explosions, and probably sinking the warship. A third plane dove into another carrier, setting additional fires. A fourth plane plunged into a cruiser, causing a tremendous explosion which sank the vessel immediately afterward."

It was a young lieutenant Yukio Seki who became the world's first official human bomb when he led that famed *Kamikaze* attack on Leyte Bay. Seki, only married a short time, was approached by his superiors and asked whether he would accept the honor. For a moment he had hesitated, just long enough to glance down and run a hand through his hair. Then, slowly he looked up into the eyes of his inquisitors, and gave a quick nod. "*Hai!*" he said abruptly, "I am profoundly honored to be considered worthy."

The attack, as indicated, was an astonishing success. The pilots had all been relatively inexperienced, but four of the five Zero fighters, each carrying a 550 pound bomb, had struck their targets according to escort observers.

Although *Tokkotai* was the designation for all suicide fighters, each group went under a different name. *Kamikaze*, however, the first attack corps, named after the "Divine Wind" that swamped Genghis Khan's invading fleet in the Thirteenth Century, became the popular term. The name *Kamikaze*, therefore came to represent our entire suicide onslaught, one inflicting the heaviest losses in the history of the United States Navy, scoring hundreds of direct hits on its vessels.

Thus it was that by the end of October 1944, *Kamikaze* had become a rallying cry. Whereas the God of Heaven had once hurled the raging elements at our enemies, he would now hurl bomb-laden planes, piloted by living human beings. There was no denying our new-found power. Under the continual bombardment of Japanese propaganda agencies, optimism was kindled. Only a minority, an objective few, permitted themselves to suspect that *Kamikaze* was a telling indication of Japan's desperate status.

Chapter Fifteen

High Rendezvous

The **first American** air raid on Tokyo had occurred more than two years before, and attacks against key Japanese strongholds had increased ever since, but it was not until my fighter training that the bombs hit Hiro.

By now the loss of such vital bases as Indonesia, Burma, and Sumatra had greatly reduced our fuel supply. Already, in fact, the shortage was severe enough to prohibit engaging the enemy in lengthy air battles, even with our best fighter planes. Radar stations on our main islands warned of enemy approach. If their course was from Nagoya to the east or Oita the opposite direction, we relaxed. If they headed for Osaka between the two, we took to the sky, fearing that they might veer toward Hiro. Already it was mainly a matter of preserving our aircraft in virtually any manner possible.

It was just before noon one day in November that Hiro's air raid sirens shrieked for the first time in earnest. Rushing to our trainers, we scrambled in, thundered down the runway, and headed for the clouds. Upon our return a short while later, the base was still in tact. A flight of fighter-escorted B-29's had bypassed Hiro and assaulted nearby Kure. For several days afterward the situation was repeated. Sirens keening, our scramble for the frantic take off, and cautious return. Each time Hiro remained unharmed.

Before long our training increased, and I graduated from my trainer to the *Hayabusa* 2, becoming a full-fledged fighter pilot, something I had dreamed about much of my life. Our furtive hide-and-seek tactics with the enemy, however, had disillusioned me terribly. Yasuo Kuwahara was not the invincible *samurai* of the skies, not the noble and glorious fighter pilot who would perform stunts over Tokyo on the Emperor's birthday or on National Foundation Day. Instead, I was compelled to flee at the first sign of danger, to hide like a coward.

The situation filled us all with disgust and humiliation. Simultaneously, it was depressing and alarming to realize that our country was in such dire straits. True, we were assured by our leaders that our elusive tactics were only temporary, that Japan was prepared for continual enemy encroachments, that at the right moment it would counter attack with overwhelming savagery. But such propaganda had acquired the odor of decay for many of us. True, *Kamikaze* had taken its toll on our enemies, but it had not turned them back.

One day we returned from the clouds to discover that the games of our recent past were over. Hiro was belching smoke, one of its hangars enveloped in flame. Several Liberator bombers had appeared with scant warning and assaulted us, tearing up part of the airstrip, destroying much of the fighter assembly plant.

Fire fighters were battling frantically while a repair crew hastily struggled to fill in craters along the runways. It was more than two hours before, fuel running low, we were able to make a precarious landing. Having given our reports in the orderly room, we wandered aimlessly about the base, surveying the destruction. A bitter and dejected group of young fighter pilots.

Nakamura and I plodded slowly along the gray-white runway, hands in our pockets, heads down, except for an occasional glance about to assess the damage. So this was what bombs could do to a base, and it was only a small taste of things to come. We both knew that, and stared for a time at the charred hangar with its ruined aircraft. "Fighter pilots that can't fight," Nakamura sneered. "Ha!"

Later that day I visited Tatsuno. He had made his solo flight in the *Akatombo* and was doing well thus far. With the bombs now striking Hiro, it was unlikely that he and his companions would undergo a full apprenticeship. "You might be flying the *Hayabusa* before you know it," I said, "maybe any day now."

For a while Tatsuno offered no reply. We were seated together on the tail section of a badly damaged bomber near one of the hangars watching the repair work still underway along parts of the air field. Eventually, he turned and eyed me searchingly. "Maybe it will be the way we always hoped, Yasuo. It seems too good to be true, and yet. . . ." He hesitated, frowning. I watched him, sensing that he was about to say something I didn't want to hear. "Well, I never expected things were going to be like this."

"Like what?" I asked, feeling a bit angry for some reason.

He shrugged. "I don't know, but if we're really going to win? When do we start? The attacks are getting worse all the time. And if we can't stop them now, how can we expect to stop them a month from now, or a half year from now? What's the secret? What are we waiting for?" Tatsuno's voice was quiet and strained.

"Things usually get bad for both sides before a war is over," I said.

"Yes, but what are we doing? Are we really hurting the Americans? Are we bombing California, New York, and Washington?"

"Those places are too far away right now," I countered.

"Of course," Tatsuno said, "and we're too close. That's the whole problem. They're too far and we're too close; they're too big, and we're too small! Do you realize that California alone—just one of their forty-eight states—is the size of our entire country?"

"Aw, that can't be right," I mumbled..

"It is right!" he insisted. "Don't you remember our geography class? California is as big as our four main islands combined."

"Maybe," I admitted, "but it's not just size that wins wars. It's the spirit. It's determination and courage."

Tatsuno angled me a glance that seemed a bit scornful. "So aren't they determined and courageous too? They've got to be to have us taking it on the chin like this. When are we going to strike back and make the

Americans retreat? Once they've dumped their bombs on every city in Japan and taken over the Emperor's Palace?"

I offered no answer. There was none. Eventually, I arose. "I'd better get back to the barracks," I said.

"Already?" He looked rather sorrowful. "You've only been here a few minutes."

"I know " I replied uncertainly, and began to walk away. "But I've got a lot to do. I haven't finished studying for my test on navigation." Once I glanced back. Tatsuno was still sitting there, leaning forward on his knees, gazing out across the runway. I waved, but he barely lifted his hand.

That afternoon I was in the air again—five of us flying above the Inland Sea at twelve thousand feet somewhere between Kure and Iwakuni. Clouds were forming rapidly below us, literally before our eyes, and falling steadily behind like shredding cotton. Far off, beyond the mountains, a spectral moon hung faint and gray, and occasionally I glanced downward at the sea, its endless, undulating surface, wrinkled, patched with shadow and alternating expanses that dazzled the eye.

At the moment it again seemed very strange to think that throughout the world men were caught up in a cataclysmic struggle of death and hatred. Slightly ahead and above me was Lieutenant Shimada, a veteran combat fighter whom we all greatly respected. Shimada had fought in many a battle going back to the early days when our planes had so badly outclassed the American P-39's and P-40's. He had known the taste of victory, and more than one enemy had fallen victim to his guns.

Sunlight gleamed on his cockpit, revealing at times the man within. I could see his leather helmet, the goggles resting upon his forehead, and my heart brimmed with admiration. Slender and unassuming, he spoke very little, but he fought with great talent and valor. Occasionally Shimada's head tilted slightly from side to side as he surveyed the waiting sky. But even those motions, the very line of his shoulders, conveyed precision and vigilance.

The vast reaches of the sky, the water and receding landscape and the waning moon all imparted serenity. I shifted in my seat, glancing back and downward over my left wing at the ocean. Winter would soon be upon us, and once more, gazing toward the distant shores of Honshu, I recalled my walks with Tomika, the fishermen at their nets—bare toes in the sand and the sense of its fading warmth, the sound of their voices and occasional laughter. The laughter of fishermen and their wives was not that of the bars or the crowded streets. It was a part of nature itself, mingling with the sigh and rush of the waves and the cries of sea birds.

Had the war changed all this? Erased it forever? Suddenly I wanted desperately to turn toward Onomichi. I would land on some empty stretch of shore, taking comfort in my very aloneness. The fish shacks would be vacant now, even the nets gone, but I would pause and listen, listen for the last faint strains of haunting laughter.

My earphones crackled, snapping me back to reality. "Enemy, two o'clock low!" I peered anxiously, saw nothing, then shot a glance at our leader. He nodded, pointing downward at an angle with his finger, and my eyes followed. This time I saw them—formation after formation—a tremendous swarm of Grumman Hellcats, and they were headed directly for Hiro!

For a moment I lost my breath. No, this could not be happening; it was an optical allusion, a fantasy. I checked my oxygen mask nervously, and all was in order. But the enemy was still there. Still afar off, though increasingly substantial—an immense swarm, too numerous to count.

Of course, I told myself, we wouldn't attack, not with only five aircraft. No, that would be sheer lunacy, and fortunately they were apparently unaware of us. It would be better, regardless, to perfect our flying skills. Air fights? Later, when we were more experienced. I glanced back off my right wing at Shiro Hashimoto, a recently acquired comrade, caught his eye, and pointed toward the enemy below. Then I opened and closed my hand rapidly. Hashimoto nodded, actually grinned.

And now, to my surprise, Shimada was turning, angling toward them. Automatically, the rest of us responded, following close behind. He was definitely tracking the Hellcats. Could this be possible? Attack? No, I told myself. We were merely observing to determine their intentions. Nevertheless, I checked my guns. It was always good to check, because one of these days when the odds were better, we'd be using them.

My ears buzzed, and I flinched. Incredible! We were going to attack! What should I do? Already I was forgetting everything I had learned. My mind had gone blank. I was on the verge of panic! Release auxiliary gas tank! Yes, that came first. Otherwise a single bullet could blow me into the next world. Tanks from our four other planes were already tumbling downward, and we were closing fast. Again I adjusted my mask. Again I checked my guns.

What now? Just follow Shimada—no other choice. Yes, just follow Shimada. Do everything he does and it will be all right. Remember how you followed The Mantis? Follow Shimada, only not so close, not so close! Don't tense up! Don't freeze. Relax, Kuwahara, relax. Your back is like a gate post. All right . . . better now. Breathe calmly. You can't fight the enemy if you're fighting yourself. Shimada's beginning his dive, so follow. Over you go, Kuwahara, over you go.

Shimada has peeled off, seeming to lift slightly, balancing it seems for a full second on his wing tip, then dropping away with increasing speed, his nose angling toward the enemy. I am following his swiftly vanishing tail, and the Hellcats are in full view, growing larger at every second. At first, just minutes earlier, only toy planes, but now they are actual aircraft, formidable looking fighters, with men inside. Americans!

It is absolutely clear now. We will strike at their rear then fan off rapidly, hit and run. Too many for anything else. The enemy is still unaware of us. Should I begin firing? No, wait for our leader. Do everything he does. But why doesn't he shoot? We can shoot now, spray them en masse and drop a dozen or more. Yes, yes! I'm sure we can. Nearer. . . nearer. . . rapidly closing. Shimada is opening up! Ripping off short, deadly bursts . . . swift red trails from the tracers, fleeting away with diabolical speed, seeming to arch and curve, heading for the enemy.

The Hellcats are aware of us now. Rolling off, no doubt in their minds. Fire, Kuwahara— fire! I haven't even squeezed the trigger. Wildly I blaze away. Compulsive, attenuated blasts . . . all consumed by the sky. Then a Hellcat flips crazily, rotating belly up, veering off, angling downward. A remarkable maneuver, but no—he's hit. I hit him . . . got him!

No, no . . . Shimada has done it. My own tracers are swallowed again and again into an endless void of deepening blue. We flash on past the stricken aircraft, banking and climbing, eager for altitude.

The entire tail of the Hellcat formation has scattered, the rest far ahead. Half a mile or so below, Shimada's victim is spiraling downward in its death throes, vomiting black smoke, smoke as black as tar. Flames lapping savagely with a kind of awful glee all along the fuselage.

Fascinated, I watched its waning death plunge, gripped simultaneously by exultation and frustration. I had never known it would be so gratifying to see an enemy destroyed. But why couldn't I have been the one to do it? Just that one Hellcat when the chance was so perfect. But perfect opportunities, I soon discovered, are rare and very brief, usually only seconds, even for the most skilled. At the time, though, I didn't even remember having him in my sights. I had just fired away compulsively hoping to score a hit by spraying enough sky.

By now we were fleeing for home, and I caught a gleam of silver from the corner of my eye, above and off my right wing tip about four hundred yards away. Then another and another, flashing and vanishing, flashing and vanishing, among the wisps of cloud. Once I glanced down and caught my breath. A short distance below and to my right three Hellcats were keeping pace. I had always supposed that the *Hayabusa* 2 could outdistance most other aircraft including the enemy's, but the American fighters were keeping up, and we were going all out, full throttle. Maybe, I thought, they have better fuel, higher octane.

No time then for further reflection. Three more Hellcats—apparently the glints of silver I spotted seconds earlier—had materialized, diving at us head on from a thousand yards above, descending with terrifying speed. Strange ripping sounds within the top of my cockpit, but I failed to comprehend the cause. Holes appearing strangely along the trailing edge of my right wing. Instinctively I glanced to the rear and glimpsed a single enemy plane, closing at three hundred yards—sporadic red lines, tracing the space that separated us, and fleeting past my cockpit.

"Cut right, cut right!" The voice of Shimada just ahead, as he performed a tight, rolling bank. The rest of us followed, and shortly thereafter I was on the tail of an enemy. Another chance, and this time I wouldn't betray it. I had him in my range finder now and fired off a calculated burst. A bit too high. Two more . . . lengthier but more precise. The bullets were going home!

It all had a dream-like quality . . . the roaring of my motor, the fierce, staccato thumping of my guns, the whitening sky. . . . But the Grumman was wounded, trailing wisps of smoke. Ramming my plane into a steep climb, I glanced down, following its path, saw the pilot bail out. The chute trailed him, and for an instant I thought it had malfunctioned. Then it popped open, bringing with it recollections of the Mantis that day over the mountains of Fukugawa.

Suddenly I realized that I was no longer with our leader. There was nothing left of our formation, nothing but Americans and a few badly outnumbered Japanese scrambled throughout the clouds. Then, without the slightest warning, I heard the voice of Lieutenant Shimada. "I'm wounded . . . burning . . . going to crash. Save yourselves! Return and report!" Simultaneously, I spotted his plane. It curved across my line of vision just ahead, caught in flame, a virtual fire ball. Then a wild explosion as he struck the American Hellcat broadside, and the two planes were plummeting downward in flame and smoke, disintegrating.

Now my own craft was vibrating strangely, coughing and trembling, the prop roar becoming hoarse and gravelly. My head felt light. I was not getting enough oxygen. Tearing off my mask, I dived steeply, saw the ocean's approach, and glanced at my air speed indicator. It didn't register, and the wind was screeching through my new bullet holes. I stared at the fuel gauge, and my fears were confirmed. Little left. I'd never make it to Hiro.

For now, however, there was no sign of the enemy. It was as if the destruction had spawned a wind to sweep the heavens clean. Gradually, nervously alert, I gained my bearings and limped onward toward Kyushu. The enemy's 50-caliber machine guns had created more havoc than I'd realized earlier. Even my compass was gone, but it was impossible to miss Kyushu, one of our four main islands there below the southwestern tip of Honshu.

Twenty minutes or so later, my motor still sputtering at times, gas tank nearly empty, I was nearing the air base at Oita. Still no sign of my companions, and it was impossible to believe that Shimada was gone. I had observed his fiery death close hand, perhaps the only living witness, yet I could not make it register. My mind was numb.

Now the landing strip was in sight, rapidly growing, and I circled, calling in for authorization to land. Moments later, as I made my approach, a warning sounded from below. "This is the control tower: Do not land—your landing gear is not down!" My pulse rate surged. "Re-peat—do not land! Your landing gear is not down!

Pulling back on the stick, I began my ascent, circling, I pushed the button again and again. "Your landing gear is not down!" Frantically I searched my instrument panel, knowing that only minutes remained, if that long, until my fuel was gone. Then, groping about beneath the panel, I discovered that the landing gear connecting wires had become separated, perhaps severed by a bullet. Fortunately, it was a simple mat-ter to rejoin the ends, and this time as I pushed the button, my wheels lowered into position.

Within a few seconds I was again making my approach, landing with a slight jolt and screech of rubber, taxiing slowly toward the main hangar. My first air battle was over.

Chapter Sixteen

Honor and a Lost Cause

Upon returning to Hiro, I learned that two others of our group had made it to safety. My friend Shiro Hashimoto had been shot down but had survived with a badly shattered leg, A few days later, Oka, Yamamoto, Nakamura, and I visited him at a hospital in Hiroshima and were depressed at what we found. Hashimoto's leg had been amputated and he had attempted suicide.

Antiseptic odors assailed my nostrils as we entered the room, and I began to wish we had never come. What could we possibly do, even say that would help? Simultaneously, I was strangely fascinated by the scene.

Hashimoto seemed to be a different person, wraith-like there in his white bed. His skin was ashen. Only the burning eyes revealed what was happening inside. The cotton blanket dropped away starkly where his leg should have been. Our greetings were uncertain, trite, somewhat embarrassed. "We brought you some magazines," I said, humiliated at the triviality of such a gesture.

"Thanks, Kuwahara," he said," but I don't feel like reading anything right now."

"Well . . ." I replied hesitantly, "maybe we can just leave them for you . . . until you're feeling better. I mean . . ." I persisted, "I'm sure you'll be improving in a few days."

Hashimoto shook his head, gasping a dry laugh. "How do you improve when a leg's been blasted off? Grow a new one?"

I made no reply, and we all simply stood there, wordless and stupid. Yet something had to be said. Why were they leaving it all to me? I was becoming irritated and eventually blundered onward. "We know it's very hard for you right now," I said and patted his hand, groping for an intelligent thought. "But you have fulfilled your obligation to the Emperor. You are a true *samurai*, far more than the rest of us. And, from now on you will be able to do as you please, even find a wife and get married." I knew that last was a mistake even before I said it, but the words had simply tumbled out.

"Oh yes!" Hashimoto rasped. "Wonderful! Maybe I can find a good strong one—one like an ox who can carry a cripple on her back."

Still, I kept talking. "I know how you feel, but lots of people are being wounded in this great war, and that doesn't mean they can't marry. Think of Lieutenant Shimada. He'll never—"

"Would to God, that I had followed Shimada!" Hashimoto croaked, actually struggling to sit up as if he might attack me. Then he fell back with a moan, closing his eyes, barely breathing, it seemed. "What good am I?" he sighed. I could scarcely hear him. "To anybody?"

Silently cursing myself, I glanced at the others. There was no accusation in their own countenances, merely vacuity. Yamamoto shook his head and stared at the floor. Then Oka, with a slight toss of his head, indicated the door. Reluctantly, I started to leave, but turned back for an instant, patting his shoulder. "We'll see you again soon," I said, knowing that we might never see him at all. It was too painful.

Just then footsteps sounded in the hallway. A man and a woman entered, obviously Hashimoto's parents. After we had exchanged introductions, the woman turned to her son without speaking and laid her hand upon his brow. Long delicate fingers, slightly tremulous. "Here," Oka volunteered and slid the room's only chair her way. Thanking him, she sat down and continued to stroke Hashimoto's forehead.

Again there was silence, and again we were ready to leave, but now the woman was speaking. "Why must people fight? Why must they hate and destroy each other? Why?" Her voice was surprisingly rich and low, filled with incredulity. She was shaking her head now, eyes half closed. "Oh, the senselessness of it all! The stupidity! Why can't. . . ?" She hesitated, eyes closed for an instant, collecting herself. "Shiro's father and I did not rear him so that he could lose his leg. Nor did we rear his brother Joji to die in some awful jungle on Guadalcanal."

Hesitantly I informed her that I had recommended her son for the medal of valor, but that too was a mistake. Obviously the only way to avoid further idiocy was to keep my mouth shut.

For a moment I gazed out the window across Hiroshima. Little did I comprehend how ironic her comments about death and destruction would become in the days ahead and how applicable with respect to that city. At the moment, I devoutly wished that we had never come there, that I could simply vanish.

"I did not mean to hurt your feelings," she said, "or to appear un-grateful, but there is something I must tell you all before you go. Look at me all of you," she commanded, and we glanced at her in surprise. "Listen to me carefully, my sons." Our astonishment increased. Her voice was harsh and dry, almost guttural, yet somehow very appealing, and her eyes possessed a kind of passionate fluidity.

"Your minds are filled with strange ideas," she continued, "much that is false and malevolent. Ideas about honor and glory, dying with valor. These and many related matters." Her face was solemn, remark-ably commanding, etched with many lines but also beautiful. Her hair contained a startling streak of white as though it might have been splashed with acid.

"But I advise you to forget such things. Seek only to preserve life—your own and those of others. Life alone is sacred." Her eyes held us hypnotically. "There is no honor, my sons, in dying for a lost cause."

I stared at her in disbelief, shot a glance at her husband, expecting him to rebuke her. As though reading my thoughts, she eyed him sharply, but he remained silent. "Fathers feel no differently about this than moth-ers do," she persisted, "not deep inside."

Suddenly I recalled with great poignancy how my own father had looked into my eyes months earlier and inquired, "Do you know my heart?"

Shortly afterward we said goodbye, but all the way back to Hiro I kept hearing the words of Hashimoto's mother: "There is no honor in dying for a lost cause." A lost cause? An indescribable feeling was settling, infusing the very pores of my skin with hopelessness. Throughout the following days those words persisted. The feeling increased, and gradually I became indignant. Who was that woman that she could presume to speak such heresy? A mere woman! And her husband—he must have been a small man. Indeed, a very small man! Obviously, she was in command of that household. She controlled him! Heresy in and of itself.

But my indignation often left me as rapidly as it had come. Always the cold and frightened feeling returned, increasing. I had not seen much of Tatsuno the past few weeks. Both of us, of course, were heavily involved in our military duties, but gradually I came to realize that he made me uncomfortable in much the same way Hashimoto's mother had. What had he said during our last actual visit? Something about the secret. Yes, what was the secret? What were we waiting for?

I had no answer, none at least that I could accept emotionally. Surely the words of Hashimoto's mother and Tatsuno did not reflect the attitude of our people in general. And yet . . . I could not deny it. The disillusionment was growing, and at last I began to face the facts.

Japan had been driven back three thousand miles across the Pacific. MacArthur had returned to the Philippines, entering Luzon and vanquishing our forces at Leyte Gulf. This I had learned through the winds of military rumor, but the winds had now attained gale force. Although I did not realize it initially, that loss had virtually eliminated Japan as a naval power. Even then, however, I knew that it had exerted a serious impact on troop morale. For many months the Americans had taken very few captives, but now we were surrendering in substantial numbers.

Of course, there was *Kamikaze*. The suicide attacks had increased on a grand scale, and from all that we could learn they had been highly effective. For a time, in fact, they had fanned the flames of hope, yet still . . . would *Kamikaze* actually stop the enemy? If so, it would require far more human bombs. Colonel Okamura's estimate that three hundred suicide planes could alter the war in our favor was obviously much too small.

Nevertheless, a part of me clung to the fraying branches of hope. If a "Divine Wind" had saved our country once when her plight was just as desperate, why not again? Was not the Imperial Way the right way after all? The best way, ultimately, for the world? Was not Japan divinely destined for leadership? If indeed there were a God—one of truth, reason, and justice—was it not only right, but also eminently logical that he should come to our rescue? Possibly our present trials were the final test, one of our courage and worthiness. So maybe, just when our plight looked the most bleak, as night was closing in, our circumstances would improve.

But how many human bombs would it require? Many of our men were still willing to lay down their lives. To many, in fact, it was no sacrifice. To some, honor and duty were, in very deed, heavier than the mountains, death lighter than a feather.

In any event, the Divine Wind was steadily mounting, and as it increased more and more of us would be drawn into it. Only a matter of time, only a matter of time. The clouds were darkening above Hiro. The first gusts were coming.

Chapter Seventeen

Death Greets the New Year

On New Year's day 1945, fighter pilots from Hiro's Fourth Squadron held a testimonial ceremony for those of our number who had died. Captain Yoshiro Tusbaki, the squadron commander, delivered an impassioned speech declaring our moral obligation to avenge those deaths. And later we visited Hiro's military shrine. Not many had died yet from Hiro. In fact, all my close friends were still with me. There was one name, however, that I will never forget, that of Lieutenant Jiro Shimada who had died and taken an enemy with him in my first air battle. For a long time I gazed at his name plate there on the base of the shrine. One of the fallen valiant.

Again I saw his plane like a flaming meteor, the crashing and billowing explosion . . . the two aircraft, fused as one then decimated . . . the blackened, smoking fragments dropping toward the water. Japanese and American, united even in the midst of their disintegration. Falling, falling, falling down and away. "No more New Years for you, Lieutenant Shimada." The words were not spoken, mere pulsations in my mind. "You have fulfilled your obligation to the Emperor." Then, very slowly, I turned and walked away.

What sad attempts we made, our words of "Happy New Year" falling like frozen clods to the earth. No doubt all of us were thinking of

New Year's Day at home somewhere in the dreamscape of the past. I recalled with a sudden twinge of nostalgia how Tomika and I had run through out home on that same day years before, jubilantly scattering beans about to drive out the evil spirits.

The spirit that entered Hiro that New Years afternoon in 1945, however, could not be driven out by scattering beans, even by the shedding of blood. It was then that Captain Tusbaki called a meeting unlike anything I had experienced before or since.

It was then that Hiro's first *Kamikaze* were appointed. "Those of you unwilling to lay down your lives as divine sons of the great *Nippon* Empire will not be required to do so." Such had been his words, his promise. Then . . . the ultimate, dramatic pause. His eyes like burning cinders. "Those incapable of accepting this honor will raise their hands now!"

Ah yes, to be a suicide pilot, a *Kamikaze*. That would be the honor of honors. Had not everyone said so? But six men had raised their hands during that meeting in response to the Captain's promise of exemption, men I knew well. Afraid enough, or perhaps brave enough, to admit what most of us secretly felt.

They had chosen life and been given death, a dubious honor.

A few months earlier, men at other bases had volunteered with apparent alacrity. Now, it would seem, many had to be compelled, even tricked! Stern evidence that *Kamikaze* was already considered a failure, a futile death, by ever-growing numbers. Daily the Allies were becoming stronger. There was no denying it now. Moving ever closer, with more men, more ships, more aircraft. The B-29 Superfortresses, ominous grumbling monstrosities that they were, had begun to clot the heavens, leaving swaths of fire and destruction. The American naval forces were closing in a terrible juggernaut.

How I hated to admit it, fought against the very idea, but it would not be denied. Japan was losing fast. How long, I wondered, would our people be able to hide behind a crumbling facade of propaganda? How much longer could anyone remain in denial? Six at Hiro had refused to, and now, ironically, would forfeit their lives in consequence. Early in January, only days after our meeting, they left Hiro for suicide training.

Periodically from then on, men were selected from my squadron and transferred to Kyushu for their final preparations, never to be heard of again.

For nearly a year now we had been carefully conditioned to accept the inevitability and glory of death in battle. For thousands, actually; it was a part of our historic philosophy. But now, suddenly, the tentacles were reaching out, relentlessly taking and taking. With each departure our sense of doom expanded. Sometimes it was a leaden feeling in the gut, sometimes a clotting in the throat. Increasingly it was both, often accompanied by waves of sadness, nascent tears and a kind of crying of the heart.

On the other hand, I had come through several air battles now with a second enemy plane to my credit, and that had at least increased my confidence as a fighter pilot. Flying over the inlet between Kure and Tokuyama, six of us had jumped two American fighters, and it had been surprisingly easy. Approximately one thousand feet above them, we veered off, diving at terrific speed and struck from the rear, almost before they were aware of our existence. All six of us opening up simultaneously with cannons and machine guns.

The nearest American virtually disintegrated under our combined onslaught and went down in a sheet of flame. The second attempted to escape, performing a sharp bank to throw us off, but two of us had anticipated the move, and within seconds I had him in my range finder. It was almost that simple. Three or four fierce bursts, and he folded, plummeting downward in a smoking tail spin. How different from my first encounter with the enemy. I almost felt cheated.

So, I was becoming a capable pilot rather quickly, as also was Nakamura with one plane to his own credit. Yet no matter how skilled we might be, no matter how many adversaries we might vanquish, the supply seemed unlimited. Indeed, relentlessly, growing, almost fiendishly. Doom was omnipresent like an oncoming tidal wave. Only one hope for survival now, a tenuous wisp which I scarcely dared contemplate. The merest acknowledgement, in fact, spelled disloyalty if not cowardice. It was February 1945, and the enemy was attacking Iwo Jima, just over 650 miles from our capital, so perhaps the war would end before long. Most of us, I suspect, prayed for this. Not directly, perhaps, for the defeat of our country but rather for a cessation to hostilities. Truly a strange and paradoxical form of denial. Many of our civilians still had faith that Japan would prevail, but we who lived within the inferno had to be either naive, fanatical, or both to expect triumph now.

Within only a few weeks my conviction regarding Japan's impending fate had become a kind of groundswell. And gradually, my fears of compromising myself began to evaporate. Now that surrender was only a matter of time, irrevocable, I was praying for it with increasing fervor and frequency. It had become the classic race against the calendar, perhaps even the clock, and ironically only the enemy could save us.

Some of us at least had greater hope than others. Most of our fliers at Hiro were inexperienced, and already I was among those ranked as top pilots. Such men would be preserved as long as possible to provide base protection and fighter escort for suicide missions into the Pacific. We would return and report in detail upon their success.

Consequently, our poorest pilots died first, causing the enemy to conclude, initially at least, that there were no skillful *Kamikaze*. In the words of American Admiral Marc Mitscher: "One thing is certain: there are no experienced *Kamikaze* pilots."

Regularly at this point, orders from the *Daihonei* in Tokyo were sent to key air installations throughout the four main islands, specifying how many pilots each base would contribute at any given time. These larger installations, in turn, drew men from bases within their jurisdiction. The one at Hiroshima, for example, drew from nearby Hiro, our own base, also from Kure, and Yokoshima—all on the main Island of Honshu. Men were then committed to special suicide bases including Kagoshima, the largest, on the southern inlet of Kyushu.

In general *Kamikaze* attacks were mounted in waves of fifteen or twenty planes at thirty-minute intervals. Some of those pilots were allegedly sealed or locked into their cockpits, but I never witnessed such things. Nor, in my opinion, was there any reason for it. Once it all began, there was no turning back except for a rare few who returned, having been unable to find the enemy. Frequently, in fact, our *Kamikaze* actually opened their cockpits and signaled with flags or scarves upon sighting the first American ships—a final show of bravado, a last gesture to boost one's courage before the plunge into oblivion.

No one living will ever comprehend the feelings of those men who covenanted with death. Not even condemned murders, not fully. The murderer is atoning for the ultimate crime against god and humanity;

justice is meted out. Of course, men throughout the world have died for their countries, sometimes knowing in advance that death was inevitable. But where, before or since, has there ever been such massive and pre-meditated self destruction as occurred with the *Kamikaze*? Where have thousands of men diligently set about their own annihilation, training methodically, relentlessly, mulling over all the details for weeks, some-times months?

Neither the Shintoistic concept of a post-mortal existence as a guard-ian warrior in the spirit realms nor the Buddhistic doctrine of nirvana has always provided solace. The "mad, fanatic Jap" was often a mere school boy, snared in the great skein of fate, not above weeping for the arms of his mother in many cases.

Not that there weren't fanatical Japanese fighters. Some wanted nothing but to die gloriously, to honor the Emperor, to gain revenge. Even the subdued, bespectacled student, browsing through some Tokyo library, might be molded by circumstances into a flaming soul dedicated to death. And there were some who seemed to approach the end as though it were only a morning stroll.

In general, however, we pilots moved along two broad paths. The *Kichigai* (madmen) were fierce in their hatred, seeking honor and immor-tality, living for only one purpose—to die. Many of these came from the navy air force which contributed a far greater number of *Kamikaze*.

As time passed, I personally allied myself more closely with a sec-ond group whose sentiments were basically the opposite though rarely expressed openly. These men, mainly the better educated, were referred to as *Sukebei* (libertines) by the *Kichigai*. I should stress, however, that the *Sukebei* were not unpatriotic, not, at least, in their own view. I would die for my country today if necessary, as I would have died then. But life was decidedly dearer to us. We saw no purpose in death for death's sake alone, and at times now our country's fate welled ominously like the seething crater of a volcano as viewed through endlessly shifting vapors.

Certainly, also, there was a middle ground, and each man's attitude fluctuated to some extent from hour to hour. There were times when I longed for revenge. Or when I considered that by destroying an Ameri-can ship I might save many of my people . . . then my own life seemed insignificant.

How often I had struggled for a certain attitude toward death—a special, indescribable feeling of acceptance. What was it that made men unafraid? Was it courage? What was courage? "We are expendable!" That was the cry. "Be resolved that honor is heavier than the mountains and death lighter than a feather." Countless times I had repeated those words, repeated them obsessively. With some men that conviction seems to have been innate. With me it was ephemeral; I was always fighting to re-kindle the flame.

All of my friends were still with me, Tatsuno now a fighter pilot. Ah, to be a fighter pilot, to be with my friends against the enemy. That had always been my dream. But it was a tattered and fading dream already. Some of us were bound to make our final, one-way trip soon, no matter how good we were. Who would be first?

Daily I went through our routine suicide practice. Methodically I performed each dive— with absolute precision now, near perfection, but little satisfaction. Mechanically I performed the exercise, beginning with a leaden feeling in the stomach that swelled throughout my throat, expanding into dread. More than once the words came: "Go on, go on! Don't stop! Crash! It will all be over in an instant. No more fear, no more waiting, no more sorrow." And always I would pull out, calling myself a coward.

In addition, there were the occasional air battles, most of them only quick scraps or sorties, in which we struck swiftly and fled. Invariably, the enemy outnumbered us, and our lives were now dedicated to something more vital than a mere air skirmish. Japan was like a man dying in the desert with little water left. The remaining drops had to be used sparingly, saved for the hours when the sun would burn its fiercest.

As the months faded, Japan began to reel, losing her grip on eastern China. The heart of Tokyo had been demolished, and our entire homeland was being ravaged. Millions of tons of our merchant shipping had been sunk, and by the Emperor's birthday in April of 1945, the enemy was assaulting Okinawa, Japan's very doorway.

It was a crucial time. Premier Suzuki had told the Japanese cabinet, "Our hopes to win the war are anchored solely in the fighting on Okinawa. The fate of the nation and its people depends on the outcome." Okinawa fell. Eighty-one days of violent battle.

The months squirmed by, and one day in May it happened—Oka and Yamamoto. I had returned from a flight over Shikoku and heard the news. I hadn't seen either of them for two or three days because we had been flying different shifts on reconnaissance. And now it had come, what I had been fearing all along but never fully accepted. The orders had been issued suddenly, and my friends and been transferred within the hour to Kagoshima. Oka and Yamamoto, gone! I could not believe it and rushed to their barracks. Surely they could not have been swept away so quickly!

The door creaked as I entered, and I gazed down the long line of cots. The bedding was gone from two of them, the thin, worn mattresses rolled, leaving only the barren springs. There was something ghastly about those beds; the naked springs cried out. I opened their empty lockers and heard their hollow clang, a death knell.

Dazed, I slumped down on one of the empty cots, feeling it sag. It was as if Oka and Yamamoto had been carried off by a sudden gale. How could such a thing have happened? No time, no notice, but of course it was probably best that way. I sat there alone, and for a while there was nothing but silence, not even the sound of motors. For several minutes I stared at the floor, on through it. Saw nothing, felt nothing. It was too much to comprehend. The place was a void.

No telling how long I sat there, insensible. Eventually I actually dozed for a moment then startled awake as a hand rested on my shoulder. Nakamura. I hadn't even heard him enter. Without speaking, we looked at each other. Someone was with him. Tatsuno. I extended my own hand uncertainly, and he gripped it.

"You know," I managed at last, my throat parched. "I had the strangest feeling sitting here. It was as if . . ." My voice cracked. "It was just as if everybody had left. This whole base empty—nobody, nobody anywhere. It was crazy! Have you ever had that kind of feeling?"

"They said to tell you *sayonara*, Yasbei," Nakamura said. (My friends were often calling me after the *samurai* now.) "Still joking, even when they got into the truck." Nakamura gave a strange laugh. "You know what Oka said—his last words? He said, 'You and Yasbei take good care of all our girls in Hiro!'"

I also laughed if only because of the release it provided. Neither of us, or Tatsuno for that matter, ever went to Hiro or the nearby cities. We rarely drank and knew little of the city women with whom our extrovertish friends had consorted.

For an instant I recalled my times with our two departed, remembering how we became well acquainted that winter night so long ago when I'd found the warm shower. They had been joking then and never stopped. Even in combat they joked, two of a kind, always together. Ironically they would die together, perhaps already had.

"But why did they go so soon? Good pilots, both of them!" I asked.

"Yes, pretty good," Nakamura replied, "but lone wolves, maybe a little erratic. The days of the lone wolves are gone."

"I know, Nakamura," I said, "but look at some of the other pilots in this squadron—not half as good, not half as good!"

"Maybe they're putting the names in a hat now," Tatsuno suggested. "That way it's more entertaining. That way, you don't know whether it will come in five minutes or five months."

"Let's get out of here," I said. "Take a walk—anything."

PART FIVE

Chapter Eighteen

Wind Among the Lanterns

At times even now the terror of *Kamikaze* fluctuated, even seemed to fade. After all, we reminded ourselves, there were many ways one could die. The bombs were coming often now, and we were learning what it was like to scramble like rats for our holes. Sometimes the enemy would sneak through our radar screens, and the alarms would scream providing little or no warning. Now we knew what it was to feel the ground shudder with explosions, to cower in dust-choked craters, while the slower men were often blown apart. Once I had seen two laborers running, frantically, the bombs dropping directly on top of them. I closed my eyes then opened them. Nothing remained but new craters.

Regularly now our hangars and assembly plant were being strafed and dive-bombed by Hellcats, P-51 Mustangs, and light bombers. Then one fatal day in June an immense flight of B-29's pulverized Hiro and nearby Kure Navy Port. The warning had sounded thirty minutes beforehand, and because of their numbers, every available pilot had taken off to preserve our remaining aircraft. But after that bombing there was virtually nothing left of Hiro, no base to which we could return. Consequently, we had to make the long and sorrowful flight to Oita Air Base in northeastern Kyushu.

It was there that I became a suicide escort. Today very few of us remain—the only ones who can testify to what happened out there with the American ships in the Pacific, who can describe how the doomed pilots acted and probably felt at the final moment.

Life at this base became increasingly grim, yet even so it was fascinating to note individual reactions. The punishment of earlier days was over. Tested and proved, we were among the elite of *Nippon*'s fighting airmen. As such, we were given extra money and told to enjoy ourselves during off-hours. Men who had rarely touched liquor took to heavy drinking, and many who had never even kissed a woman joined the lines at the prostitute's door—ten minutes a turn.

Women and drink had long been considered vices as far as fighter pilots were concerned–not exactly immoral as some other cultures might view it, but wrong because pilots had a duty to perform, a monumental obligation which nothing should hinder. The Imperial Rescript itself contained stern warnings about succumbing to creature comforts and self indulgence. In our own case, however, greater license was granted. We were the men with numbered days, and everywhere the sense of finality was growing. People who would have condemned others for such actions now said nothing. Life was short, and the airmen, especially fighter pilots, were highly esteemed, almost idolized by most of the public.

To some, religion and the pure life became all the more meaningful, and several of us hiked into the nearby mountains to feel the caress of nature, to escape, to meditate. Occasionally Nakamura, Tatsuno and I went together as comrades, trying to cast aside the grimmer aspects of life as completely as possible. On one occasion, we sat together and reflected upon life rather profoundly for people our age. Tatsuno was the real philosopher, though, always probing deeper into the mysteries of existence than most people do. Despite all he had seen of death and sorrow, Tatsuno believed that life had a purpose, that it was the ultimate school of schools, that even the most terrible physical pain or mental anguish, had a place in the eternal scheme.

Once the three of us sat on a knoll, gazing across the ocean to where the clouds were creating a resplendent sunset of orange, gold, amber, and blazing red like the heart of a blast furnace. Between the clouds stretched the horizon in a narrow, irregular expanse of pale green. Above it all the sky was a royal blue, deepening into purple, and a single star pulsed the color of mercury. "Some day . . . ." Tatsuno mused and paused.

"Some day, what?" Nakamura asked.

Tatsuno waited for a minute or more. "Maybe it will all fall into place." He shrugged, twisted his head. "Pain and sorrow. Maybe none of that will really matter except in terms of how we met it. Some people come away stronger . . . better. Or death. Some see it, and they are destroyed. Others seem to gain a greater appreciation for all of life, a greater reverence. It's as if the spirit itself has been polished and refined. Maybe that sounds crazy, but I think that's the idea."

Nakamura was frowning. "Yes, but whose idea?"

"Somebody's" Tatsuno replied at last. "Maybe just mine. Maybe whoever's in charge."

On other occasions my walks were solitary. Alone one Sunday morning, I wandered past small, well-tended farms toward the mountains. On either side of me stretched the rice fields, dotted at intervals with farmers, some with yokes over their shoulders carrying buckets of human waste, others irrigating or at work with hoes. Those farmers were artisans, their crops laid out with patience and devotion, with drawing-board precision.

Old women were also scattered throughout some of the fields, pulling weeds. For hours they would bend in the traditional squatting position, nothing visible but their backs and umbrella-like straw hats.

These aged brown *obahsan* of the earth lived to toil. For them work was more than mere expediency. It was life itself. All had known hardship. Many had lost sons in the war. Many had been forced to sell their daughters. But always those weathered faces were ready to form cracked smiles of greeting and welcome. For them, life emanated from the rice where the sun warmed their backs and the mud oozed up between their toes. Another woman nearby sometimes to converse with, and easy laughter. That was life and it was enough. Never before had I envied old women. Respected them, truly, as I did our elderly in general, but never envied them until then.

Walking slowly up the long, dirt road, I passed an ox with a ring in his nose. He was tied to a tree, switching his tail occasionally at the flies. The ox seemed very calm and resigned. That was his life, there beneath the tree and he accepted it. The hole in his nose had formed a scarred lining long ago. The ring did not hurt now. Remove it, and he might wander vaguely, I decided. Probably, though, he would remain where he was, flicking his tail. That was enough. So, in the end, conditions didn't matter nearly so much as perspective. Acceptance, resignation—that was the important thing.

Near the foot of the mountain, the lane fanned into a broad, graveled road, extending a hundred yards to a stone stairway. The steps ascended in tiers, passing beneath several great, wooden *torii*. Midway, a woman holding a bright yellow parasol was climbing upward with a baby in a carrying cloth upon her back. Even from that distance I knew that the baby would not be dangling limply. It would be hugging her back like some tiny arboreal creature, bright dark eyes incredibly luminous, peering alertly over her shoulder, drinking in the world, the universe. Reflecting them.

Passing beneath the final, upper *torii*, I emerged in a clearing where temples and shrines lay in a half moon, their walls covered with intricately carved designs, their eaves curving upward at the tips. Part of one facade was carved with golden dragons, another with red and green lions possessing strangely human faces. Still another was adorned with flowers, exotic plant life, bending reeds, and low-flying waterfowl.

At the entrance to the clearing an aged man and a young girl, probably his granddaughter, were selling amulets. All alone, those two—just the old man and the little girl. There where sunlight and trees filigreed the land with light and shadow, where a breeze played intermittently along the lattices and the ancient buildings.

Having purchased one of the charms, I strolled ahead toward the buildings. At the entrance to the main temple were many lanterns, the center one—red, black, and gold about six feet in diameter. I was surprised that so few people were present, but reminded myself that this was a remote area. It was still early. Once I glimpsed the yellow parasol gliding among some trees before vanishing behind a pagoda.

Climbing the temple steps very slowly, meditatively, I paused at the entrance and gazed into the darkened and hallowed confines. It required a few seconds for my eyes to adjust to the dimness, but gradually the faintly burnished wooden floors materialized, then the darkened corridors, all of it simmering with reverence and quiescence, faintly echoing the ages past. No bombs had fallen here; nor, I devoutly hoped, would they. Here the war did not exist, and everything within seemed expectant, gently beckoning.

I removed my shoes and hesitated, caressed suddenly by the cooler temperature. Looming a short distance before me was an immense, rounded statue of Buddha, towering perhaps fifteen feet into the gloom. It was a pale, gray green like oxidized copper, yet it seemed to emanate a steady, subtly expanding glow. Automatically, I knelt, gazing upward into its face. What a countenance! How indescribably benign and imperturbable! How removed from the petty cares of the world!

The longer I gazed, the lighter it became, and the more it seemed to convey . . . what? Almost a smugness at having so fully transcended the mundane. But no, not smugness, I decided, for it had transcended that too—all such concerns, all triviality, all vanity. It was, instead, the very quintessence of tranquility.

For perhaps an hour I sat there, my legs tucked beneath me, meditating. I did not comprehend all the differences between the religion of Buddha and national *Shintoism*. Nor did I understand how it was possible for a person to embrace both simultaneously as many in my country actually did, for their doctrines regarding an after life seemed utterly antithetic.

On the one hand lay ultimate transcendency, ultimate liquidation of individual identity and absorption into the grand and universal "soul", much as a drop of water enters the ocean. On the other, the perpetuation of personality and of human relationships. For our fighting men, those who died valiantly in battle, the honor of being guardian warriors in the realms beyond.

As present, however, differences in theology were irrelevant. For the moment I was already in another world. "If death is anything like this," I thought, "then perhaps it won't matter much how it comes as Tatsuno says, only in terms of how we face it. A few years one way or another, in reality, for all of us. Then it will come as surely as the setting of the sun, as surely as cherry blossoms fall by the roadside. And, after that? What it was I did not know, yet there had to be something, an outcome that was correct and in keeping with the grand and proper order of things.

Something about that temple impelled me to linger on and on. There in that remote sanctuary I was safe, and the world beyond the mountain was unreal. For a time I actually believed that I had found the solution. I would stay here forever beyond all harm, all strife, all sorrow. Ere long I would become a priest. Yes, that was my answer. Here where antiquity hovered, absorbing the present and the future. Here in this eternal fourth dimension, this place of sweet sadness, and attenuated nostalgia, of kindness . . . of ultimate reconciliation.

How long I remained there, I am uncertain, but the sun had crossed its zenith, and the shadows of afternoon were expanding. At length I arose and left, turning my back upon the great Buddha, feeling the persistence of its vibrations, and entered the waiting day. Sitting upon the stairs a short distance below was a man in a white robe, his head shaven bald and faintly gleaming. His hands rested in his lap, and as I drew closer it appeared that he was totally relaxed, remarkably in tune with his surroundings, much like the Buddha itself. His gaze was directed at the distant sky and ocean.

As I passed by, his voice came warmly, with remarkable resonance: "Good afternoon, young airman!"

"Good afternoon," I replied uncertainly.

"You have come from Oita?"

"Yes, revered sir, from Oita." I hesitated, angling a furtive glance, fearful that either refusal to look his way at all or a direct stare would be disrespectful. Simultaneously, it occurred to me that his hair was actually very dense, the dark roots sheening through his scalp like an abundance of iron filings.

"Do you have a few moments?" he continued, "or must you now return to your base immediately?"

I hesitated, unaccountably embarrassed. "I must . . ." I began then reversed myself. "I have a few minutes, revered sir."

"Good," he said, giving a quick nod. "Come and sit down. We shall enjoy the trees and beautiful vistas together."

Bowing, I introduced myself and sat beside him as directed. Strangely enough, the uneasiness swiftly receded. After all, I reminded myself, the season is late. Why waste it on timidity? It was good now simply to be in this man's presence, to converse, or remain silent.

Soon, however, he began to ask me questions—where my home was, how long I had been a pilot, how long at Oita, and at last: "What is you present assignment?"

"Fighter pilot," I said. "In a few days I will be flying escort missions."

"*Ah so!*" The words came quietly, politely, the eyebrows barely elevating, "for the *Kamikaze?*"

I nodded. "Yes, revered sir."

For a time, he offered no reply, merely nodded faintly, contemplating the horizon. Eventually he spoke, inquiring thoughtfully and at length regarding my background and family, and all the while I wondered when he was going to speak to me officially, with formality, as a Buddhist priest and as my elder. He never did.

Clouds were collecting about the sun, now, enhancing the shadows and the breeze. Its tendrils were playing over us, stirring trees in the valley below. "Wind is a strange phenomenon," he observed quietly, "is it not?" For an instant I regarded his profile, one a bit like my father's. "We don't really know its point of origin, nor can we see it."

"That is true," I acknowledged.

"Yet it is always present somewhere, always manifesting itself, always moving. No doubt it is one of those things that will always be." He paused. "Do you believe that the spirit of man itself might be somewhat similar?"

"Perhaps so," I said.

"You and I," he continued slowly. "I mean the essence—that something which makes you and me who we are—I suspect that it will always be, much like the wind. Always somewhere, moving, doing its work, becoming manifest."

"My friend Tatsuno feels that way," I told him. "I . . . I greatly want to also."

"*Ah so!*" Again the exclamation with the same subdued politeness, and he regarded me curiously, earnestly. "There is not one thing that ever reduces itself to mere absence," he said. "Even the human body." He held out his own hands, strong looking hands with pronounced, widely branching veins. His fingernails were impressively well groomed. "Destroyed most certainly!" The fingers closed, forming fists, "But not annihilated!" I glanced at him. Those last words had come with a kind of passion. His face was fiercely resolute.

Then his manner became more mild once more. "Changed, yes, in remarkable ways, but not obliterated. Matter, energy—they have always existed. They were not woven from an empty loom. They will always be."

I nodded. "Perhaps so, revered sir."

"And thus, my friend. . . ." His hand actually settled upon my shoulder for an instant, "although the spirit can depart this frail tabernacle called the body, that should not concern us unduly. It is all a part of the grand cosmic order, and we continue. The wind has left these lanterns now. It is far away, quiescent for the moment perhaps, but the air itself is everywhere."

Soon it was time to go, and I departed, offering much thanks and several bows of respect.

"I hope that you will return, Airman Kuwahara," he said.

"I likewise, revered father," I replied.

Then I left the clearing, descending the long stone stairway beneath the *torii*.

Chapter Nineteen

The Miracle of Life

After that visit I began to view the world, life and death, somewhat differently. The temple, and the great, emanating Buddah, the priest . . . and the wind among the lanterns. I had accepted the priest's philosophy, and although it transcended my sense of reason, it also appealed to it. Even more, it somehow resonated within my being.

Nevertheless, no philosophy, even the most sustaining, could fully vanquish what I experienced during my first escort flight over Okinawa or what I felt in the aftermath. Never before had I seen men, indeed my own companions, plunge to their death in that manner.

After my first escort flight, I tossed in near delirium throughout the night, the images of that mission flashing through my mind in endless and chaotic array. At times I would awaken, wrenched upright into a sitting position, clasping my brow with both hands, hoping to exorcize it all by a concerted act of will. Determination! I told myself, If you have enough determination, you can turn it off and have a little peace. But inevitably, at the first approach of sleep, it returned with diabolical insistence. I could not escape.

Over and over, I was accompanying our fifteen *Kamikaze*, watching as the dives commenced, two or three transformed into savage eruptions of flame and smoke, flames the color of molten lava, smoke black as the fur of a panther. At times I was alone with only the boundless water below. Endless water in endlessly varying tones—indigo blue, darkening gray . . . and subtly glowing pearl . . . turquoise and brilliant, spring-rice green.

And water alone was all right, yet asleep or awake, no matter how tightly I clenched my eyes and willed it otherwise, I could not exclude the vision of that first ship . . . and another, and another.

Then, inevitably, the entire enemy convoy—dozens of battleships, carriers, destroyers, and other vessels, sullenly balanced there upon the face of the sea, methodically—imperceptibly, it seemed, at first view—gliding forward, leaving their widening white wakes. The ships swiftly enlarging, the tracers streaking wildly in straight red lines, and the proliferating death blossoms of the flak.

Always at that point, I would escape the nightmare with a jolt. It was the falling sensation that nearly everyone experiences at times on the threshold of sleep but greatly intensified. Then . . . lying there shuddering, afraid of wakefulness, yet more afraid of sleep.

During that night and the days to come, I wondered increasingly what might become of my body at the end of my first and final one-way trip. If I accomplished my mission and struck an enemy ship, what would the explosion be like? No doubt, only a shattered second of remaining awareness . . . unless by some fantastic quirk of fate I were to survive. No, no—ridiculous. No one could ever survive such contact.

What, I wondered, would become of my head? Would my head be blasted from my body? I could almost see it at times, a charred and featureless blob sinking to the floor of the ocean. How deep was the ocean, there off Okinawa? A mile? More? I thought of the Mariana Trench therein the West Pacific. Six miles deep, the deepest spot in the entire ocean.

In my mind I saw a leg—my leg, tossed on an immense wave. I saw one of my arms. Would my arms and legs provide food for the sharks? My fingers . . . would my fingers seem strange to some fish? I saw a fish, its round eye staring impassively at fingers lodged in a strand of kelp. The fish was canary yellow with brilliant stripes of blue, its fins gently wavering, almost transparent. I saw it nibble tentatively.

If I struck an American ship, however, I might take many others with me. What wonderful irony, to find my burial in intimate company with the enemy. Ah yes . . . I shook my head, actually feeling the insinuation of a smile. Death, the grand and undeniable equalizer! What remarkable impartiality! What a curious camaraderie it bestows upon us all!

Often on those sultry nights my mattress became so damp from my own sweat, so hot that I arose and walked to the window, hoping for a mere trace of breeze, the faintest whisper. Usually nothing came, but I would stand there long enough immersed in thought to let the mattress cool a bit. Sometimes I would turn it over because the underside was cooler. Having removed the sheet, I would waft it up and down in the humid air hoping to dry it a little.

Over the past few weeks I had acquired a heat rash on my chest and upper arms that sometimes itched insanely. But no matter, I told myself; all such concerns would soon be of no consequence. Often still, I thought poignantly of home. I wrote few letters now, though, because they were being censored, and several of them had apparently never arrived. Therefore, even this final and tenuous link with my past had been reduced to a few trite words, abstract sentiments that could scarcely be conveyed.

Nevertheless, both my mother and Tomika wrote me faithfully. The first bombs had now fallen upon Onomichi, but thus far our immediate neighborhood had been spared, perhaps because of its sparser population and inconspicuousness upon the verdant mountainside. Happily, none of our family or immediate neighbors had been injured, but now after so many months away it had all become a fond dream, and even the dream was waning, for I would never return.

Now that I was a fighter escort, Nakamura, Tatsuno and I did not see each other as often, and our barracks were some distance apart. At times Nakamura and I flew the same mission, but that provided little opportunity for close association, and Tatsuno, with less experience, was only flying reconnaissance at present.

Throughout it all—the anxiety, fear, frustration, sorrow . . . the fleeting hopes, we escort pilots were learning something valuable, learning what was necessary for a *Kamikaze* to die effectively and with honor. We knew, better than anyone else, what it required to sink an enemy ship. I personally knew the best strategy, having witnessed some successes and far too many failures.

To the novice, diving into an American ship might seem relatively simple. In reality, however, it had become increasingly difficult. First, there were the ever-vigilant enemy fighters. In addition, each vessel fired off an astounding barrage. The combined output of anti-aircraft, heavy caliber machine guns, and other weaponry, created a virtual lead wall at times.

Moreover, the moment they were under attack, the ships began to zig-zag erratically, so that many of our pilots missed their targets completely, plunging into the ocean. Often, as well, it was easy to become confused in pre-dawn attacks or storm. One *Kamikaze* from another base, in fact, was reported to have mistaken a tiny island for a battleship during the early hours of morning. A billowing eruption against the gloomy shore had revealed his error.

In my own estimation, the best procedure was to descend from a height of ten to five thousand feet, the sun at our tails. The dive angle would vary from forty-five to sixty degrees, leveling out about five hundred yards from the target and roaring in as low to the water as possible.

Thus an approach would occur below the angle of the bigger guns. That way also the ships were in danger of hitting each other with their own weaponry, and a strike at the waterline greatly increased the likeli-hood of a sunken vessel

Despite our most desperate and ingenious efforts, however, the aver-age number of hits was now only ten to fifteen percent. A sad contrast to those first impressive results at Luzon.

Chapter Twenty

Women of the Shadows

During **my months** in the air force I had spent little time in the cities. Unlike most of my associates I rarely entered the bars and never once patronized any of the numerous brothels. In consequence, I received a lot of teasing. It is difficult to explain why some of us abstained. As I have indicated, however, sexual relations out of wedlock were viewed by my people somewhat differently than they were by those of various other cultures. Despite the Imperial Rescript, the satisfying of physical appetites was not considered immoral in the traditional sense as long as it did not interfere with one's duties and obligations.

My own attitude was partly the result of pride. Having come from a wealthy family of high social standing, I did not wish to debase myself by association with the lower elements of city life. In addition, I was still very young and shy. Women made me uneasy. It was even hard for me to converse with those outside my own family.

In any event, I did not consider the purchasing of sex, like meat across the counter, especially admirable. Certainly it was no achievement. One man's money was as good as another's. Frequently, as I noted with scornful amusement, men whom the average woman would never have offered a second glance in civilian life were coming to view themselves as great and captivating lovers.

On the other hand, I did suffer temptation. Sometimes at night, outside the base, I heard the feminine voices, laughter—occasionally warm and comforting, more often brazen and seductive. And often those sounds filled me with frustration. "The time is late Kuwahara," I told myself. "Better live life to the full. Go find the best in town. You've got the money."

Occasionally as I strolled through the city with Tatsuno and Naka-mura, the prostitutes who approached us were amazingly aggressive. One in particular—a woman, perhaps in her early thirties, with large, jutting breasts, makeup so heavy her face appeared embalmed, and a lavishly painted mouth. She had actually seized my arm and tugged me toward a shadowed doorway. I could smell the musky odor of her body blending with the cloying scent of tobacco breath and perfume. How well even now I remember the throaty voice: "Come along, young airman, I can make you happy all night long for only a few *yen*!"

Simultaneously excited and disgusted, I had shaken her off, stam-mering, "No, no thank you."

How Tatsuno and Nakamura had laughed. Then they had almost roared when in mock anger she shouted, "Oh, so you don't like a good woman! You are not a man yet, correct? Just a baby. Come back when you are a man, *akachan*; maybe I will give it to you free!"

Now that we were allowed overnight passes, only a few men slept in the barracks. On those hot nights, sometimes only two or three of us there, I tossed, even talked to myself. Wiping the sweat from my brow and upper lip, I would hear the words: "Come back when you are a man, baby dear."

Once, about midnight, I sprang from my cot and began yanking on my clothes, nearly tearing them. Damn that leering face! That smug, brazen. . . . Damn that sexy, ogling countenance, that pliant smirking mouth! Damn those large, impertinent breasts! I would show her! She would never call me a baby again—not when I was through with her.

She'd moan, weep, plead! That's what she would do.

I stubbed my toe and swore aloud, then blundered into my open locker door and swore even louder. "What's the matter, Kuwahara?" a voice drifted from the far end of the barracks.

Stifling a desire to shout, "Shut up and mind your own business!" I stood by the locker, clenching my fists but offering no reply. What was there to say? For a long time I stared into the locker's confines as though it were the void, letting its darkness fill my head, letting it absorb and dissolve the faces and the voices, allowing its emptiness to enter my soul and blot out everything.

Finally, I lay down again, heaving a sigh. At last a slight breeze was sifting through the barracks. I remembered how I had reacted, seeing girls—some no older than thirteen or fourteen—standing in the shadows, along the darkened facades of buildings and the alleys. Many of them were no different outwardly than girls I had known at school.

Then, too, I reminded myself that a visit to one of those places would not be very enjoyable anyway. Nakamura had tried it, just once, and had returned to the base sickened and disillusioned. In the pallid light of morning he had awakened to reality, gazing upon the woman beside him. The paint had worn from her mouth except for a few remaining flakes, and her eye shadow was smudged like ashes. Her hair was disheveled and ratty, the breath rasping from her open mouth. Nakamura had retreated swiftly, suddenly aware that he might have contracted gonorrhea, or syphilis.

No, I would never make Nakamura's mistake. At least, I would go out with my self respect in tact. Then, however, a thought surfaced. There was one thing I could do in the time remaining, something to ease the endless anxiety and frustration, at least make life a little more bearable. There were night clubs in many of the towns run by our military, places, I'd been told, with a rather pleasant, home-like atmosphere, where one could simply order a meal or a drink. And, of course, there were girls, girls to dance with or merely visit.

What was the name? I wondered. The one nearest our base there in Oita? The Tokiwaya Club—that was it. Yes, I would go to the Tokiwaya just to see what it was like. Perhaps it would help take my mind off Okinawa. Perhaps I would not wonder quite as often when my death orders were coming.

Chapter Twenty-One

Toyoko

An evening in June found me sitting at a table in secluded corner of the Tokiwaya. My friends had gone elsewhere, and I was there alone, idly contemplating the froth in my glass of beer. Other men were on hand from the base—too many, laughing boisterously at times, dancing spastically, even idiotically in some cases. Or so it seemed to me.

This was definitely not what I had hoped for. Such frivolity only depressed me. Sitting there, staring into that glass of beer, I decided that it looked, even smelled, like urine. How long had it been now since I had visited my family? I was struck more forcibly than ever that it had been more than a year. Now it would take a miracle, the miracle of miracles, for me ever to see them again.

Why had I come here in the first place? Pushing the glass of beer aside, I leaned on the table with my face cradled in my arms. Yet where else could I go? Where lay escape? Only in that final, fatal dive. The rest was simply a matter of waiting . . . waiting . . . agonized waiting.

Several minutes had passed, and I was actually almost asleep when a hand touched my shoulder, very gently. "Are you ill?" the words came. Startled, I glanced up. The voice was incredibly soft, the face, heart shaped with high, gleaming cheek bones, the eyes dark and fathomless. Her expression? It reminded me remarkably of my own sister's in times of greatest concern. Inquisitive, yet gentle and compassionate, not the expression of that woman of the streets.

"Is everything all right?" she inquired. What fantastic sweetness! There is no other word. "You don't look very well."

Momentarily it occurred to me that she couldn't really be interested, not in my personal problems. After all, she was being paid to be nice; it was simply part of her job. Yet there was something about her eyes now, a kind of wistful light that belied such explanations. Her gaze had captured my own almost hypnotically, but suddenly, highly embarrassed, I glanced down at the table. "No, not . . . I'm not sick. Just . . . well, thinking."

"*Ah so*," she said, softly yet with strange wonderment, as though my thoughts must have been quite profound, eminently worthy of her attention. The smile flowed, this time with a tinge of mischief, but again the ineffable sweetness. "Would you care to dance?"

Forcing a twitching smile, I shook my head. "I'm afraid I'm not very good." Then I was stammering again, terribly humiliated. "I don't even know how, in fact."

"That's all right," she replied and hesitated. For one desperate moment I feared that she would leave, vanish from my life forever. "Would you mind if I sat down for a while? Here with you?"

I glanced at her again and reddened. Still the same expression. She had never once averted her gaze from my face. "Yes," I said, "I mean, no. I'd be happy to . . . have you sit down. I mean, if you aren't too busy. If you really want to."

'Thank you," she said.

We sat in silence for a moment, her eyes still upon me while I stared at my hands, gaze flicking up once or twice to meet her own but unable to maintain contact. "Could I buy you a beer?" I asked, "some dinner?"

She shook her head. "No, but that's surely nice of you. Thank you very, very much." Yes, she was like Tomika, not so much physically as the expression, her entire demeanor. I cast furtive glances at the intricate flowered designs on her *kimono*—silver and gold—and let my gaze descend to the soft white *tabi*, stockings with a separate sleeve for the big toe. Everything about her was neat and delicate, her hands like those of a ceramic *geisha* as were her feet in their woven *zori*. Yet she possessed those feminine fluid contours that any normal man would regard with fascination.

Vainly I struggled for something to say. Conversation with my friends had never been difficult, but now with this woman simply sitting there, steadily watching me . . . it was a strange situation indeed. "Well . . ." I managed at last, "I supposed I should be getting back to the base." Intending to sip my beer, I began to stand, lifted the glass, and accidentally took too large a gulp, half choking.

Her eyes were full of amusement, the mischief increasing, and her hand reached out to touch, even press, my own. "Wait, please!" Mystified, I sat down again, this time finally staring at her directly. Could it possibly be that she was infatuated with me, maybe—for some weird reason—even in love? Vain, foolish idea, but what was the answer? "Would you mind greatly if I asked you a personal question?" she inquired.

"Ah . . . yes, I guess so." The imbecilic stammering again. "I mean— no, I don't mind!" I blurted, wondering why I had said the simple word "no" so loudly. People were even looking at us. "It's all right."

"Good," she said, "and please don't be offended, but I can't help wondering how old you are."

So that was it. I felt myself becoming angry. Almost gruffly, I replied, "I—I'm twenty, twenty years old. Why? Why do you ask?"

"*Ah so desuka!*" She sounded as if that were a marvelous achievement, very respectful. "Is that true? Twenty?"

"*Hai*" I replied even more abruptly. "Why do you want to know?"

"Oh, you really are angry, aren't you?" For the first time, she glanced down. "Please excuse me for my extreme presumption." For a few seconds I thought that she was going to cry. "The reason I asked . . . I just had to because . . . you remind me so much of my younger brother, so very much I can hardly believe this is happening." Again, Tomika—especially that unique pleading quality in her eyes the night she had learned of my enlistment. The tear falling on my photograph. "He was killed in Burma."

"Oh," I said, suddenly feeling sick—sorrow for her, but also a sense of dread as though it were an omen. "I am terribly sorry."

For a time we simply looked at each other, immersed in a great sense of pathos, of tragedy—in a strange kind of rapport that I had never experienced before. "I am so sorry," I said. "You must miss him very greatly."

She barely nodded. For a minute or two we remained there in silence. Then at length she reached out, pressing her hand against my own again, and I could feel the emanations of life. Somehow it all seemed very natural.

By now, however, it was closing time, and we were saying farewell. Beginning to leave, I paused, glancing back at her. They were turning out the lights, and her face in the gathering darkness was remarkably luminous and phantom-like. "I'm so very sorry about your brother," I repeated and hesitated. "I lied to you about my age, because I was ashamed. I am only sixteen too. Well, almost seventeen," I added.

'Thank you," she said, "for your compassion, and for your honesty. A tear glistened in the corner of her eye, and she barely touched it with the tip of one finger. "Will you be coming back?"

"I hope so," I replied. "I want to."

The following evening, having flown another escort mission, I returned promptly to the Tokiwaya, ordered a second noxious beer and sat down at the same table. Minutes crawled by during which time I feigned interest in my drink, once even raising the glass and sighting at the colored lights though its contents. A blue light turned it green, red light a dull orange. At least that was an improvement, but in reality, of course, I was only looking for one thing: that remarkable young woman from the night before.

Eventually, I arose and crossed the fringe of the dance floor, greeting a few friends along the way, to obtain some peanuts and packet of fried squid. That too, however, was only a pretense. For perhaps twenty minutes I had been looking everywhere, covertly but also obsessively, to no avail. Then I returned, and sat there absorbed in the dark surface of the table with its slurred and amorphous motions of people dancing. Perhaps the idea was not to look for her at all. Maybe then she would materialize magically as on the night before and lay her hand upon my shoulder.

Another fifteen minutes elapsed, and I was rapidly becoming more restless, even irritated. Each time some girl passed by, I angled a glance, but never a sign of the right person. Once I thought I saw her dancing with an airman I knew, and my heart squirmed. But wrong again. She was not there.

Dismayed, I stood, ready to leave, offering the Tokiwaya one final, panoramic overview. Gone . . . non existent. A mere dream. So now, another hot, nightmarish siege in the barracks. A girl passed by carrying bowls of *soba* noodles, sloshing the contents of one in her haste. Surprising myself, I called out to her, but she continued with her tray, barely casting me a glance and murmuring something I didn't catch.

Then she returned. "What would you like?"

Suddenly I realized that I didn't even know the other girl's name. "That person I was with last—" I was almost stammering. "The one sitting here with me last night for quite a while. At this table. Do you know which one I mean?" She merely looked confused and shook her head. "The girl with the long hair," I persisted. "Very pretty." My face was flushing absurdly. "Long hair, tied in back."

"I'm sorry," she said, "but I just started working here."

"All right, thank you," I said dejectedly, got up and walked toward the exit.

I closed the door behind me hard, shutting out the music and the laughter, then wandered slowly down the street, hands in my pockets, watching my feet move steadily with a life of their own. Maybe a little walk around town. Maybe I would go see a prostitute, after all. That would serve her right—asking me to come back, then not even being there! I spat in the gutter, and my mouth felt dry. Simultaneously I heard the clop-clop of wooden *geta* approaching rapidly behind me.

"*Ano!*" It was the same girl I had just queried. Breathlessly she accosted me. "That girl you were asking for—it's her night off." I offered my thanks profusely, even bowing, and she giggled, clearly embarrassed. "You're welcome." Then she was clattering off again.

"Wait!" I called. "Normally I would never have asked the next question, but now it seemed imperative. "What's her name?"

She hesitated. "Her name? I don't. . . ." More hesitation. "Maybe it's Toyoko. I think it's Toyoko."

"Do you happen to know where she lives? I'm supposed to give her an important message," I added lamely.

"I don't really know. I couldn't say for sure." Clattering off into the dark again. "I have to get back."

"All right! But just tell me where you think she lives. It's very important that I talk to her."

I jerked a ten yen note from my pocket, running after her. "Wait!"

Again she paused, casting a quick backward, almost frightened, glance. "No, I don't want any money."

"Take it," I insisted, now face to face. "I know you can use it. Just say where you think she might be. That's all you have to do, and I won't tell anybody."

"All right!" she said looking distressed, and took the note. "I think she lives down by the beach in the Miyazaki Apartments, but I don't have the exact address. Don't blame me if that isn't—"

"Thank you very much," I interjected and was on my way.

"I'm not sure, remember!" her voice trailed, sounding like that of a grade school girl. I made no reply.

It took me several minutes to find the place, but at last I was standing before the Miyazaki Apartments, squinting to read the sign in the blackness. Fortunately the place was not very large, probably only a dozen units, located behind a white and slightly crumbling stucco wall covered with vines and fragrant flowers.

The time was only ten o'clock, and some of the windows were dimly lighted. Moments later I entered the gloomy alcove of the first and peered at the mailboxes. Six of them—two without names. The last one, however, read, "Toyoko Akimoto," and my heart skipped a beat. Yes, that had to be it! Slipping off my shoes, I mounted the stairs swiftly, almost stealthily, and paused before the door of room six.

A soft light gleamed beneath the entrance, and my pulse quickened. Taking a deep breath, I knocked and waited, fairly burning inside. No answer. I hesitated then knocked louder. Perhaps Toyoko Akimoto was asleep. Or maybe someone was there with her. The very thought dismayed me greatly.

I waited uncertainly for some time, then on impulse tried the panel. Ever so cautiously, I felt it catch, then glide open an inch, squeaking softly. Two small rooms, the second raised slightly above the first, opening onto a tiny balcony. "Toyoko?" I called softly, surprised at the sound of my own voice. "Miss Akimoto?" All a dream. Crazy. Suddenly a panel opened noisily below giving me a start, but it was only someone leaving. Again I hesitated, then slid the door open a bit farther. Definitely a woman's residence. It smelled faintly of perfume, and several *kimono* hung on the wall. One was pink, another violet. Yes, the very atmosphere seemed to emanate femininity. The only furnishings in the main room were a round, lacquered tea table the color of molasses, a charcoal burner and two dark red cushions with gold brocade. In the raised room beyond, a single *futon* was laid out for sleeping. Another folded on top with two sheets and a white nightgown.

Entranced, I slid the door even wider, I could see a child-sized dresser on one side of that room near an open window. Across its top was draped a pair of silk hose—a real rarity. A faint, tentative breeze was filtering through the window, lilting the tips of the stockings and billowing the curtains off an open balcony.

I knew that I should leave, felt the guiltiness of a thief in the night. What if this belonged to a different Toyoko? Or what if that wasn't her name at all? The girl who had given me the information merely supposed she was called that, hadn't even known her last name. What excuse could I give if the person who lived there should suddenly appear?

Uncertainly, I had turned, on the verge of leaving, unmindful that I had left her door half open. Simultaneously, I heard a faint tinkling sound. I turned back listening. Yes, coming from the balcony . . . a soft, silvery, clinking—a sound that made the hot night a little cooler. It was a sound from my past—glass chimes, suspended from the overhang there on the balcony, the breeze running its fingers through them. I craned my neck, peering, saw fragments of glass barely trembling and oscillating, reflecting vagrant gleams of light like miniature stars.

Enchanted, I lingered, listening then gave a start at the sound of a door opening below. *Geta* clapped against the concrete floor of the alcove, one after another, echoing. Then someone was padding rapidly up the stairs toward me. No escape now! What would I do? What could I say?

Wearing a *yukata* of midnight blue, bent low over the stairs, she failed to notice me before we nearly collided, then glanced up with a gasp of astonishment, placing a hand to her mouth. I struggled to speak, but my vocal cords seemed shriveled and parched. For a moment we simply stared at each other. She had a large white towel over one arm and looked different enough without her make-up that I was badly confused. Her luxuriant hair was not tied. It flared down her back, still slightly rumpled and damp, smelling of scented soap.

"Oh," she murmured, "It's you! You frightened me."

I opened my mouth, gagging the words out by sheer force of will. "I'm sorry," I stammered. "I didn't mean to frighten you. I was just leaving." Making no sense whatever. "I mean I only wanted to—"

"It's all right," she said. "It's just that I wasn't expecting you." This followed by a little rill of laughter that tinkled like the chimes. "I just got back from the bath."

"Yes, I can tell," I said, all the more embarrassed. "I can see that this is a bad time, though, so I'd better be leaving. It's just that we're flying a lot of missions now, and. . . ." Again the groping.

"Oh, no!" She shook her head, and her eyes met mine as on the night before. Her hand reached out, the fingers barely tracing my arm. "You aren't . . . Aren't going for good?"

"No," I replied with greater confidence, "not for good—not for a while yet."

"I'm so glad" she sighed, "please wait just a minute, please." She slipped inside, closing the door, then immediately opened it again for an instant. "Don't go away," her voice came, "I'll be right back!"

Minutes later the door opened all the way, and Toyoko was standing there in her pink *kimono*, wearing lipstick and rouge as she had the night before. "Please come in," she said.

"Are you sure it's all right for me to be here?" I mumbled, feeling more foolish than ever.

"Of course it is," she replied and her tone was quite motherly. Then she handed me a cushion. "It's much nicer out on the balcony, Yasuo. A breeze is coming in off the sea." The chimes were more insistent now, more melodious. "And we can look out upon the water."

A wide, tiled overhang slanted downward beneath the balcony, below which lay a courtyard, and beyond that over darkened alleys, roof tops and trees rolled the ocean. Its surge and roar was gentle but insistent, gradually increasing, and we could see the ragged fringe of white surf welling inward along the beach then subsiding, reviving again with the next breaker in a long and crashing sigh.

"Do you like the sound of the ocean?" Toyoko inquired.

"Yes, very much," I replied.

Tilting her head back and closing her eyes, she murmured, "Hmmm, I love it. It smells so wonderful. And the sound. No matter what the problem . . . well, it somehow helps."

"Very true," I said, "no matter what the problem." For a moment I reflected upon the fact that soon the ocean would solve all my problems, felt the simmering of soul. Then it subsided with the next dying wave, and for a time I was at peace.

"I like those chimes," I said. "They remind me of the ones in our garden at home. Where did you get them?"

She smiled, a fleeting expression of fond reminiscence. "They were given to me, by a friend. By the way, why don't you take your socks off and dangle your feet over the edge the way I'm doing."

"That's all right," I replied nervously. "This way is fine."

"Oh, come on," she said and actually began tugging at my toes, pulling the socks off. Meanwhile, I found myself laughing nervously but also feeling grateful that I had showered using lavish amounts of soap before leaving the base, donning fresh underwear and stockings. At least, I didn't smell bad, and Toyoko smelled wonderful.

Then she was rolling my trouser cuffs up slightly as well. "There now, doesn't that feel a hundred times better?"

"*Hai,*" I laughed, "it really does." In some ways she was like a little girl, amazingly natural and unaffected. Yes, I was beginning to feel at ease. My instincts had been right after all. Either that, or I had been extraordinarily lucky.

"Last night," I said, "you asked me a question—remember?" Toyoko looked uncertain. "About my age. I told you that I was only sixteen." She nodded, watching me. "Is it all right if I ask you the same question?"

"Oh, that! Why not? I'm almost twenty-four. I'm an old, old woman," she said, and we laughed together.

"You told me I reminded you of your brother," I continued. "That was interesting. I mean, I was surprised to hear you say that because you remind me of my sister, Tomika."

After that we visited for nearly two hours, talking about our pasts. Toyoko had left a large family in Nagasaki when she was eighteen and supported herself ever since, working in bars and restaurants, once as a maid in a mansion. She had even traveled for several months with a troop of dancers and modeled for large department stores occasionally. For the past year she had been a hostess at the Tokiwaya.

"It's been good, Yasuo—talking to you," she said as I left. "This is the first night that I haven't been lonely in months. Will you come back soon?"

"Yes, yes, any time," I replied, "if you really want me to."

Her smile was utterly enchanting. "Are you free tomorrow night?" she inquired. "I'll be off at ten, and I was thinking we might go for a walk along the beach."

That night I returned to the base happier than I had been for many months. Even the flights loomed less sinister, the entire future. Maybe, I told myself, the war would end soon—soon enough to save me. For the first time in my life I was actually feeling a close kinship with a woman outside my own family. I decided, in fact, that living with men only, year in, year out, could be terribly deadening.

Almost every night the following week I met Toyoko at her apartment, and as the days passed I began taking her rations from the base. Food of almost any kind was hard to obtain now, and it made me very happy to help her a little. When no onions were available for our *sukiyaki*, Toyoko used cabbage. Even cabbage was rationed but usually still available at some of the markets.

Occasionally also I brought clothes for her to wash. Despite my reluctance, she had insisted and clearly took delight in doing things for me, watching with an almost maternal expression as I consumed great quantities of her cooking.

Late one Saturday night as I prepared to leave for the base, Toyoko eyed me inquisitively. "Yasuo. . . ." she said and hesitated.

"What is it?" I asked.

Reaching out, she placed her hand on my arm. "Do you really have to go?"

"Well," I replied uncertainly, "it's getting late; I can't keep you up all night."

Her glance softened. "Why not stay here? It wouldn't be any problem at all." Excited but also confused, I merely mumbled incoherently, and she continued. "I have two *futon*—and two sheets; we could both have one." Again, the humiliating embarrassment, the fumbling for words. "Oh, why not, Yasuo? I'll sleep here and you can sleep in the other room by the balcony—in where it's cool. Look, we can even draw the curtains for complete privacy." She gestured gracefully at the diaphanous, white veil next to her, barely tracing it with the backs of her finger nails.

Toyoko's so-called curtains would obviously afford little privacy, but I decided not to argue the point. By now I was her most willing captive. "All right," I said, "that is very kind of you." It took only a moment to unroll the *futon*, and I stretched out upon it in the dark, my forearm across my brow, hearing the whisper of cloth as Toyoko undressed in the adjoining room. The chimes tinkled entrancingly almost over my head, and in one of the distant lanes an itinerant noodle vendor tweedled his flute.

Chapter Twenty-Two

Chimes in the Night

I was staying with Toyoko Akimoto regularly now, and it was almost as natural as being with my own family. Despite our age difference, we had much in common, and usually needed little more entertainment than the sound of each other's voices. Sometimes we sat at evening in the rear garden and leaned against a large, lichen-covered rock by the wall.

Overhead curved the flowering branches of a tree clustered with fragrant yellow blossoms, and occasionally their petals fluttered down upon us in gentle celebration. Often Toyoko placed a stick of incense in a rusted urn nearby, and we would savor the odor, eyes closed for the moment while freshets of night air flirted the smoke into tendrils and sudden swirls.

As much as I wanted to be with Tatsuno and Nakamura, there in those final days, I wanted to be with Toyoko more. I could not, in fact, stand to be away from her for a single night, and the days without her were growing torture. Simultaneously, I was often insecure, wondering how she could possibly be content to spend her free time with one so young as I . . . such a natural relationship in one respect and yet so strange I often seemed to walk in a dream.

My friends, of course, were beginning to make remarks. It was, I realized, inevitable, and more than one flier had begun referring to Toyoko as my "woman". Several, unable to disguise their envy, began plying me with questions. Upon returning to the barracks for morning formation, I was met with many a joke and inquiry. "How was it, Kuwahara? Terrific, right?" or, "Hey, lover boy! How come you never live in the barracks any more?"

Most of the men, however, were unaware of my absence, having abandoned the base by night themselves. As for the others, I made little effort to clarify the situation and usually managed to change the subject. For one thing, few of them would have believed me had I told the truth, and those who did would have ridiculed me mercilessly. Furthermore, I thought too highly of Toyoko to open her private life to the crassness of the army air force.

With Tatsuno and Nakamura, on the other hand, it was a different matter. They deserved to have the facts and understand how I felt about the situation. "For your information," I told them, "This is not at all what people think it is. We have a relationship that's impossible to understand unless you've experienced it. She reminds me a lot of my older sister, and I remind her of her younger brother who was killed in Burma."

"I believe you," Nakamura said, "but seriously now . . . you actually mean to tell us that you can spend night after night with a *musume* like that, almost on the same *futon*, and not—"

"We sleep in separate rooms!" I retorted, becoming a bit angry.

"All right, all right!" Nakamura held up his palms in mock surrender. "But she must like you a lot, so maybe you're really missing out."

"I can see what Yasbei means, though," Tatsuno said, subdued and reflective as usual. "I'd give anything for a situation like that—just someone special to be with and talk to. Most of the people around here can't even carry on an intelligent conversation. Nothing but foul language."

"That's the military," Nakamura said.

"True," Tatsuno replied, "but that doesn't mean it's worth anything."

"I know it doesn't, but I'm just saying—"

"It's not only degrading, it's trite; it's an insult to anybody with even half a brain."

"I agree!" Nakamura said pointedly. "I'm on your side. But still . . . a woman like that? And nothing but talking?" He rolled his eyes. "Not me!" I began to reply, but he continued. "It's none of my business. That's just the way I look at it." He shrugged and shook his head, actually looking a bit sorrowful. "No, I'd never take on one of those sluts in town again, but you've got something special."

"I know," I said, "that's why I don't want to ruin it."

"Yes, but getting physical—that doesn't mean you have to ruin it. It's how you go about the whole thing. It's not just you; it's whether she wants it too, and I'll bet you my next month's pay she does." He shot me a glance. "Look, Yasbei—none of us have much time left. When a starving man is offered a first-class dinner, he doesn't just sit and look at it forever." He clapped me on the arm. "You're going to kick yourself, Kuwahara!"

"Don't try to propagandize him," Tatsuno said. "He's found something good, and he knows what he wants."

Nakamura's advice merely left me sad and uneasy, and it also made me very lonely. At the time, Toyoko had taken a trip to Fukuoka to visit some acquaintances. Consequently, I spent the empty evenings with my friends and proved a poor companion. With Toyoko away, life was suddenly more bleak than ever.

Nights in the hot, humid barracks were like a lone and dreary wasteland, and before long, first as a form of escape, I began fantasizing about Toyoko, about making love to her. But if it ever happened, I told myself, it would be all right because she would have become my wife. Yet in between each fantasy, I felt the growing dread. The day of destruction loomed more and more ominously.

Toyoko returned after less than a week, but I was nearly frantic to see her. That night as she opened her door, I simply stood gawking for a moment. "What's the matter?" she laughed. "Don't you recognize me?" As on my first night at her apartment, she had just returned from the bath and was wearing the midnight-blue *yukata*. "Yasuo-*chan*?" Toyoko tilted her head sidewise. "Is something wrong?"

"No, no, not at all," I said. "For some reason you look different, and . . . well, I've really missed you."

"Well," she said consolingly and held out her hands. "Here I am—I'm back." Instinctively, I reached out, extending my own hands inward beneath the broad sleeves and laid hold of her upper arms. It was the first time I had ever touched a woman that way, and her arms were smoother, softer, more slender than I had ever imagined. Suddenly I realized that I had grown a lot the past few months.

Clumsily, I pulled her to me and found her lips with my own. One tantalizing instant. Then she ducked her head, twisting it slightly to one side. "Yasuo!" she murmured, sounding far too much like a mother.

Drawing her still closer, I kissed her exquisite neck, repeating, "Toyoko, I've missed you."

Again, I sought with only partial success to kiss her. "You'll never know how alone I've been."

As we separated, her eyes were wistful. "I've missed you too, Yasuo—Immensely."

Simultaneously I remembered. I had bought her a present, a rare and expensive bottle of perfume, *Kinsuru*. I had hunted a long time for it.

"Yasuo-*chan*. How wonderfully sweet! How remarkably considerate and generous!"

Suddenly more flustered than ever, I replied, "No, it is nothing at all. It is a most miserable gift, really. I just wanted. . . ." Opening the bottle, she sniffed, half closing her eyes in an expression of exotic delight. "Oh, yes, *Kinsuru* . . . How utterly fantastic!" Tilting her head provocatively to the side, she dabbed the tiniest amount with utmost grace behind one earlobe, then extended her finger tips, fragrant and faintly tremulous, for me to smell.

Later that evening, however, as we strolled along a mild bluff beside the ocean, Toyoko seemed strangely taciturn. "Are you sad?" I inquired at last. She paused, gaze sweeping the horizon, sighing almost inaudibly. "Didn't you have a pleasant time with your friends?" I persisted.

I watched her chest rise and fall. Then she glanced at the sand beneath our feet. "Let's sit down," she said at last. "I need to tell you something."

"All right," I replied, but my voice quavered. As we settled down upon the sand, I felt a sense of dread, almost as though I were on the verge of receiving my final orders. "What is it? What's wrong?"

"Promise me first that you won't be angry," she said.

I glanced at her strangely. "How can I promise you that when I don't have the vaguest idea what you're going to say?"

"Oh," she sighed, "you are angry, aren't you?"

The very words she had used that first night in the Tokiwaya, and for some reason they vexed me considerably." Only because you're making me angry!" I retorted. "Just tell me what's going on and quit playing games."

"All right," she sighed, "maybe that's what I've been doing. It's just that. . . well, that trip to Fukuoka wasn't merely to see friends."

She waited so long I was becoming desperate.

"So?" I demanded. "Whatever it is—just tell me."

Another sigh. "It was to see a man I've known for a long time." I waited, holding my breathe. "He's an army officer."

Wonderful, I thought bitterly, A sixteen-year-old corporal competing with a grown-up man, an officer. "What rank is he?" I asked, despite myself.

"He's a lieutenant," Toyoko replied. So, it could have been worse, but still . . . "He used to be stationed in Hiroshima, and a year or so back we were going to be married. But after he was transferred a few months ago he changed his mind. I guess, in fact, that we both did. The relationship was very good at times . . . very bad at others." She folded her arms, shook her head faintly and gazed into the gathering night.

"Anyway, about two weeks ago he sent a letter asking me to come visit. I debated whether I should go, but finally decided I had to, had to give it one last chance." Again, I waited in mounting agony. "After we were back together again, though, it became all the more evident that we needed to go our separate ways."

"So you mean you definitely aren't getting married?" It was a stupid question on the surface. She had already told me, and I was immersed in a wave of relief. Nevertheless, I had to be absolutely certain.

"Yes, that's what I mean. It's good that I went so there would be no question, but it's all past now. And I had to tell you."

My heart was resuming its normal rate now, but I was still perplexed. "Why?" I asked at last. "You could have just come back and said you had a nice visit with your friends, let it go at that."

"Because," she replied, "I want to be an honest and trustworthy person, especially with you."

After that, neither of us spoke for a long time, and I leaned back upon one elbow, wondering, wondering. Why, honest with me? Only because I was so much like her brother? Before us lay the sea, breathless at the moment yet very much alive, filled with faint yet portentous stirrings within its ever darkening vastness.

"I'm honored if I have become a brother to you Toyoko," I said, "but if that's all I am then maybe you'd be better off with your lieutenant after all. Before long I won't be here either." Suddenly, unexpectedly, we both began to cry, uncontrollably, clinging to each other like the last survivors on the ledge of a crumbling world.

"No, Yasuo, no!" she wailed. "I won't let it happen!" Our tears mingled together, coursing down our cheeks. Yet strangely I could distinguish the taste of her tears from my own, salty as the sea, yet somehow sweeter, far more pure. "I will not let it happen!" Toyoko repeated and pressed her jaw against my temple, almost painfully. "The war will end! The war will end in time!"

Eventually we fell asleep clasped in each other's arms, but dimly aware at times of the occasional sprinkling of warm raindrops. We awakened, cold and shivering to the leaden tones of dawn in the far east, a sallow smear of yellow more like imagination than reality. Toyoko's hair was damp and gritty with sand, and the waves were lambasting the shore on a rising tide, its lacy, white fringes sizzling near our feet. A great strand of kelp with bulbs and tentacles the color of iodine neared and withdrew, neared closer and withdrew. Tiny spider crabs pranced, skittered, and vanished into the sand as though vaporized when we arose and headed toward the apartment.

The hour was nigh for my return to the base.

For a time my life remained in strange suspension. The flights continued, but I only lived for my nights with Toyoko. Somehow the prospect of my own demise seemed less real, not quite so inevitable whenever I was near her. Vagrant rays of hope, subtle yet distinct, like the coming of that morning on the beach. For now I took refuge in Toyoko's insistence that the war would end, end in time, partly because it was so passionate, partly because I believed what I wanted to believe.

The strip of beach we frequented was a relatively safe one for swimmers, and on nights when the sea was calm we sometimes entered it, occasionally swimming out beyond the breakers, rising together upon the gentle swells, feeling perhaps that somehow we might be transported far away on those warm, moon dappled waters to some enchanted isle of respite, far far away to a place of perpetual happiness, magically liberated from all danger, from fear and sorrow . . . a place where the war would never come.

Late one night after just such a moment, we returned to shore, strolling hand in hand back to her apartment, smelling the tang of salt and seaweed mingled with ozone on the breath of a nascent storm. Back in the apartment, with no light but the glowing coals in the *hibachi*, we changed into our *yukata*. Once I glanced at Toyoko, seeing a faint, red-orange glow against the bare curve of her thigh and shoulder. The rest was in shadow.

Then we went out onto the balcony and sat listening to the bird-like wheedles of the *soba* flutes. Even now, with the war nearing its very nadir, people had to make a living. Somehow, inevitably, life would go on. "There are a lot of lonely people in the world tonight, millions of lonely women," Toyoko murmured.

"Are you lonely also?" I asked.

"No," she said and pressed my hand. "Not with you, Yasuo. It's just that . . ." Her hand withdrew.

"Just that what?"

Her eyes closed, and she took a deep breath. "Oh, I don't know, I don't know. Why couldn't you be. . . ."

"Be what?" I was becoming angry again. "Older? Less like your brother?" She made no reply. I began to tremble. "Am I such a baby to you still?"

"No, not a baby."

"I'm almost seventeen, Toyoko. Maybe that seems awfully young to you, but age isn't merely a matter of years. I've seen things. I've done things! I know things that other men—millions of older men—don't know. Things they won't know if they live forever!" The words had simply erupted spontaneously, and I was surprised at them, at my own emotions.

Nevertheless, they were undeniable, suddenly overwhelming. "Toyoko, I have to tell you . . . I can't go on like this. It's driving me crazy. Yes, you were a sister to me at first but no more, not now! I want you!"

"No, Yasuo-*chan*, please!" she murmured. I was stroking her face, her neck, pulling her to me, kissing her eyelids, her ears, her entire face. Capturing her mouth, I held it fiercely against my own, and for an instant she relented, her lips moving and fluid, incredibly tender and pliant . . . uninhibited. Then, I crushed her to me tightly, bearing her down and she began to struggle. "No, Yasuo—please don't."

"But why?" I agonized, "when will it be right? Never? Or only when I'm dead and gone?" Reaching beneath her *yukata*, I began to stroke her thigh, and the skin was fantastically smooth, beyond belief, so hot it seemed to burn my hand. "Toyoko, I need you—we need each other! Let me prove to you that I'm a man!"

But now she was thrusting my hand away with greater determination than ever. "No, Yasuo, no, no. It's not right, not for either of us, not now!"

"But why?" I implored. "When?" Her *yukata* had fallen open in our struggles, revealing her breasts. I had never seen anything so sweet, so exquisite, so tantalizing. I sought them with my mouth, my hands, my face, consumed in their remarkable softness, but she gave a smothered cry and thrust a knee against my ribs, throwing me off balance.

Now we were rolling wildly about, grappling, sobbing, suddenly finding ourselves against the brittle railing of the balcony. Several of the rails loosened from the impact, and two or three of them fell off to strike the tiled roof, clattering on the paving stones of the courtyard. Somewhere a voice called out, full of irritation. We were literally upon the brink of destruction.

Gasping, I stared into Toyoko's face, pulling her back to safety. She was crying like a child, inconsolably. Sick at heart, I released her, pulling her *yukata* tight about her waist. "Toyoko, please forgive me!" I pleaded. "I'm sorry, I'm sorry, I'm sorry!" I buried my face against her shoulder. Now, once again, both of us weeping. How much weeping we were doing of late!

The plaintive flute calls had subsided when at length we entered the apartment again, stretched out in our separate rooms on our separate *futon.* Occasionally, I could hear Toyoko sniffling, still catching her breath. Once a tide of anguish and sorrow such as I had never experienced inundated me. "Toyoko, I'm so sorry," I called. "Please forgive me. At least don't hate me!"

No reply—only the echo of my own voice, dying and forlorn. That and the omnipresent sighing of the ocean. Well, the words came, It's over now. Nothing now but going back to that immense black hole called Oita Air Base. Volunteer for your orders. Maybe they will grant your request early . . . for surely, there is nothing left.

Within moments, however, I heard sounds of activity. Toyoko was dragging her *futon* into my room, laying it out quietly . . . smoothing its surface with the palms of her hands . . . stretching out beside me. Then her hand found mine, our fingers intertwining. "I don't hate you, Yasuo." Her voice was still thick with emotion, very frail. "I could never hate you, and there's nothing to forgive. It wasn't your fault."

"It was," I protested. "I was the one who forced things."

"No," she whispered, "no, shhhh!" Two fingers pressed against my lips. "It wasn't your fault; it's really mine, and I don't think you're not a man. You are not simply my little brother either. It's just that we've had something so wonderful and special, I don't want to destroy it. Do you understand what I'm trying to say?"

"Maybe," I replied. "I hope so."

"I haven't always been the person I wanted to be, Yasuo, but I'm trying to change. I want to look at Toyoko Akimoto in the mirror and know who she is—to know that she is worthy of her own respect. I want to look into my own eyes and see someone of. . . ." She began to cry again, this time almost inaudibly. "Someone of value. Not simply to be like most of those girls at the Tokiyawa, and the ones who walk the streets."

"You are of value," I insisted. "More valuable to me than my own life. And you are not that way, not that way at all. I never for a moment thought of you in that connection. It's just that . . ." I paused for a long time, trying to collect myself, wondering how to explain it, then scarcely explained it at all. "Just that I got carried away, and I'm sorry."

"Shhhh!" she intoned, ever so gently, again pressing her fingers to my lips. "There's nothing to be sorry about. Let's just be together and at peace. Together and at peace; that's good enough."

"Yes," I said and waited for some time. "But I have to tell you something, Toyoko," I continued more calmly. "If I don't I can never be at peace."

"Tell me," she said. "Whatever you need to."

I hesitated a long time, summoning my courage, for such words are not easily spoken by people of my background and culture. Indeed, scarcely ever given voice. "I love you," I said, "more than I can possibly say."

Her hand tightened upon my wrist, and I could feel my own pulse. Her breath came in long, shuddering sighs merging with the faint roar of the rising surf and the miniscule clink, tinkle, clink of the wind chimes. The rain was settling lightly again, little more than a dense mist.

"I love you too, Yasuo," she said. "Ever since that first night." Something seemed to be flowing from her hand into my wrist, into all my veins and arteries, tingling in my skin. Both pulses now beating in unison. "And that first night, Yasuo, we were so lonely." Our breathing was deep and tranquil now, slow and regular. The chimes and the sea would carry us quietly away. "So lonely," she repeated. "So lonely."

Chapter Twenty-Three

Ashes for the Family Shrine

At seven that morning I awakened. Toyoko was sleeping serenely, and I dressed quietly. Before departing I knelt beside her, gazing into her countenance. They say love blinds one to the defects of the beloved. Perhaps so, but I had never, from our first encounter, recognized any defects with Toyoko, inwardly or outwardly. To me, she was very near perfection.

She was wearing her white nightgown, one with delicate lace on the neck, throat, and hemline, and those high burnished cheek bones were glowing more strongly as the morning light expanded. I had never realized how long and thick her eyelashes were, how intensely black, yet the growing light was turning her hair to tints of auburn. Her breasts rose and fell gently with each breath, but now I only felt an ineffable tenderness.

Lying there in the lap of slumber, she looked very much like a mere teenager. Only the very faintest lines at the sides of her lips and outer corners of her eyes belied that illusion. In that final moment, I could hear the sound of her breathing, the soft, slow inhalation and exhalation. Even the sound of her breath was perfect. Suddenly it seemed very important that I imprint her entire image within my soul, etch it deeply there forever.

Bending over her, I placed my cheek ever so gently against her own, barely traced my lips across her brow. For an instant Toyoko stirred, her own lips forming the faintest smile, happiness and sadness, wistfulness and mischief, secret things woven from the depths of a dream. Then I arose with infinite caution and left, casting a final backward glance. Sliding the door shut carefully behind me, I descended the stairs with utmost stealth to keep them from creaking.

The streets and lanes were quiet at that hour, largely untraveled, and clouds were digesting the eastern sky, gradually excluding the light. In the fields and between the houses, tiny whirlwinds captured dust, dried leaves, and bits of paper. A cold front was moving in from the ocean, bearing the odor of dead kelp and fish along a stretch of backwater. It was one of those rare summer mornings, those curious reminders, even in the midst of heat and greenery, that winter will come again.

Nearing the base, I felt the empty tingling in my loins, that inchoate sense of excitement and dread that marked the onset of another mission. Once again, the escort flight, fighter protection and monitor to the demise of my companions. It was a strange calling, and with the completion of each fateful journey, my spirit inflated more fully with apprehension, indeed, with a sense of doom. Fate would play its unassailable hand, and I was caught up in it, along with my companions, like bubbles on the incoming tide.

Who would it be this time? I wondered. Another fifteen or twenty men, but lately I hadn't been checking the names. It seemed better that way. Somehow, I had convinced myself that as long as I did not view a name on the roster, it did not exist, just as people tell themselves they are not ill until condemned by a doctor's diagnosis. In any event, I had no close friends there at Oita except for Tatsuno and Nakamura. It was better that way.

At the base entrance, I held out my pass to the MP, a mere formality now, and he waved me on with barely a glance. The place was beginning to vibrate, and overhead, almost out of sight, a plane cried. I walked faster. It was almost time for formation.

The formation was over promptly with the usual, now sometimes suspicious, "all present or accounted for" reports from our flight leaders to the commanding officer. Next, I hastened to the chow hall, planning to eat quickly and give my fighter a final inspection. I was more cautious in this regard than most, almost punctilious, always wanting to be sure that the mechanics had left nothing undone. At least I was confident by now in my own flying ability and was determined not to leave this world because of some trivial oversight. When I left the world it would count for something.

Months of grueling practice were behind me—a series of dog fights, mostly hit and run affairs on our part, but several battles worthy of the name. No longer was I the green and timorous pilot of that first encounter. I now had two enemy planes to my credit, and at Oita I had been promoted to corporal, a rank not easily attained then by Japanese enlisted men. Now, grim though the task might be, I was an escort, leading and protecting our *Kamikaze*, defending them against the enemy to that final, fateful dive, then returning to give my report. That was my job. Who else, I asked myself, had a more important one?

And at night . . . there would be Toyoko. Toyoko had said she loved me, and that was enough. She had promised me that the war would end before it was too late, and I took refuge in those words. Never mind that they were tendered in the crucible of emotion, in a moment of desperation. Still, I clung to them, strongly immured in the household of denial.

That was the only way by now that I could survive psychologically. Yes, yes—something would happen to save me. Not only would the war end in time but something highly extraordinary would occur. Occasionally, in fact, the feeling pulsed strangely at unexpected moments, even within the onset of my dreams. It was a kind of prescience that generated a strange effervescence throughout my veins, my entire epithelium. Even now, though, my moods fluctuated. Doom still hovered and often overflowed the boundaries of my little sanctuary.

Today, in fact, it was encroaching strongly. Today Nakamura and I were flying together. I had spotted him in the chow hall, ahead of me in line and followed him to a table.

"*Yai, tomadachi,*" I said and roughed his head playfully. Simply an informal greeting, an effort to release tension. "Seen Tatsuno this morning."

Nakamura glanced up at me, but the familiar grin was gone. "Yes, I've seen Tatsuno," he said.

"Well, what's the matter? Where is he?"

"Getting ready," he answered.

I felt the sudden chill but hoped for the best. "Going with us? Escort now?"

"Going with us—yes. Escort–no."

Something filled my chest like cold sludge. "He's lucky," Nakamura said. "No more worries, not after noon today. You and I . . . we're still waiting, still on the tines of a pitchfork."

I placed my chop sticks on the table very carefully as if that simple act were of utmost importance. "When did he find out? Why didn't someone tell me earlier so I could have at least been with him?"

"It only happened yesterday," Namamura said coldly. "And you haven't exactly been the most available man in the world this past month. You should try reading the orders sometime, Kuwahara. You don't want to miss your own."

"Really?" I retorted, angry over my very guilt. "So what are they going to do? Shoot me?" Then, riddled with contrition, I bowed my head, eyelids clenched and locked my hands together. "You're right. I haven't been a friend to him at all lately. Not to you or anybody else." Fiercely I bit my knuckle. That was the only thing I could tolerate for the moment, my teeth cutting into the skin and bone.

"I did try to tell you, incidentally," Nakamura said. "Went to your girl's apartment about ten, but you weren't there."

"We were down at the beach "

"Nice! Lots nicer than being with—"

"Stop it!" I banged my fists on the table and grated my chair back, igniting glances of surprise from those nearby. Then I stood, leaving my food untouched, and blundered my way out of the chow hall. Everyone, it seemed, was staring at me. Where was Tatsuno? I had to find him, tell him we'd go down together. To hell with waiting for orders. I'd cover him all the way, end this madness together. My dearest friend would not go alone.

Without realizing it, I was running, hearing Nakamura's voice yet not hearing it. Three hundred yards to Tatsano's barracks, and I was running at top speed, feeling the blood pound in my temples, hearing my breath rasp in my lungs, vaguely aware that the intense physical conditioning of basic training had diminished somewhat. Then, abruptly, I stopped. Tatsuno and his company of the damned would not be in their barracks now; they would be undergoing their final briefing.

Bleakly I turned and shambled off toward my own barracks. Two hours before takeoff time–an hour before my own briefing. Nothing to do but wait. I wouldn't even check my *Hayabusa* now, not until time to go. It would either fly or it wouldn't. All was in the hands of fate.

Nakamura was waiting when I entered the barracks, lying back on one of the bunks, hands locked behind his head, staring at the ceiling. He sat up at my approach, and I settled down beside him, hearing the springs squeak. "Don't feel bad, Yasbei," he mumbled. "I apologize for what I said because Tatsuno wouldn't have wanted it otherwise. Not for you. You've found somebody worth spending time with, all the time you've got left. I was just envious."

"But I haven't even seen him for a week," I said. "Do you know how long he and I have known each other?"

He nodded. "Ever since you were about four years old—Tats told me. But what good could you have done him hanging around here? None of us know when its coming. We'd probably just be getting on each other's nerves." He shrugged. "I haven't seen him that much myself. He's been up to the mountain, visiting that priest you told us about."

For a long time we remained there. Silence, except for a faint and constant ringing in my ears like the sound of a distant locust. "I have a strange feeling about today," Nakamura mused. His words were scarcely audible. "Today maybe we'll all go down, one way or another. Pay our debt to the Emperor."

Somehow the remaining time passed, more as though it had suddenly evaporated. A blank space, a void without dimension or recollection. Then Nakamura and I were there on the airfield, suited up, ready to fly. Sixteen pilots all told—four of us escorts, the remaining dozen never to return. They had grouped now for final directions before an officer holding a large map of the Pacific.

Minutes later it was time for the last formation, and we all stood at attention, hearing the parting words of our commanding officer. From the corner of my eye I could see Tatsuno, but he didn't look quite real, more like a pallid facsimile of the person he had once been. His spirit had perhaps already gone like the wind among the lanterns.

Around the shaved skull of each *Kamikaze* was bound a small flag, the crimson rising sun directly over his forehead. These departures were never conducted in a perfunctory manner. Instead, there was much ceremony, toasts, valiant speeches—most of which I had already almost learned by rote.

Boys and girls, drafted from school to work on the base, were permitted to assemble with the squadron on these occasions. Among the fringe of onlookers several girls began to cry then grew quiet as our commanding officer, Yoshiro Tsubaki prepared to address us. His voice commenced in a kind of nasal whine, droning on and on, mingling with the heat waves, occasionally descending to somber guttural tones . . . then, at last, reached its conclusion: "And so, valiant comrades, smile as you go . . . There is a place prepared for you in the glorious and esteemed presence of your ancestors, where you will attain unto everlasting honor. *Samurai* of the skies . . . guardian warriors, we bid you *sayonara*."

Now, at last, it was time to sing the parting battle song:
"The airman's color is the color of the cherry blossom.
See, oh see, how the blossoms fall on the hills of Yoshino.
If we are born proud sons of the Yamato race, let us die,
Let us die with triumph, fighting in the sky."

So now, at last, the final toast, the *sake* glasses raised and the resurgent cry: "*Tennoheika Banazai*! Long live the Emperor!"

Our *Kamikaze* are saying *sayonara* now, laughing and joking nervously like student athletes before a race. Climbing into their obsolete aircraft—antiquated fighters, even trainers. The old planes don't matter greatly. After all, it is their final trip as well.

The smiles? Perhaps they will remain on some of those faces to the very last. For others, the smiles will die as they settle into their cockpits. Perhaps for some, very few, the serpents of fear won't strike until the enemy ships appeared. And what is courage? A question I have never fully resolved. Who, in fact, is the most courageous—the man who feels the least fear or the man who feels the most and still fulfills his obligation?

But now, there is only one man, a very young one, little more than a boy. Yes, now with Nakamura, the two of them walking toward me. He does not look real, his face pallid, almost transparent. Yes, yes—the spirit has gone ahead. His body will mechanically but faithfully fulfill its duty. What a strange and haunting smile carved upon that waxen visage, the secret perhaps to some immense enigma that the rest of us have yet to fathom.

Tell him! Tell him! Tell him you'll cover him all the way, that you will die together! But no, that is not what he seeks, and something strangles any words. Your time will come soon enough, Yasuo Kuwahara, the time that fate has ordained. That is right. By repeating those words, I retreat from the groundswell, the sorrow and the guilt. I am no friend, though; I haven't been for weeks. No friend. And never once has he presumed to tell me the truth.

The lead in my chest is solid now, crushing. The words emerge painfully under much pressure. "Tatsuno . . . I—" We reach out, and our hands clasp fiercely, but despite the heat of the sun his fingers are cold. Of course, of course; the spirit is elsewhere. Nakamura, a better friend than I, accords us this final moment.

"Remember, Yasbei. . . ." the words came, almost subliminally it seemed. "How we always dreamed of flying together?"

"Yes," I said. Our gazes had blended inseparably for the moment. The ultimate searching of souls.

"Well," he murmured, and the smile increased. "It has come to pass. We fly together today."

"Yes." Muscles on one side of my face were twitching. "I will follow you soon, all the way. Perhaps this very afternoon."

Then, unexpectedly, he extended the other hand. It was wrapped in a meager bandage, and the bandage was turning red. "Here, Yasuo—take care of this for me. It is not much to send, but you know what to do."

Swiftly, I looked away. Tatsuno had just given me the little finger of his left hand.

Our *Kamikaze* almost always left a part of themselves behind—a lock of hair, fingernails, an entire finger—for cremation. The ashes were then sent home to repose in the family shrine. There in a special alcove with the pictures of their ancestors. Once yearly, a priest would enter that room to pray.

The first motors were beginning to cough and rev, and suddenly I flung my arms around Tatsuno crushingly as though somehow I might preserve him. Preserve, at least, all that had gone before, all that we had meant to each other. For that instant we clung together on the edge of a great chasm. Then we broke apart, and somehow, following another blank space, I was seated in my *Hayabusa*, fastening the safety belt, feeling the controls, adjusting the goggles on my forehead. The entire base was grumbling now on the brink of departure.

I checked the prop mixture, pressed the starter button, and one cylinder caught in a high coughing explosion, then another and another. The motor surged ravenously then adjusted in a steady, powerful roar. One by one, we were moving out—lethargic, winged beasts awakened from their lairs. Uno, a veteran of five kills, was in the lead, and I was close behind—signals coming laconically from the control tower. Already the onlookers were in another world, withdrawn. A ring of sad faces and waving hands, fading as the prop blasts hurled sand, bits of straw and paper.

The commanding officer, the remaining pilots, the students, the mechanics come to bid farewell to the ships they had nurtured for a season . . . all shrinking now as the air field fell away beneath us.

Chapter Twenty-Four

The Divine Storm

It was good flying weather. The seasonal rains had at last subsided leaving the skies a splendid morning glory blue. Within moments we were over the mountains, and more than ever it seemed to me that Japan itself was essentially an endless conglomeration of mountains-great, rolling remnants from the past when islands reared volcanically like stricken monsters, when fires burst from nature's hidden furnaces to be quenched at last by time and the sea.

We left the ancient shores, the shores of our four islands, the clangorous cities and quiet rural villages that were home to more than seventy million people.

Thirty minutes after take off we landed to refuel at Kagoshima on the island of Kyushu— for twelve men, most of them still mere boys chronologically—the final glimpse of their homeland. For twelve men the three-hour flight onward to Okinawa would be all that remained, their last short hours upon the earth. Oka and Yamamoto had departed three weeks ago, gone forever, blazing their way into history and the infinite regions of oblivion. Mere dream figures now, their eyes, their forms, their voices fading, fading . . . etherizing, echoing ever more faintly into the past.

Minutes from Kagoshima we spotted a flight of B-29's escorted by Grummans, traveling toward Shikoku. Altering our course slightly, we faded into a skein of wispy cirrus clouds then continued steadily, steadily onward into the day. Far below, rolled the Pacific . . . an immense, ever-wrinkling green, brilliant and dazzling under the sun in places like a billion holiday sparklers.

My mind was teeming with memory now. Home, like my vanished friends, was a poignant fantasy that pulsed and subsided, pulsed and subsided. And always, irresistibly, the face of Toyoko. As the minutes fled I saw her countless times in countless ways. Occasionally merely the face of a phantom tinged with subtle tones of silver and ivy in the shadows, ethereal in the garden moonlight, or softly luminescent beneath the red-orange glow of a lantern gateway. Sometimes her clear dark eyes flowing with inquiry or sweet appraisal, the inevitable tint of loving mischief, of motherly empathy and amusement.

At times our glances had locked so closely and unwaveringly that I could descry tiny replicas of my own face within her pupils. How often I had found myself entranced by the phenomenal, dance-like fluidity of Toyoko's movements as her fingers traced the strings of a *samisen* or lilted back her long and fragrant hair from the nape of her neck. How I cherished the way she walked in her tight *kimono*—such precise and exquisitely dainty steps, one foot placed directly before the other.

Yet always, there was the great expanding void within me, and increasingly, at last to the point of obsession, the words of Nakamura, his fateful augury only a short time earlier in another world: "Today, maybe we will all go down . . . pay our debt to the Emperor." Once despite all, I shook my head half smiling. Kenji Nakamura! What an irrepressible spirit! Nakamura, the recruit who had first befriended me during those soul-ravaging days of basic when it seemed as though our entrails were being wrenched from our throats with grappling hooks. Nakamura, my loquacious comrade—faithful and highly practical in many ways, but who also lived with remarkable abandon.

Even more, increasingly, I thought about Tatsuno. I remembered a day long ago when we had run laughing through the streets of Onomichi swatting at each other with our school caps. How young, how childlike and innocent, back then, two years into the past. Tatsuno, forever my best friend—sometimes playful, a prankster, yet loyal unto death, often introspective, harboring deep and stirring thoughts. "Tatsuno . . . Tatsuno. . . ." I repeated his name many times, shaking my head and fleetingly closing my eyes . . . droning, droning onward, ever more entranced by an unyielding sense of immensity.

Clouds were forming intermittently now just beneath us, whiter than the purest snow, casting shadows of dun and olive on the waters twenty-thousand feet below. Suddenly my radio receiver issued a sharp reaming, startling me from my reverie. A blare of static that pained my ear drums. "One hour remaining," the words crackled. Ahead and slightly below at a fifty-foot diagonal to my right wing tip was our flight leader, Sgt. Motoharu Uno. His head slowly pivoted, constantly surveying our surroundings, and upon catching his glance I held up my gloved fist, responding with a single nod.

Age twenty-six, Uno was one of the old men in our squadron. Squat and sinewy, he had known little except rice farming until the war, but he was highly intelligent with remarkable strength and coordination. Awesome courage. He also possessed uncanny vision and was known by his friends as *Washi*—Eagle. Soon, if Uno survived what lay beyond, perhaps because of it, he would become an ace.

Ahead the clouds were enlarging, darkening slightly like dirty cotton along their undersides, extinguishing the sun-dazzled expanses below. Our *Kamikaze* were traveling in sections of three—each a lethal arrow slicing undeviatingly onward toward the enemy. On and on and on. . . the harsh, strangely comforting vibrato of my motor rising and falling, rising and falling, against the gathering afternoon.

Miraculously, time itself had faded like vapor on an immense mirror. As we neared our destination the dry-plaster feeling in my mouth increased, a feeling that inevitably occurred at such moments. And, as always, my head began to throb, an aching throughout my upper eye sockets and brow, gradually asserting itself within the base of my skull as well. My gloved hands clenched the controls, and I opened them flexing my fingers. Beneath my leather aviator cap a drop of sweat trickled slyly down my temple . . . then another.

"Too tense, Kuwahara," I warned, "too taut!" Ironically, the words came with great intensity. Again the finger flexing followed by the massaging of the back of my neck and scalp with one hand, the rotating of my head. "Loosen up, Kuwahara, loosen up." Shoulders rising, rotating along with my head, falling. Swift painful glimpses of my past, my home and family . . . of Toyoko. Toyoko embraced in slumber, Toyoko in her white nightgown with the lacy fringes. Her brow and cheek bones graced with light, lips touched with their faint entrancing dream smile, impossibly far away and long ago now, in some lost dimension.

Strange how so many thoughts, all irrelevant to the question at hand, continued to beset me. Perhaps they were a part of my defense mechanism, sedatives against the rat-like gnawings of fear. Soon, though, very soon, those sedatives would wear off completely.

Long ago it seemed (or was it only moments?) we had passed the tiny islands of Yaku and Togara, and now with Amami dissolving in our wake, we saw the first dim outlines of our fate. Okinawa! An electric shock in my right neck cord, a fierce burning that nearly welled beyond containment. Yes, Okinawa, sprawling there on the ocean's bosom like an immense and slowly writhing sea monster.

Then came another jolt as Uno waggled his wings. Far off I saw their faint silvery wakes . . . and now . . . the first American ships. *Ichi, ni, san, shi.* . . . I kept counting. Twenty five in all, and there no larger than cucumber seeds at first, directly in the center of the task force, was our quarry—four aircraft carriers, closely attended by battle ships and a wider perimeter of cruisers and destroyers.

Again Uno waggled his wings, and we began our descent. At ten thousand feet we leveled off, and our twelve *Kamikaze* forged ahead of us at full power. Now time was suddenly in ruthless acceleration, the ships growing . . . growing . . . growing at a rate that was literally stupefying. Now they were opening fire! A great, spasmodic concatenation of reflex actions from their giant guns, each followed by explosive puffs of black smoke and spouts of dull orange from the ships engulfed in cloud shadow.

So at last the waiting was over. I even welcomed the fear, for with it came the wild rush of adrenaline and sense of inevitability. Whatever our skills might be, however valiantly and cunningly we might perform, we had now entered the portals of Fate, and there was no turning back. Simultaneously, the strange yet familiar voice inside, continued to assure me that death happened only to other people. Soon, somehow, it would all be past. I would returned unharmed and make my report as always.

Ahead, the first suicide formation is diving now at forty-five degrees, followed methodically by the next . . . and the next. Tatsuno is leading the final section in an ancient navy aircraft, ready to fall apart long before its last take-off, a Mitsubishi, Type 96. Now the fated twelve are opening their cockpits and their silken scarves are fluttering in the wind, a symbol of their willingness to die for the Emperor, their final acknowledgment of that grand and ultimate honor. Always the wind, the Divine Wind.

The American fleet is less than a mile ahead, and I am sweating profusely, watching, watching, my mind roaring, and the sound within is somehow far greater than that of my *Hayabusa*. The lead *Kamikaze* plummets, screaming almost vertically into the flak. He'll never reach the carriers; that seems certain. Instead, he levels and veers sharply to the right making for a cruiser near the convoy's perimeter. And for a moment it looks as if he'll succeed. But no—he's hit, virtually wrenched apart, all in the fraction of a second. Only a yellow flare remains, rapidly disintegrating . . . fading, fading to ashes, to nothing.

Everything is a blur now—a mixture of motion, sound, and color— the variegated green of the ocean, the stark, hard gray of the ships, the unremitting belches of black as their five-inch rifles fire deadly bursts of shrapnel, periodic flashes of orange from the shadows, and a virtual maze of white-hot red from the tracer bullets leaving their 20 and 40 millimeter anti aircraft guns . . . tracers that seem to arch almost languorously. Two more planes explode simultaneously, but a fourth wails unscathed through the entire barrage, leveling beneath the flak umbrella only twenty feet above the surface. . . .

A hit! He has struck a destroyer directly above its water line. It shudders as if assaulted by an immense battering ram, and I actually seem to hear the bellowing explosion, then another and another, above the endless roar of my motor. It's good! It's good! The vessel is already in its death throes. Water gushing in through a monstrous hole that has nearly torn it apart, surging and plunging over the bow. As I follow my flight leader, climbing and arching along the battle's perimeter, the destroyer up-ends, stern black and ominous in a curious state of suspension as though attesting to its own demise. Then, almost instantaneously, it is gone . . . swallowed . . . non-existent.

Already I have lost track of the flights. They have been scattered like dragonflies before a gale. The two trailing formations are knifing downward through the lethal blossoms of flak. Everywhere, incredible violence and confusion. One of our planes is roaring low across the water, machine guns kicking up countless spouts all around him. Headed straight for a carrier, closing the gap at tremendous speed with less than two hundred yards remaining. Straight in . . . he'll score a direct hit! My entire body surges with an awful jubilation. But no-no, they stop him, blowing off a wing and most of his tail section. Veering lamely, he collides with the ship's bow inflicting little damage.

The enemy defense is almost impregnable; only a gnat can penetrate that fire screen. Two more suicides lance at the second carrier, and one disintegrates fairly splattering the water with its remains. The other bursts into flame like a monstrous blow torch, makes a half roll and arches into the ocean upside down.

So far, I am certain, we have sunk only one ship, and already, within mere minutes, we have few aircraft left. Hard to know where they are now, even discern them because of the swelling murkiness of the horizon, but at least two planes have temporarily secluded themselves there—and now, unexpectedly, they materialize a mile to our left. We circle high above, watching. . . . Two planes, an advanced trainer and a Mitsubishi fighter are completing a wide turn, heading swiftly back toward us. I squint, and the realization seizes my innards. That Mitsubishi, it's Tatsuno! Yes, definitely! Tatsuno was in the last section—our only navy plane.

The two of them climb at full throttle then begin their dive, charging toward the convoy's heart. The trainer, however, is rapidly falling behind, and seconds later he is ripped from the sky by enemy fighters. His wings are savagely torn away, the entire plane almost rent in half, and he corkscrews insanely downward leaving a silver-gold waterspout in a brilliant patch of sunlight.

Tatsuno is alone now, still unscathed, making a perfect run, better than anything they ever taught us in school. Tatsuno! Tatsuno! Fire spouts along his tail section, but he remains on course. A tanker wallows just ahead like a vast, sullen whale. The orange tatters along Tatuno's fuselage extend with devilish exultation, and his plane is an all-devouring flame. Tatsuno! He's closing! A hit! A HIT!

An enormous explosion bellows upward, rocking the sky, vomiting thick, black smoke that momentarily seems to swallow the very flames generating it. Then comes a staccato series of smaller bursts, stupendous eruptions of brilliant orange, and one last, mighty blast that seems to shake the sea like canvas in a wind. The tanker is going down along with my dearest friend.

No trace now but the widening shroud of oil.

Our *Kamikaze* were gone now—all twelve to another world. We had sunk one destroyer and one tanker, wounded a cruiser, also severely damaged a battleship, something I didn't learn until later. But there was no time then to ponder our success or to mourn our loss. The fighter fifty yards ahead and to my left waggled its wings in warning. My friend Nakamura, and he was jabbing with his finger toward a flight of Grumman Hellcats swarming in above us at four o'clock.

I had spotted them fleetingly earlier, streaking from the carriers—hornets angered at having their nests invaded—then lost sight of them in the melee. Now, fantastically, three Hellcats were on my tail with startling speed and determination, firing savage bursts from only three hundred yards. Two more behind them, slightly lower and about half a mile to the right, were veering my way, maneuvering into firing position.

Lead chewed my stabilizer, sheared off the tip of my rudder, and a fifty-caliber slug pierced the canopy only six inches above my head. Simultaneously I spotted Uno, emerging from a skein of clouds just beyond. He was easing into a tight right curve, and I followed, rotating in a half roll and banking into a radical turn.

Now, within seconds, I had reversed positions with my enemy and I was on his tail, trying desperately to center him in my gun sights. Momentarily we seemed to be on opposite ends of a teetering balance scale. Then it adjusted, and I was tracking him, blasting away with my nose cannon . . . missing! Angrily I opened up with my machine guns but in my eagerness failed to aim with precision.

Only two Hellcats discernible now, and they flared frantically in opposite directions, my quarry swerving to the right. The other bore strongly to the left only to draw fire from a *Hayabusa* coming at him head on. Nakamura! The two planes screamed past each other almost colliding, the Hellcat taking lead, and I glanced fleetingly over my shoulder to see it casting slender streamers of flame as it distanced against the sun.

Meanwhile my own foe was climbing rapidly, and I roared after him firing a series of short, rapid bursts. Realizing his predicament, the Hellcat angled off to the left, dropping away, spiraling nose over wing tip, into a shallow dive. I had anticipated him, however, and followed doggedly, opening up again with my guns. This time smoke began to billow from beneath his engine cowling, so thickly, I barely saw the cockpit open as the pilot struggled free and rolled off the wing next to the fuselage. He then plummeted downward like a rock for some distance before pulling his chute, and the canopy popped, blossoming white, drifting against the deep blue of the water.

Only seconds later an enemy plane was attacking me broadside from about two hundred yards. I could see the lethal sparkling of his fifty calibers against a large soot-colored cloud. Then, incredibly, the Hellcat disintegrated in a blinding starburst the color of the sun. One of our *Hayabusa* was cutting a high, wailing arch along the cloud's upper border, etched triumphantly against the dazzling sky beyond. The contrasting light was so intense it hurt my eyes, and I squinted painfully just as the *Hayabusa* vanished into the mounting darkness ahead. Not, however, before I had glimpsed the pilot's profile through the glint of sunlight on his goggles, the fierce, determined tightness of his lips.

Uno! I shook my head in admiration and amazement. He had blasted it directly in the fuel tank with his 25 mm cannons. His wartime total now tallied six confirmed kills and at least three or four probables. My own score now stood at three as did Nakamura's.

"Run for it!" His words crackled in my headphones. "Too many— head for home!" Abruptly now, the enemy was materializing from almost all directions. Everywhere . . . blue wings, white stars and blunt, belligerent snouts—all avidly bent on revenge. My friends were nowhere in sight, and I slammed the throttle to the firewall, roaring north toward home and the secrecy of the clouds. Several Hellcats were still streaking after me, diving head on. Instinctively, I hit the stick pivoting left, and all of them overshot me but one flying higher in the rear.

Torquing radically the opposite direction, I descended in a gargantuan, groaning barrel roll, feeling my entire airframe shuddering as the G-force slammed, squeezing the blood from my head and eyes. My enemy followed with fiendish tenacity only a hundred yards or so behind, somehow actually closing the distance. Sledge hammer sounds, and I flinched, feeling my heart lurch. I'd been hit. . . but for the moment no discernible damage, and it was time for even more desperate measures.

Again I rolled, angling now into a steep vertical dive . . . down, down, down . . . the air shrieking past my cockpit, gradually spiraling, spiraling downward, seeming to rotate with the very earth . . . then rolling more widely. Ships growing amid the broadening sprawls of smoke, revolving as if the ocean itself had become a vast, cosmic whirlpool. Long hours of suicide practice had honed my skill in such maneuvers, but soon I was in reach of the surface fire again. A battleship along the convoy's periphery was opening up with his heavy rifles, and the flack was collecting close about me.

I pulled from my dive in a monstrous, shuddering, gut-wrenching groan, barely above the water, feeling as if the flesh would rip from my bones, losing my vision and sense of direction, blacking out, as though my head had been dragged into my shoulders. The tenacious Grumman Hellcat, however, was less fortunate—accidentally blasted apart by his own ships at the very nadir of his descent. Glancing wildly at my wavering compass needle and trembling gryo horizon, I somehow reoriented myself and hurtled on north scrambling for altitude.

The American ships were still salvoing at long range while one remaining fighter plane continued to fire at me from several hundred yards away. For an instant I felt a smug sense of triumph. Simultaneously I heard a series of feral pinging noises followed by a clank. My heart squirmed, pounding, and my throat constricted as I waited for the flames, the smoke . . . the explosion. For several agonizing seconds the motor faltered then blessedly caught hold as the Hellcat swiftly drew closer.

Ahead, a short distance to the northwest, the clouds were mounting to awesome heights in gray-black anvils—cumulonimbus, and I headed for them full throttle, blending my will with that of my plane, uniting all our remaining strength in a final bid for emancipation. Faster Kuwahara, faster . . . holes appearing supernaturally in my right wing. . .

more pinging. . . . Then I was engulfed in darkness.

I grinned triumphantly into the gloom, convinced now that I had made it. The enemy had battled ferociously—every thing in his power, everything upon the face of the ocean, everything that he could hurl into the sky. The enemy had failed. Our own forces, on the other hand, had inflicted substantial damage.

Not far ahead, lightning crackled lividly fracturing the walls of darkness which reunited almost instantly with an ominous concussion more powerful than all the guns below combined. Close, very close. But at least, I told myself, the elements were impersonal. Now, though, my cockpit had filled with the odor of burning rubber and super-heated metal, and the anxiety soon returned. No way of knowing how much damage I had sustained earlier, and I was also faced with another problem. Rain was slashing my wings and cockpit, mounting gusts that often left me blindfolded except for the incessant flashes of lightning, each accompanied by a stunning jar as if truck loads of lumber were being dumped against me from every side.

I had encountered storms before but never one like this. Clouds converged about me like a herd of angry elephants, transforming to monstrous proportions and colors from gray to India ink . . . roiling, incessantly roiling, in an ominous maelstrom. The winds and rain lashed savagely, slicing through the jagged holes in my greenhouse.

Again my motor coughed, windmilling, and I held my breath, practically igniting with tension. Yet once again it caught, and the burning smell was abating, probably because of the deluge. Temples throbbing, I squinted painfully, praying for the return of day. Off somewhere lay the afternoon, yet there near the storm's gullet it was fast approaching midnight. Each flash of lightning spawned crashes of thunder reverberating off in stupendous chain reactions, numbing the very atmosphere. My sense of direction was gone, decimated, and with each concussion my compass needle gyrated erratically. My turn and bank indicator was useless, stunned! No matter what awaited me out there in the daylight, I had to escape fast.

But where? Far off to my left was a pallid smear of yellow-gray, and instinctively I headed toward it like a moth to lamplight. The glow was increasing when suddenly the belly of my plane, seemed to collapse. It was like a blow to the sternum, and I clutched in desperation at the controls as my *Hayabusa* dropped a hundred feet within the next second, prop clawing helplessly. The motor rattled as if it would tear loose, and the entire frame vibrated frantically.

Then the pressure subsided, and I was blasted upward, shaken and tumbled hopelessly. Dazed, head spinning, I battled for equilibrium, some semblance of control, yet there was none. Slam my rudder to the left, and I could as easily be hurled to the right. Wrench my elevator upward, and I might be rammed toward the sea.

Instruments battered and dying, my motor steadily becoming more asthmatic, I was desperately tired, both body and soul. Minutes before, I had welcomed the storm, all but laughed in its face. Now I was growing numb, arms nearly paralyzed. Even the inside of my plane was revolving dizzily, my vision so blurred I could no longer even tell whether it was raining or not. Again, time had ceased to exist. Once, strangely, the winds abated, and I found myself drifting in a kind of vacuum, blinking at the blue flashes and hearing the reverberations with strange curiosity. Like an automaton, I was flying with only one purpose—to continue . . . on and on until the great light was born again.

Then the winds came raving back. The flashes illumined a vast cloud with magnificent tones of peach and rose, its countenance forming a diabolical leer as greater darkness ensued. No longer were the elements impersonal. The lightning was not crackling; it was laughing maliciously, and the thunder bellowed, hammering with its fists. The wind, above all, hated me—cursing, buffeting, wrenching, and now I knew that I had been betrayed with the promise of sanctuary to my destruction. Even nature was with the enemy.

An abrupt volcanic eruption of air and cloud confirmed the fact, catching my right wing tip and hurling me in a series of huge, erratic gyrations as agonized groanings burst from the bowels of my aircraft . . . down . . . down an endless cone of blackness to my doom. Death . . . death . . . all very swiftly now. Oblivion.

Yet even then, far off down that final passage, something willed the battered, shuddering entity that had been my fighter back to life, exerted effort against alien controls.

Astoundingly, I was flying level, waves the color of molasses curling at my belly, scudding with froth, and I was once more in command. As from some remote distance, sounds of the motor rose and fell, and my aircraft actually seemed to be skimming the very wave crests. Momentarily I had recollections of my first glider competition, being towed for that first breath-stifling takeoff across the turf at Onomichi High School.

So low now, so very low! The mere, slight tilting of one wing, only a few degrees, and the ocean would have me forever. And why fight it? The great waters had taken my friends, taken Tatsuno, always taken whatever they wanted. Only a few slight ridiculous degrees . . . But my fear had evaporated, giving way to perversity.

Yes, now I would taunt the ocean, making it wait, tantalizing the endless, hypnotic waves, dipping my wing tips boldly . . . but never quite close enough . . . not until the appropriate moment. No doubt they would have me in time but on my own terms—not until I had laughed and humiliated them as the lightning and thunder had laughed and roared, humiliating me.

Suddenly the water flashed green! An instant later it transformed to the color of white-hot slag temporarily blinding me. First by the darkness and now by the light. I squinted painfully, blinking, seeing only strange, amoeboid forms that welled in blend of dark maroon and irregular, ever-melting fringes of saffron. And gradually the pain eased. Gradually, sight was restored. I was in a world of dazzling green and gold. The heavens above and beyond were completely cloudless, supernally blue.

Cautiously, very gradually, I ascended to a thousand feet as my body and mind, my very spirit, relaxed. No ships, no planes, only the endless water and the endless sky as I droned steadily onward alone, the only living soul in the world—lost amid the lonely reaches of sun and sea.

The motor sputtered, and I glanced at my fuel gauge: a mere twenty-five gallons—little time left. Apprehensively, fearing the American ears listening somewhere beyond the horizon, I began to signal. No answer. I waited, holding my breath, tried again. Still no reply. My fighter was winging onward, staunch and true once more. Wonderful creature! How I loved and admired it! But now . . . after everything, to run out of fuel—to expire helplessly like a strong man whose wrists were slashed. What a grand and ridiculous irony!

Hopeless . . . but I had an obligation to do my best. Like my *samurai* ancestors, I might ultimately die yet never be vanquished. I adjusted the fuel control to its thinnest mixture, cut the propeller cycles down to the minimum—below 1,500 rpm's. Any less and my plane would stall.

Again I signaled, caught my breath and waited . . . static . . . then a voice! Faint and dry initially, the buzzing of a wasp trapped in a jar, a voice from the regions of the dead. But a voice—an answer! China! "This is Nanking. . . ." I had made connections!

A few degrees to my left and straight ahead was the island of Formosa, and at last I could discern its outlines—like a mere translucent watermark at first, the faintest lineation on a broad pastel of gray and green. Soon, though, it became more substantial, seeming to rise and fall on its gathering tides like an immense ship—a ship . . . a carrier of colossal dimension unlike all others, one that offered hope. Sanctuary.

My *Hayabusa* purred steadily onward, constant and true, and once I looked back. Something warned me not to, a profound sense of superstition, that even the subtlest glance might welcome the tentacles of fate. Nevertheless, I looked. Somewhere off in that golden afternoon lay Okinawa and the enemy task force. Only twenty-three ships instead of twenty-five. Somewhere drifted the remains of our twelve *Kamikaze*, the remains of my friend Tatsuno.

And there—hanging slumberous now—far behind, lurked the storm. The Divine Storm had saved me as it had saved my people centuries before.

Chapter Twenty-Five

The Lonely Place

A short while later I covered the remaining distance to Formosa, and landed at Taihoku, the main base. Then, with scarcely a moment's rest, and only a perfunctory inspection of my wounded aircraft, I flew as directed to a smaller base close by near Kiirun. There I remained for nearly two weeks because of insufficient fuel. Yes, conditions were now that desperate. The bases in Formosa consuming their final rations. Barely enough fuel for the suicides who left each day.

Despite my exhaustion, however, my first concern upon landing was my aircraft. During the months, and now especially, I had developed an affection for that ship. My *Hayabusa* had become a living creature, a loyal and faithful friend I not only understood but also loved. Somehow along the way it had acquired a soul. It had helped me vanquish my enemies and, even when all appeared hopeless, it had persevered, prevailed against the storm.

Parts of the tail assembly and the tip of my right wing had been sheared off, and several bullet holes in the fuselage had left gaps two to three inches in diameter where they exited. The motor itself had stopped lead but amazingly, merely faltered for a time.

In addition, there were two holes through my canopy. One bullet had gashed the dome, and another had pierced the glass only an inch or two above my head. How close, how very close! What a slender, wavering path we tread between life and death!

My plane, in any event, was still functional, seemingly almost invulnerable, and upon landing at the assigned base I rested beside it for a time in the shade of some palm trees on the airstrip's edge. Never, even during my most arduous days in basic training, had I been so exhausted. I would make my report in due time when I felt ready, but at the moment I seemed to be dissolving.

Two mechanics were approaching in the distance, and across the concrete runway preparations were underway for the next day's mission. Obviously, the area had been bombed a short time earlier, and crews were still filling in the remaining craters, packing the dirt down with antiquated steamrollers. Drained now, almost to the point of stupor, I lay back at the jungle's edge, my head resting upon my folded flight jacket, waiting for the mechanics.

The air was hot and humid, and I was already covered with sweat. What would it be like, I wondered vaguely, to be a mechanic, simply to repair planes instead of flying them? Not so long ago the very thought had filled me with scorn. Lately, though, I had begun to view the matter quite differently. What a simple, pleasant life, freed from the eternal stress and anxiety, the constant gnawing of fear. The chance to live! For a moment I actually resented the two men approaching me. What a luxury—the right to live!

I closed my eyes, and saw the face of Toyoko, the smile and her own eyes filled with that incredible tenderness and compassion. I heard her words: "The war will end! The war will end in time!"

Merely a forlorn hope, or was she on a special wave length, incredibly intuitive? Perhaps, all I needed was faith, to be in tune with Toyoko. Had I not only hours ago been miraculously preserved? "Toyoko," I murmured her name, "Wait for me, Toyoko."

Suddenly I heard the roar of planes, approaching at tremendous speed, and seconds later the keening of an air raid alarm. Without the slightest additional warning, Hellcats came thundering off the jungle roof, swarming upon us in waves of five. I bolted upright, staring as the two mechanics dashed my way heading for cover. The distant construction crew scattered in every direction, but they were too late. Already the first flights were opening up, spraying the area voraciously with their guns.

I watched as bullets stitched and spattered the concrete, casting up lethal little puffs of dust, overtaking half a dozen fugitives, reducing them to shattered corpses in an instant. Suddenly, aware of my own vulnerability, I struggled to my feet and staggered blindly into the jungle. Hurling myself to the earth, I lay there panting, peering back in time to see one of the mechanics plunging into the underbrush nearby. The second was less fortunate, trapped in a hail of lead just short of cover, upended and rolled violently for several yards as though hit by a truck.

Four men, including the two driving steam rollers, had escaped the first two waves and were feigning death in the middle of the field, but their ruse was futile. A third wave of Hellcats, bellowing low across the strip, ravaged them unmercifully with their guns. I saw the bodies writhe and roll, one of them half rising to twist and sprawl face down convulsing.

The enemy fighters cavorted about, uncontested, blasting everything in sight, having a marvelous time. Not the slightest protest or most feeble attempt to retaliate. A hanger was flaming now, disgorging billows of brown and black smoke. A line of obsolete *Kamikaze* planes and several escort fighters were ripped to shards, some exploding and burning.

Finally, their ammunition spent, the enemy planes circled, arching above the flames and through the rising smoke, climbing triumphantly into the blue, sunlight exploding and scintillating like immense blow torches from their windshields.

Furtively, I crept from the undergrowth to inspect my *Hayabusa*, but it had escaped detection there in the shadow of the jungle. Then, weary beyond all measure, so weary the destruction on every hand scarcely registered, I wandered across the field to make my report. Who I would report to or where, I didn't know. Perhaps there was no headquarters left.

Tomorrow there would probably be more attacks, more deaths, more aircraft demolished. But now I wanted only one thing—to report in and be assigned a place to sleep—anywhere. Eventually, I discovered the orderly room, still in tact, and half an hour later, dead on my feet, I collapsed on a dirty cot against a wall between two rusty lockers. Nearby some men were playing cards at a table, laughing boisterously at times as if the war had never come. The room was thick with cigarette smoke, blue swirls so dense I could scarcely discern their faces. It didn't matter. The entire base still reeked with smoke. Nothing mattered.

How long since I had seen her? Days? Weeks? Surely not that very morning. Tatsuno? I saw his gray and faded countenance, the enigmatic smile . . . his *Mitsubishi* knifing downward. . . the wounded ship, wallowing and swallowed in the waves. The leering giants of the storm. But where was Nakamura? Who knew? Gone forever perhaps . . . the feeling in his bones. Uno and Kimura and the rest of our escorts. Gone?

I sighed, flung my forearm across my brow, dreamed deliriously, mind and soul resonating with sound and violence, swirling irresistibly on the vast and drifting panoply of the ocean, horizon upon horizon, always the beyond and the beyond and the beyond.

Once I surfaced upon the rim of some immeasurable significance, moaning and mumbling incoherently, pleading for the answer. I remember emerging, bathed in the stifling dampness, my body fairly steaming, and hearing a voice: "Take it easy, fighter pilot. Just relax." Someone was wiping my face and arms with a damp cloth. "Just relax." Now he was actually fanning me with a towel, and I drifted off again, this time into blessed emptiness.

For two weeks I remained at that remote spot as an instructor for their *Kamikaze*. What a unique and dire assignment, actually teaching men how to die. The rationale behind it all, the great and mysterious "Why", I left to others. No longer could I find a respectable answer. It would require the ultimate miracle of miracles to reverse the fortunes of war now, a miracle beyond the most fantastic imagination. The handwriting was upon the wall, and the wall was crumbling rapidly. We were merely dying for the sake of dying.

Honor? What honor? Why? Increasingly now, images returned of my friend Shiro Nomoto, there in the white hospital bed, his leg gone, seeing the face of his mother, and hearing her words: "Listen to me, my sons . . . there is nothing honorable in dying for a lost cause."

But daily the condemned men left to perform their own execution. Another and another . . . and another. . . . I bade them my pathetic farewells, watched them rise above the burning concrete, above the dark and secret jungle, circling the field and waggling their wings in a last *sayonara*.

Two hours after their departure, signal men at the base would listen for the high, long-drawn beeping noise swelling their eustacian tubes and piercing their ear drums—signals that the attack was underway. Then, often in less than a minute, like scissors cutting a taut cord, the sound would end. Silence . . . oblivion. *Sayonara*, you loyal hopeless sons of Nihon. Mere memories now.

I did not learn what had become of our other escorts, my companions at Okinawa, for several days. Uno was the only one who had returned to Oita. Nakamura and Kimura had vanished, and I had also been reported missing in action initially. Uno had seen me plunging toward the convoy, Hellcats close behind, and had assumed the worst. Appropriately, for the worst had only seemed reasonable. There was still a remote possibility that Nakamura and Kimura had escaped as I had, perhaps landing on some island along the Ryuku chain extending southwest below Kyushu. But very doubtful.

Nakamura. At my last glimpse of him, he was gunning down the enemy, but something beyond mere assumption told me that he was gone now, gone like the true *samurai*. Yes, truly, gone. My sorrow? It was only an ongoing numbness. Perhaps some day the numbness would subside, blossoming into the black flower of pain.

So all my friends had entered the unknown now, and I waited alone in the sultry afternoons of Formosa, watching daily as our *Kamikaze* departed, some of them pilots younger than I with little training or skill. Death hovered in the very atmosphere, in the odor of smoke, gasoline, and oil that never fully dissipated, in the coppery smell of newly flowing blood. Or was it only there within my brain cells? No matter, it was always present.

Always there, even on those afternoons as I wandered an empty beach, sometimes swam in the ocean, wondering if the tide might take me out beyond the point of no return. Drowning itself seemed a mild and uneventful death these days, almost pleasurable. At times I sat upon the shore, letting the tide glide up about my feet, fading in its endless and fizzing, miniscule bubbles, each bubble transient like life itself. But always, the odor of death.

Unending thoughts of Toyoko. In all likelihood she thought I was dead now, or perhaps she had checked with the base and discovered that I was still alive. Again, maybe she had decided I was indeed far too young, that it would be better to end things. After all, nearly seven years separated us in terms of age. Perhaps she had returned to her lieutenant in Fukuoka and worked things out. How strange to think that we had known each other only a few short weeks, that we had known each other at all. It was only part of the fond and foolish dream, a mirage lost far behind in the ocean.

The day before my departure eight suicides racketed into the sky, wheeling broadly, dipping their wings, and headed out. Then, strangely, one of them circled back, angling it seemed for a landing. For a moment I thought he was experiencing engine trouble, but I was wrong. "He'll never make it!" a voice cried. "Coming in too steep! Too fast!"

"Heading for the hangar!" someone else yelled. "Do something!"

"Do what? I shouted angrily.

"Fire engines!" Another shout.

An instant later I hit the concrete as the plane ripped into the hangar in a deafening, brain-numbing explosion, erupting in a huge, red-orange fireball. In mere seconds the entire hangar was a ablaze, belching smoke black as the pit and vanquishing the sun. Sirens wailed. Men scrambled, shouting and swearing. Within only two or three minutes a fire truck was on hand, spraying the flames with a long, arching stream of water, but it was like trying to extinguish a bonfire with a squirt gun. The entire effort, in fact, seemed almost farcical.

I watched calmly, disdainful of their clumsy efforts, but suddenly the adjoining hangar erupted as well in a whole series of explosions, and the fire crew staggered back, stumbling over themselves, over the hose which, freed from their grasp, lashed about like a wounded python, spraying everything in sight, knocking men from their feet, even as they struggled to arise.

Fantastically, the detonations continued—fireball after fireball, fiendish in their brilliance and ferocity, and already the smoke was so intense the day had become night. Thousands of gallons, almost all that was left of our fuel reserves were going, and now our remaining fighters. Never yet had I seen or heard anything like it, and for some reason I was feeling a remarkable sense of exhilaration, literal jubilation!

The fire and smoke gradually subsided a bit but persisted for nearly two hours, and when at length the sun reappeared, it looked wan and surrealistic, the color of tarnished silver.

Afterward, a note was discovered which the dead pilot had left in a sealed envelope with one of his companions as he departed, instructing him to read it an hour later. Penned that morning, it contained some terse observations regarding Japan's hopeless plight and the futility of war. The conclusion read as follows:

"My fellow comrades, by the time you read these words I will be gone. Please do not judge me harshly or in anger. What is done is done for good reason. Perhaps someday our leaders and people everywhere will come to understand the insanity of war. For now, I pray that my own miserable efforts will enable others here to live. Our country's surrender is at the doors, and by the time you read these words there will be fewer planes for men to waste their lives in and far less fuel for any who remain."

Fortunately or unfortunately (I will never be sure), my *Hayabusa* had been repaired and fueled before the grand destruction, parked, hidden with several others to escape enemy detection within a fringe of trees and undergrowth near the spot where I had originally landed. The following morning I winged off over the jungle, leaving that wretched, lonely place forever.

PART SIX

Chapter Twenty-Six

Lighter than a Feather

I**t was the** last of June, 1945, when I landed again at Oita. I had flown back through China, crossing over the East China Sea to avoid American fighters.

Frantic to see Toyoko, I rushed to the orderly room to report in. How would she react upon seeing me? Had she discovered that I was still alive? Perhaps, but Oita had merely received an official communication regarding my survival, one that might not be revealed to anyone outside the base. Furthermore, as I had discovered a day or two earlier, none of my personal letters to her or to my family had ever left Formosa. The mail in that area was largely inoperative.

The desk sergeant glanced up indifferently when I entered as though I had never left the base. "You're to report to the commanding officer immediately, Kuwahara," he said.

I stared at him. "Immediately?"

"Yes, immediately!"

Dumbfounded, I turned and shuffled out the door. My excitement had changed to dread, but there was nothing to do except clean up and change as quickly as possible.

There in the barracks countless thoughts surged through my mind. I had supposed that Uno's report two weeks ago was sufficient. What more could I tell Captain Tsubaki than he had already learned? Soon I was striding across the base at an ever increasing pace. What could he want? Not even giving me time to catch my breath? Didn't the man have any idea what I'd been through? That I had just flown all the way from Formosa?

Upon entering Tsubaki's office, I found him deeply preoccupied with a great pile of paper work, and for a moment he failed to acknowledge my presence. Nevertheless, I reported crisply in the prescribed manner and held my salute.

Seconds later the Captain looked up, gazing at me a bit oddly as though we had never met before. Then, peremptorily, he returned my salute, barely fanning his eyebrow and turned back his papers. "Be seated, Kuwahara," he said. Eventually he regarded me again, and this time his expression was somewhat different, intensely searching, unnerving. Where, I wondered, had I seen that look before?

"How are conditions in Formosa?" he inquired. Momentarily I was tongue tied, wondering what he expected.

"You mean, Honorable Captain . . ." I mumbled.

"Planes, ammunition, fuel . . . morale! What's going on there?"

For a second or two I struggled with the urge to be evasive, then decided on bluntness. "There is little left of anything," I said. "Anywhere. Kochi, the base where I was stationed this past two weeks, is dying. Day before yesterday, in fact. . . ." I hesitated.

"What? In fact, what?"

"One of our *Kamikaze* turned back and dived into the main hangar. The one next to it was full of fuel, and both of them went up along with about twenty fighters."

"Remarkable," Tsubaki mused. "But why? Did anyone ever find out?"

"Yes, Honorable Captain. He left a message insisting that we had already lost the war and that he hoped his death would save the lives of others."

"Remarkable," Tsubaki repeated, "quite remarkable." Leaning back, arms folded, he perused the upper walls and part of the ceiling as though searching for an answer. "Rather ironic as well, wouldn't you say?" I stared at him uncertainly, and he shrugged, holding out his hands. "A *Kamikaze*, attacking his own military. Isn't that a bit ironic?"

"Yes, Honorable Captain," I answered. "I understand what you are saying."

"So what is your view of the situation?" he asked. "Of the war itself."

The question shocked me, and for a second or two, I merely looked at him, feeling my throat working. "I am a mere corporal, Honorable Captain," I finally replied.

"That does not matter!" he insisted, almost angrily. "You have been there at the heart of it. What is your honest, objective view of the war?"

For a moment I faltered, groping for words. "The enemy is triumphing, honorable Captain," I said, and for an awful moment feared I might actually begin crying. Crying in the presence of my commanding officer! Literally a humiliation worse than death. "Everywhere." I stared hard at the floor, feeling my eyes sting. "Okinawa . . . Formosa . . . everywhere! Soon the enemy will be at our shores, fire bombs from the B-29's descending upon every city, as they have before upon Tokyo and other places." I felt the swelling in my throat, the choking sensation. "Nothing remains but the dying."

The captain made no reply. No sound but the distant droning of motors—omnipresent yet steadily fading, fading more each day it seemed. Etherizing.

"So what is it like out there over Okinawa?" I glanced up. Tsubaki was gazing through the window toward the ocean. Again, I struggled for a reply. "Indescribable I suppose," he said quietly.

"Yes, Honorable Captain—indescribable."

"You lost your best friend in that last attack," Tsubaki observed, and again I felt surprise. Until then I had no idea that he was even aware of my relationship with Tatsuno.

"Yes, honorable Captain. Two of my best friends—Nakamura also I'm afraid."

Yoshiro Tsubaki nodded, pursing his lips, inhaling deeply. Still the distant gaze, his eyes reflecting the afternoon light, filled with a faint but steady burning. "Mere boys." He shook his head. "Out there in the sky . . . planes falling apart, and all that fire coming up."

I waited, merely waited. What was there to say?

"And the enemy? Do you hate the enemy with a burning passion? Long for his annihilation?"

"Sometimes I hate the enemy, Captain," I replied cautiously. "Sometimes . . . ."

"Yes?" Tsubaki's face welled with perception.

"Sometimes I hate—"

"Our leaders in Tokyo?"

I took a deep breath, feeling my entire body quiver. "Yes!" My voice cracked. "I hate them for what they have done to this nation, for their eternal lies to our people! The *Daihonei*! Even after the bombs have fallen upon their very heads, their voices will swell up from the ground like sewer gas. 'All is well, oh people of Japan! Fear not, gullible, stupid people of Japan! This is all a part of the glorious plan!'" I buried my face in my hands, forcing back the sobs. "Whose plan?" Simultaneously, I was dimly aware that I had spoken rank heresy, words that might well justify a general court martial, even execution. But what did it matter?

At last I glanced up, biting my lower lip. I could feel my own face hardening with hopeless anger. But Tsubaki was again gazing out the window, and his countenance seemed to have aged, grown more haggard with each passing minute. "Mere boys and all that fire coming up," he repeated. "And I have to send them."

I waited, felt the growing sense of expectation, inevitability. "Corporal Kuwahara. . . ."

"Yes, Honorable Captain."

"You have seen a lot of war this past year. Much sorrow, much death and destruction. Experienced more than a million other men will experience, in a million years." I waited. Tsubaki sighed. "Of course, we could have sent you long ago, but you have an excellent record. You have been of great value to your country."

"Thank you, Honorable Captain," I said, scarcely able to hear my own words. "It is only a small and humble effort."

"No!" Tsubaki insisted. "It is far more than that." The sound of motors was expanding now. "But, at last the time has come." I nodded, head bowed. The motors ever louder, the locust-like ringing in my ears suddenly exploding in volume. "I would change it, if I could, Corporal Kuwahara. Believe me, I would change the entire world. But I am only the commander of a doomed squadron—what little remains. Now, however, the end has come. For everyone left."

My hands were shaking. The muscles were twitching in my arms and legs, my heart lurching. I closed my eyes, waiting, and the words came. "Are you prepared?"

As though listening to a recording, I heard my own reply, virtually inaudible through all the roaring and ringing. "Yes, honorable Captain. I am honored to be deemed worthy. I wish to go as soon as possible."

Again Tsubaki sighed. "That is commendable. You will return to Hiro within the hour." Within the hour! Incredible! "Your orders will come within a week or two."

"Hiro?" I glanced at him in surprise.

"Yes. Part of it has been restored." Tsubaki stood, unwilling now to look at me, and I also arose. The room was slowly churning. I was very dizzy. "*Sayonara*, Corporal Kuwahara."

"*Sayonara*, Honorable Captain."

Seconds later I was headed for my quarters to pack my belongings. The military never allowed a man to stay in one spot very long; never a place he could call home. Always juggling men around like spare parts. I passed the barracks where Nakamura had lived, then further on, the one for Tatsuno. Stayed but not stayed, lived but not lived, gone yet not gone. They could not be gone; they had to be somewhere, like the wind. Yet only their belongings remained and had probably been sent to their families by now.

Then a disconcerting thought struck me. What had become of Tatsuno's little finger? He had entrusted it to my care, and somehow amid all the chaos I had almost forgotten about it. Dismayed, I altered my course, heading for my *Hayabusa*. Simultaneously, visions of Toyoko surfaced in my mind for the hundredth time—alternately bright and vibrant, then like wraiths fading within the mist. My eyes blurred, and I clenched my teeth. All these stupid tears, this craven bawling. I was compromising myself badly, failing to be a man. My time had come at last, only a matter of days. Then no more worries." I trudged blindly onward, my soul grayer than the concrete. But why should I be any different than the rest? I wondered. Why should Kuwahara be exempted when thousands of others were called upon to make the great sacrifice? Why

Tatsuno and Nakamura . . . Oka and Yamamoto, but not Kuwahara? I was expendable like all the rest. In the end, were we not all expendable? All of mankind? It was only a matter of time for everyone.

"Be resolved that honor is heavier than the mountains, while death is lighter than a feather." Yes, lighter than a feather, and that I would cling to. Ahead was my *Hayabusa*, waiting stoically. My salvation, my companion in death. Waiting so steadfastly, so patiently . . . so faithfully. In moments, we would ascend skyward together once more and return to Hiro, our source of origin. Because aircraft were now so scarce, we would probably remain together as always. Companions unto the end. The thought gave me a little comfort.

Upon nearing my plane, I encountered a bomber pilot named Takahashi whom I had known casually at Hiro. He had just finished going over his aircraft with two of our mechanics. I waved and he grinned. "Checking it out?" I called.

An elaborate shrug. "Right! But who knows why? Haven't dropped a bomb in the past month." Then he regarded me more seriously. "Taking off?"

I nodded. "*Hai*, in about an hour—back to Hiro." For a second I paused, reflecting. "Still going to the Tokiwaya?"

"Right!" He held up his thumb, grinning. "Good duty!"

"You remember that girl I've been going with? Toyoko Akimoto?"

The grin widened. "*Hai*! Who doesn't?"

I hesitated. "Well, she thinks I'm . . . ." Suddenly I was feeling foolish, humiliated. "She probably doesn't know I made it back from Okinawa.

He watched me expectantly. "You want me to tell her anything?"

For a moment I wavered, riddled with indecision. What could he tell her? That I was scheduled to die? No, I'd have to decide what to do once I was back at Hiro. Maybe get her a message some way, or maybe just. . . . He was watching me curiously, waiting. "Tell her I'm still alive—that they shipped me back to Hiro the minute I got here." Again, I hesitated. "Tell her I'll contact her before long, if they'll let me."

Takahashi nodded, his face turning sober, and tossed me a half wave, half salute. "All right, Yasbei! Good luck!"

I smiled. He had called me "Yasbei"—probably the only person left who would ever honor me that way. "Thanks, Takahashi," I answered. "Same to you. Be sure to tell her."

"Right—definitely. I'll be sure to."

What I wanted to say was, "Tell her that I miss her desperately, that I love her beyond belief." But that would have to come later if it ever came at all.

A minute or two afterward I climbed into my fighter. Yes, to my relief, Tatsuno's finger was still there wrapped in a handkerchief beneath the control panel, blackened and shriveled, beginning to smell of decay, but I would see at all costs that it reached his family.

Slowly I left the cockpit, sliding languidly off the wing, and planted my feet on the concrete runway. Simultaneously, a strange thing happened. A tiny gray feather came lilting and tumbling toward me across the concrete, probably from one of the numerous pigeons that frequented the area. It caught in a rough spot almost at my feet, quivering impulsively in the breeze as though blessed with a life of its own.

For a time I watched, wondering how far it might journey. To what distant place? Suddenly, on impulse, I stooped and picked it up. Ah, Yasbei, Yasbei! How crazy you are! Crazy, yes, but I put the feather in my pocket.

Chapter Twenty-Seven

Battle with the Giants

Hiro! **Hiro again.** I had been away only two months, but it might as well have been two years. What was time? Something I would never comprehend. I merely knew that nothing was more relentless. Nothing was as relentless as time or as constant as change. And Hiro had indeed changed drastically.

Despite efforts at reconstruction, the base was badly ravaged. The main hangar and several of the barracks were charred ruins. Part of the airfield had been bombed so heavily, it was for the present beyond repair. Tumbled patches of concrete, craters six to eight feet deep. Even the water tower was gone, the tower from which one of our trainees had leapt to his death in days gone by. Where Hiro obtained its water now I did not know.

The barracks from my fighter training was gone, burned to ashes, but the one from basic remained, and after reporting to the orderly room I paid it a visit. Empty now. Wandering its length, I realized that time was relative, even to the dust. The dust of centuries lay upon the empty bed springs, upon the lockers, and across the floor.

Few things are more empty, more lonely than a moribund military installation. Yet now, ironically, I felt twinges of nostalgia. Nostalgia for the trials of basic training? Ridiculous, yet in a way I even missed The Pig and his henchman The Snake. Standing there alone, I wondered what had become of them.

No signs of basic training whatever now, so perhaps they had been assigned elsewhere. Perhaps they had been killed in the bombing. The thought afforded no satisfaction, only more emptiness.

I walked the length of the barracks very slowly, staring down at my feet, each step leaving its imprint in the dust. Where had all that dust come from? Glancing about, I saw a dozen shattered windows and immediately had my answer. Great clouds of it from all the bombing. The entire base was covered with it.

Approaching the rear door, I spotted two ball bats leaning there to my left in the corner of the room. I shook my head, felt my lips forming a wan smile. Of course, of course! The wonderful ball bats! Hefting one, I felt its smoothness, blew away the dust and gave a violent, echoing sneeze. But no one was there to hear, only the pervasive quality of absence. Through watering eyes I read the familiar inscription: "*Yamato damashii Seishinbo*"—a ball bat for instilling the fighting spirit, the spirit of *Yamato*.

So there was little to do now but wait, merely exist while the days expired. A few of our fighter pilots were filtering back to the base now, most of whom I had known in passing at Oita, all like myself awaiting the final word. In consequence, we were placed on alert, restricted to the base, and time languished in the mounting heat of July, stifling us in its vapor.

In the midst of it all, I returned to the abandoned barracks, sat down on the back steps, and wrote a letter.

"Dear Toyoko: . . ."

For a long time, I sat there, my pen suspended as though the very ink were full of indecision.

"I am still among the living, waiting for my orders—orders that may come any day, any hour. Yet even so . . . ." Again I hesitated fraught with uncertainty. "I still cling to your words the last time we were together. Remember? You said that the war would end in time. You said that something strange and unexpected would happen. What that might be,

I have no idea and don't suppose you do either. Perhaps no one does.

"In any event, it must come soon or I will be gone along with nearly everyone remaining here." My hand began to tremble, the words becoming wavery. "But always remember, Toyoko. . . ." My throat was tightening badly as though I had swallowed a handful of the dust all around me. My eyes watered, and my body shook with a strange, shuddering gasp.

"That whatever happens, I will always love you. I will always be here somewhere, like the wind among the lanterns." For a long time I wept silently, making no effort to control my shaking. The final words were badly scrawled, and the page was becoming damp.

"Perhaps some night I will come to ring the chimes on your balcony. I pray that you will remember me when you hear them ringing, and when you hear waves along the shore. Most of all, I pray that you are safe and well. I pray for your eternal happiness."

That afternoon, I mailed the letter, not knowing whether it would ever leave the base post office—or if so, whether mail was even being delivered at Oita. Yet somehow, in some slight way, putting those words on paper helped.

And somehow, also, those final days squirmed by. Each bleak hour expired, leaving its faint and fetid aftermath, dissolving at times in the fiery breath of an occasional air battle.

We almost welcomed them now—anything to relieve the curse of waiting, and we fought with great abandon, caring little whether we lived or died. Life assumes a different perspective when only a little remains, yet ironically, our very daring seemed to preserve us. Two of us downed an enemy fighter in a surprise attack near Kure one day, then fled almost before the Americans knew what had happened. As our victim plummeted toward the bay, I decided that my only answer was to hurl fear to the winds.

Do not be afraid—there is nothing to lose! It gave one a special magic. Strike the enemy hard and fast before he strikes you. Then vanish. Yes, now that there was no hope, it was easy to attack fearlessly. I knew how to use the clouds and the sun; they were my friends. The enemy could send a thousand planes—no matter. We would somehow be there, a dwindling few, to slash at their tails and send them on their way to hell.

A week passed . . . two weeks . . . incredibly, nearly a month. It was now almost August, and I was still awaiting my summons—day by day,

hour by hour, minute by minute. How does one exist under such circumstances? He exists because he exists. There is no alternative but death,
by one's own hand or otherwise. Throughout it all, however, was the
faint, pale hope that the war would end. It seemed increasingly obvious
that the sun was setting. No longer was the *Nippon* Empire The Land of
The Rising Sun. And still, as well, I clung to Toyoko's promise: "The
war will end! The war will end in time!"

What a bizarre kind of race, my own doom running neck and neck
with the doom of my country. What endless feelings of ambivalence.
And yet . . . again increasingly I reflected upon the words of Namoto's
mother: "Listen to me, my sons . . . there is no honor in dying for a lost
cause." Nor was there any advantage. What, in practical reality, could
be accomplished now, even if every last remaining one of us, by some
absurd quirk of fate, sank an enemy ship? They were limitless, implacable.
More and more now, my bitterness toward our obstinate, idiotic leaders
in Tokyo transcended my hatred for the enemy.

Nevertheless, we fought on.

Near the end of July we learned that a force of B-29's was flying
southwest of Osaka, probably slated to pummel that city, then split,
striking Matsue and Okayama. Only four of us—a Lieutenant Shoji
Mattu, sergeant, another corporal and I—were sent forth to meet them
above Okayama. A pitiful few, another telling evidence that Japan was
breathing her death rattles. Even so, we had covenanted together just
before takeoff. Today we would send one of those thunderous Superfortresses to its death.

Having calculated the time of our encounter with the 29's, I did
some additional planning. Our flight would carry us over Onomichi,
my very home. Why not stage a brief aerobatic performance for the
students at Onomichi High School—perhaps even for my own family
and neighbors? It seemed a fine idea, and my three companions were
all enthusiastic.

Shortly before take-off I sat down to write a brief message, merely a
few words of devotion to my family. Merely a few words, because I had
only seconds and didn't know what to say. What could I tell them? That
I would soon be receiving my final orders? No, no sense in it. None at all.
They would find out soon enough. Still, I had to leave them something.

It was apparent from their letters, that most of my own were not being delivered, nor had I received much word from them in some time.

After pondering the matter briefly, I scribbled down a few words, telling them that I was again at Hiro, that I was "well", that I hoped and prayed they were. Simultaneously I almost wondered whether my family still existed, whether they ever had. The aura of unreality was steadily growing more powerful. Lately, in fact, there had been disquieting moments when I could no longer conjure up their images. I was literally forgetting what they looked like.

I rolled the message up and placed it in a metal tube to which I had attached a long white streamer. It was essential that the descent be clearly visible, that someone find it and make the delivery according to the enclosed instructions.

Minutes after leaving the landing field, I was gazing down upon familiar territory—the shipyards, the shore line where the fishermen dwelt, the main buildings of town, those that remained. Many of them had been demolished, but the radio station was still standing along, as I had devoutly hoped, with my high school. My own home neighborhood, secluded within the Senkoji Mountains, still appeared to be in tact as well.

A group of students on the school athletic field gazed up as we began our descent. Plummeting down, my companions close behind, I could see their upturned faces. Seconds later, however, I glanced back, steeply climbing, and was astonished to see them scattering for cover.

Shaking my head, I grinned, even laughed. Green kids!

The lieutenant's voice crackled over my intercom. "Don't even know their own planes!"

"Act like they've never even seen them before," I fired back, then grew more serious. Very probably they had not seen any, not for a long time. Soon, though, they emerged from hiding and were beginning to wave. I could see their faces clearly, practically hear their cries. With only seconds to spare, we plunged at them, spiraling crazily, pulling out at treetop level, rocking the buildings with our thunder. On our third and final pass we arched over the field, banking hard to avoid the encircling mountains. Students had flooded from every exit and were waving joyfully. Angling, low I released my message, saw it fluttering earthward.

People were even appearing from some of the houses now, but as I passed over my own there was no sign of life, and in seconds the city was falling behind . . . fading . . . gone. What a peculiar sensation. Everything, my home included, had looked so different from the air. Once more Onomichi was only a fond illusion. I had not returned home after all.

Soaring onward toward our special rendezvous, I wondered what would become of my people, those innocent young girls? How many of them, of our women, would the enemy use according to its whims? A vanquished nation is a plundered nation, spared no cruelty or humiliation. Well, regardless of what might come, today the enemy would feel our sting.

Not long afterward we neared Okayama, and soon, exactly as calculated, the B-29's appeared—only six of them, but ominous nonetheless, forging their way eastward at fifteen thousand feet, flanked by a dozen Hellcats. The 29's were indeed awesome, considerably larger and more formidable than the 17's we had encountered earlier in the war. Six of them, lethal leviathans trailing vapor against a purple sky.

Our lieutenant signaled, and I felt my mouth tighten, the upper lip puffing with air, as we climbed and circled to their rear. At the moment our enemy was apparently unaware of us. The Japanese Army Air Force, once a formidable power, was now only a mockery, and the 29's lumbered ponderously onward. Relentlessly! Utterly remorseless. The Americans simply kept coming and coming, more and more and more, ever growing in numbers and size.

Only when we plummeted downward from the sun were they aware of us. Lining up the rear Fortress in my range finder, I began firing, and it swiftly retaliated with a vicious barrage of its own. Others were opening fire as well, and the Hellcats swarmed into action, intent on living up to their name.

Roaring downward behind our lieutenant, I saw the tracers racing toward and past us, all in an instant, all very near . . . saw them striking home. The lieutenant's plane seemed to shudder momentarily like someone taking a savage body blow. Then, casting off streamers of smoke and flame, it persisted. Portions of the fuselage were ripping apart, but miraculously he continued, slicing directly through the tail section of the lead bomber and exploding.

Helplessly maimed, the B-29 spiraled downward in monstrous and moaning, ever-widening gyrations, its severed tail dropping vertically after the blackened and fading remains of Shoji Matta.

Almost simultaneously, I levered back on the stick, pulling out of my dive at more than five G's, wavering, nearly tearing my wings off. For several seconds the blood drained from my head, and by the time I had recovered, the remaining bombers had surged onward, fanning and swerving to avoid the fate of their leader.

So suddenly, both our lieutenant and the B-29—gone! Incredulous, I followed the rapidly vanishing enemy, gradually climbing as I gained on them. The huge bombers were remarkably swift, and it required two or three minutes for me to close the gap. As I moved in on the trailing bomber it began to zigzag erratically, opening up with its tail guns, and the Hellcats were circling ravenously, coming at me from almost every direction.

I was only two hundred yards above the elusive 29 now and about that far behind. Time for the attack, and I angled into a steep dive, charging at him full bore, pivoting on my axis, aileron rolling down at well over four hundred miles an hour. The 29's turret guns, both front and rear, were opening up now. I had completed my final roll—too late to worry about being elusive—air speed approaching five hundred, firing attenuated bursts directly at its nose area.

Now the enemy was looming, larger than life, disgorging a withering barrage, graphing the air all about me with the sinister red lines. But I was flying as never before, undeterred, and the monster veered off even more sharply, undoubtedly expecting to be rammed. I watched my own tracers arch, seeming to curve, stitching their seam backward along his wing and fuselage. Making contact! The B-29 was coughing smoke, and I felt a diabolical surge of elation. Triumph! Revenge!

Now it was rapidly losing altitude, but still deadly. As I screamed past its massive rudder, the tail guns were ripping away without compromise, the hot lead ravaging my wings and fuselage. Yes, the familiar, ominous sledge hammer sounds, and a Hellcat was firing away at me from the rear. Two others were charging in from the side.

Pulling out radically, I hit the stick and rudder pedal, swerving left and climbing. Only one of the Grummans was still with me at this point. Trailing the others, he had anticipated me. I was circling hard, still bidding for altitude, and upon completing a full 360 degrees, I glanced back over my shoulder. The enemy was still there, slightly above, determined to cut inside my arc . . . banking so closely that I could distinctly see the pilot. The sun was glinting on his goggles, his white teeth bared in a triumphant grin.

A confident American, an expression I will never forget, for suddenly I was terribly afraid, afraid as never before, my veins filling with ice crystals. Not so much fear for myself actually as for another reason. Somehow that expression, that mere single glimpse, symbolized the hopelessness of our plight as nothing else ever had.

The contest was over, and I dropped away radically, barrel rolling . . . plunging straight downward for thousands of feet as I had done the month before over Okinawa. Two of the enemy, apparently pursuing my comrades, fanned off startled as I thundered by, missing one of them by only a few yards.

Down, down, down, spinning . . . at last dropping straight. Pulling out perilously near the earth, fighting off the blackness. Escape once more, and I was gunning homeward at full throttle. Momentarily, despite all, I rejoiced in our good fortune. In addition to the 29 destroyed by our lieutenant, a second had also gone down. How I wanted to claim that monster for my own, to see it hit the water! Undoubtedly, it was the bomber with which I had done battle. I had not witnessed its actual demise, however, nor had others been on hand to verify what occurred.

Later I learned that a B-29 had crashed near Okayama, its crew bailing out over the inland sea.

Chapter Twenty-Eight

Hiroshima

It was August 1, 1945, and I had returned from a reconnaissance flight near Matsue to learn that someone had paid me a
visit. "Some woman was here to see you, Kuwahara," the desk sergeant
said.

My heart surged, beating rapidly. Toyoko?

"Your sister," the clerk added. Well then, my sister. Wonderful! Surely
I wanted to see her as well.

"Unfortunately, we couldn't allow her to stay," the desk sergeant
continued, "As you know, we can't have any civilians on the base now."
I barely nodded. "She left you these," he said.

Thanking him, I hurried to my barracks, carrying the envelope and
tiny parcel. Sitting on my cot, I opened the note and began reading:

"Yasuo-*chan*, we received your message and were overjoyed to hear
from you—the first word in many weeks. We did not know what had
become of you. But now, to learn that you are near us once more—that
makes us feel so much better, even though we cannot see you.

"How proud we are, Yasuo! We know that you are bringing great
honor to the Emperor, your country, and your family. I love you for this,
my brother, for your courage, but always, even more for what you have

been to me, what we have been to each other. I speak now, as well, for our entire family. Wherever you may go, whatever you may be doing, our love journeys with you.

"Each day I pray for you at our shrine and always in my heart. Your Sister, Tomika."

Over and over, I read those words, consumed by emotion. An immense longing swept over me like a tide. If only I could have seen her—for a single, fleeting second! Just one more time! Then the tide ebbed. No, better not to have seen her at all, not to see any of them. Better that way. At last I opened the little parcel. For a long time I sat there bowed, staring at her gift, feeling its softness against my palm, gazing at its lustrous darkness. Tomika had left me a lock of her hair.

A torpid August first merged with August second. Over a month since my meeting with Captain Tsubaki. A month, and still waiting! Incredible! Why didn't the word come? Why? What were they waiting for? And now the paradox loomed even more strangely. As each day brought me closer to death it might also draw me farther away. It was a race between the death of our nation and the death of Yasuo Kuwahara.

The night of August third, I tossed feverishly, beset by endless nightmares. Death was no longer my greatest fear. Waiting itself was worse. No hope now. Desperate though our country had become, I decided that its surrender might still take months. The waiting, waiting, the abominable waiting! The strangling noose of uncertainty, growing ever tighter!

Once I awakened, muttering incoherently, my entire body slick with sweat, my hair not only damp but even wet with it. If my orders didn't come soon, I might take the easy way out after all. A sharp knife, a quick slice across the jugular vein. "There is nothing honorable in dying for a lost cause," the words came. "There is nothing. . . ." I almost choked.

I was ensnared in the great net from which there was no escape. One way or another, I would die. But die the easy way to escape the hard way? After all the struggle, end my life through cowardice? Humiliation and dishonor? Yes, humiliation and dishonor, to myself and to my family, if not for our government for which I had now lost all respect. I shook my head, sighing, moaning. No, not the easy way—not the coward's way.

Wait, Kuwahara. Wait, barely existing from one moment to the next. Grit your teeth. Clench your fists. Swear . . . Pray to God. Curse him if you have to, but wait. Do not bring dishonor. Keep me sane, keep me in the skies, striking at the enemy . . . until the word comes! Yes, fighting is the best solution now—my only salvation.

August fourth, I found myself praying many times that day, much of it virtually senseless, often utterly contradictory. I knew where a sharp knife was, waiting patiently without compromise. God send me an enemy plane. Don't make me wait. Do not leave me here!

At four in the morning, August fifth, I sat bolt upright, tearing myself from the ragged fracture of another nightmare. My mattress was again saturated with sweat, and I arose shakily to begin pacing the floor. I was seeing it all from a different perspective again. What did it matter how I died, just so I got it over with? My family? I didn't have a family. My entire past was a dream. Life itself the constant nightmare, inescapable, awake or asleep.

The wooden floor was hard and a bit slivery as I crossed it and exited through the back door. Cooler outside, the base silent and corpse like, slowly wreathing in darkness and the first bilious gleams of dawn. In a few minutes I would go get the knife, kneel there beside the barracks—dark and cool. Enter the waning darkness, the coolness, before they escaped, flee with them forever. No, no ridiculous. Not after so long a struggle. For a moment I cursed the entire world, but nothing would send me out a coward. I would have that one, cold triumph.

Now . . . go back in and lie down on your soggy mattress. Got to sleep before the feeling changes again. You'll make it to the end, Yasbei. . . somehow. Think about anything else . . . about Toyoko. No, no, better not. Toyoko makes you remember that final night together. Then think of Tatsuno–Nakamura too. You were not a true friend, Kuwahara. Yes, guilt, a rancid taste on the tongue—that only one thing can dispel. Think of someone else. Toyoko. No, not Toyoko, not . . . Think of your sister, your mother. Ah, ah yes . . . you can see their faces once more, hear their blessed voices.

An hour before reveille, I sank into a feverish sleep, a state of near coma.

And that day . . . I received my written orders. On August eighth, I would take off for the final time. At last, at last, I truly knew! A great and leaden door had swung open revealing my destiny. Okinawa . . . waiting there amid the endless waters and the swirling vapors of time.

Three days. Somehow, some way, I would cling to the melting rim of existence three more days.

The following morning I would be granted a two-day pass. Such was the Japanese Military's magnanimity to its fated sons. At first I had decided not to use that pass. I had reflected upon the matter lengthily, well beforehand, in fact, convinced that it would be better never to see my family or friends again, told myself that in effect I had died already. I had banished the idea from my mind.

Almost.

Early that next morning, August sixth, I burst into the orderly room with a frantic change of heart. "My pass! Do you have a two-day pass for me?"

The desk sergeant was owlish, slightly grizzled, wearing thick-lensed reading glasses. For a moment he regarded me strangely. "You were supposed to have signed for it last night, Corporal."

"I couldn't last night," I said struggling hard to contain myself, "Just give me the pass—I'll sign for it now."

"Well . . . all right," he replied, still stupidly reluctant. "Ummm, let's see. . . ." Fumbling his way through the file with infuriating clumsiness. "Ummmm . . . let's see: Ito . . . Kimura. . . *Hai*, Kuwahara! Go ahead, but date it August fifth, or, it will be my ass! No, not there, damn it! Right here, under Kimura's."

For a moment I had scarcely known what I was doing. It was almost as if I had never learned to write. "*Arigato*, Sergeant—thank you." With trembling hands I scrawled my signature, destination, time of departure, time of return, then fled.

Minutes later I had obtained a ride in the back of an army truck headed for Hiroshima. It would not take long to reach my home from there. Home, my place of origin, the people to whom I belonged. I should have known the pull would be too great, inexorable, like the gravitational force of the moon upon the tides. How foolish I had been.

The truck rumbled erratically forward, jolting and clattering over the pitted road, nearly jarring my teeth loose at times, but I didn't mind. I was gazing at the darkening green of the rice fields, the narrow canals, the lush, green vegetation of the mountains, the interplay of sunlight

and retreating shadow, and the burgeoning blue of the sky. Suddenly
there was a remarkable enchantment about my entire surroundings—a
beauty I had almost forgotten.

Nostalgia welled with the advancing light, and now I was remembering experiences from my boyhood: a family visit to the shrines of Kyoto,
a secluded lake miraculously high in the mountains somewhere, taking
turns with my brothers looking through a pay telescope at scenes far
distant . . . two fishermen in a row boat a mile away, unaware of our gaze
as they baited their hooks then commenced eating their lunch. A bright
river of memory flowing through my mind with scenes of enchantment
at every turn, but most of all home.

Unexpectedly I was strangely happy. Miraculously, it suddenly
seemed that the next two days would somehow be exempt from the
manacles of fate just ahead. A golden island that would glow throughout the expanses of eternity. The forty-eight hours would pass, but the
island would remain, and death would merely be a transition, a process
of purification wherein the good, the just, the truly happy would abide.
Yes in the last analysis, death would indeed be lighter than a feather.

Perhaps God, or Buddah, or fate . . . someone or something . . .
who or whatever placed us in this strange estate called mortality would
accomplish it. "Make it acceptable to me," I murmured, "please make
it all right." The words repeated themselves over and over, resonating
throughout my being, and I leaned forward, elbows on my knees, hands
clasping my head.

That way I could feel every rock and depression in the road, but it
was working. Someone or something was listening. I continued to repeat
the words but more calmly now, and my soul was relaxing as though a
clean breeze were drifting through. I glanced up. Yes, a cleansing breeze,
literally. The rice was billowing in soft green waves. And yes, the happiness had not deserted me. Two golden days, and that was everything.

I left the truck on the outskirts of Hiroshima at about 7:30 a. m.,
and a few minutes later boarded a streetcar. Impulsively, only moments
earlier, I had decided to visit briefly with a friend there in the Second
General Army Hospital before going on to Onomichi. Leaving the
streetcar, I heard it move off along the tracks, emitting a lonely tootle in
the distance. For an instant I gazed about, filled with a sudden need to

consume, somehow digest and metabolize my entire surroundings.

The sky was still clear except for a muted overcast in the west as I walked along Shiratori Street toward the hospital. Already it was growing sultry, and even at that hour small bands of children were skittering about the streets, blessedly unaware that their world was falling apart. "*Ohayo gozaimasu!*" A man passed by, carrying a briefcase, and I returned his good morning. Grocers and magazine vendors had opened the shutters to their flimsy huts, but there was little within them of interest.

Once, on impulse, though, I stopped to purchase an orange. I could feel its roundness as I continued along the street, the gratifying texture of its skin, even the pores, in my hand. What a marvelous creation, how remarkably designed! By chance alone? If so, why the consistency in oranges everywhere, the order of their growth? The pliable, rubbery skin, so easily removable yet so remarkably protective? Why the delightful, incredibly sweet, easily separable sections, perfectly constituted to delight the palate and enhance one's health? The skin glowed entrancingly, joyfully. My mouth watered, but I would wait, cherishing it until the proper time. A reward, a gift to myself. For what, I did not know. Perhaps for having simply survived so long, so miraculously.

Along my way, an old woman called to me. Her face was a mosaic of wrinkles and lines as though it had been frozen and shattered. Eyeing her curiously, I turned back, and she reached for me with a trembling hand. For a moment I gazed into her withered face, into eyes still bright and alert. "I want to know the truth, young man," she rasped. "What has become of our aircraft? Why are they no longer up there?" She hunched before me, shriveled, blinking and stoic, probably anticipating the worst, even wanting it.

Gently I laid my hand upon her shoulder, and gazed at the pavement. I wished greatly that I could go somewhere with that ancient *obasan*. Conversation would be unnecessary, only her presence. That, perhaps, and a cup of tea. "Old mother," I said, "there are few planes left. Before long it will all be over, and we won't have to hide from the bombs any more." Her claw closed upon my hand almost painfully, and I began to leave. Then I turned back for a moment. "Here, take this," I said and handed her the orange.

Minutes later I heard air raid sirens—a small concern, since two

American planes had already passed over while I was on the street car. The lone B-29 above did not seem threatening for some reason, merely patronizing. If I were up there now in my *Hayabusa* I would dive at it from the eye of the sun, all guns blazing, pumping them out from my cannons. But the old woman was right. No Japanese planes in sight. The sky was empty except for that single, stolid, lumbering monster, coursing the heavens with total impunity.

I continued to watch it occasionally, however, as I went along my way. There was something disconcerting in its very placidness, about the persistent smugness of its droning. So casual, so presumptuous. Soon a tiny white speck separated from its silver belly, and the plane moved off, picking up speed. No larger than a marble at first, the object increased to the size of a baseball, then seemed to change in form, becoming a large mushroom. A parachute, carrying a strange, dark object, tapered like a shark but blunt at one end as though the head had been chopped off. Yes. I heard the speculations of others watching with me.

"What are they up to now?"

"More of their stupid pamphlets?"

"Yes, more propaganda–more of the same old thing. Don't pay it any—"

All other mutterings were obliterated, along with everything else. Suddenly a monstrous multi-colored flash bulb went off directly in my face. Something like concentrated heat lightning stifled me, transforming my lungs into vacuums. So fast, it might have been a mere figment of the imagination.

Yet simultaneously I threw up my hands, vainly striving to protect my face from the ferocious burning. A mighty blast furnace had just been opened upon the world.

Within the next moment there came a cataclysm which no one will ever describe adequately. It was neither a roar, a boom, nor a blast. Rather, it was a combination of all those qualities with something else added   the fantastic power of earthquakes, avalanches, and erupting volcanoes. For one fantastic, overwhelming moment nature had unleashed its wrath, and the world had ruptured in a mighty convulsion.

All this within only seconds, and I was slammed to the earth as though struck by a charging rhino. Sudden darkness, all light extinguished like the flicking of a switch . . . pressure, an agonized, choking gasp . . . my body seared with pain. Then relief, utter vacancy. I did not exist. Never had.

Minutes . . . hours . . . days? Impossible to tell, but somewhere within the depths of nothingness, there came a sound. A rumbling that somehow, in defiance of natural law, restored my spirit in the depths of the void. At the time, however, these things were only dim awareness—the awareness perhaps of a worm stirring in the winter soil or an insect within its cocoon.

Another rumbling . . . then another, and the sense of awareness expanded. Carts . . . the rumbling of carts! But why? What had happened? Where was I? Gradually my sense of personality acquired clearer dimension. I was Yasuo Kuwahara, Corporal. Kuwahara . . . on my way somewhere. On my way home?

Going home to say goodbye.

Yes, recollection returning. But what had happened? An earthquake? No, a strange and impossible explosion. A bomb perhaps, a bomb of colossal force utterly beyond the realm of experience. There within the darkness I saw again the white and welling mushroom—drifting on the retina of memory, steadily transforming now, becoming a gigantic jellyfish—something dark and sullen, inexpressibly grotesque, attached to its tendrils.

But I was Yasuo—Yasuo Kuwahara, still alive, though helpless, scarcely able to move. Buried alive! The realization riddled me with horror, greater fear than I had yet known, but eventually I worked one arm free from the rubble embracing it, feeling the skin of my hand rip on something jagged. My eyes, nose, ears, even my mouth, were clogged with dirt, and for several minutes I choked and spat, blinking frantically, then stopped suddenly from pain as the grit rasped my eyeballs.

For a long time I simply lay there, gasping and groaning. My eyes were watering copiously, but eventually they cleared enough that I could detect a tiny scratch of light overhead. It seemed now that I could hear more sounds above as well, people treading about—once another rumbling noise.

Again, it died, and I was filled with terror. Buried alive. I began to writhe, groping about with my free hand and encountering the jagged board that had ripped it earlier. "Help! Help me!" I forced out the words with all my strength, but they sounded like the croaks of a frog. Again and again I called out, gradually with greater volume, also growing pain in my throat and chest.

The pressure from my waist down was also increasing, becoming unbearable. The numbness was creeping upward, entering my torso. Hours seemed to elapse, and occasionally there were more noises overhead. At times I would call out, then go down in a swoon. It was that whirlpool again that I had discovered months before during my beatings from the Mantis.

Once I surfaced, and for the moment my thoughts were lucid. A huge and terrible bomb, yes. The Americans had dropped a new bomb unlike any the world had ever known. Yes, that had to be it.

During my flights to Okinawa some weeks earlier I had heard occasional radio messages from the enemy in Saipan, warning us to surrender or suffer catastrophic consequences. Was this the ultimate realization?

What an ironic situation in any event. A suicide pilot, a noble, glorious *Kamikaze*, dying inside the earth only a short distance from his home! For an instant I almost laughed. What an ignominious way to die! On the other hand . . . why did it matter? Perhaps all of Japan was gone. Had a B-29 circled over every major city, releasing a parachute with a bomb? What a thought. No more Japan! Everything gone, in ruins. No, no, impossible.

More noise above, giving me a start. Dust had sifted through the scratch of light overhead. For a moment it widened then shrank to a mere bird's eye. More dust. The eye closed, and I yelled. Feeling as though my lungs might tear loose, I shouted again and again. No answer. Sobbing for air and groaning, I made a last feeble bid for help.

Seconds later the eye blinked once more and became a yawning mouth. "I hear you," a voice came. "Be patient—we're removing the rubble." Wonderful words, yet there in my helplessness, I wondered again whether I was now a complete cripple. The numbness in my body was increasing. How long had I been there? Days? Would I be liberated only to die moments later? Or to be hopelessly paralyzed?

The sounds above increased. At length, unbelievably, the weight was lifting, darkness changed to a blinding light. "Are you all right?" a voice inquired. "Easy, easy—better not move. Better not. . . ." But I was moving, getting to my hands and knees. Moving! Struggling to rise . . . somehow regaining my feet! But dizzy, overwhelmingly dizzy.

The world teetered in a blur. What a weird, swirling vision! Voices, insistently, warning, comforting, making no sense, and I toppled backward, the blood draining from my head, much as though I were completing a power dive in my fighter plane. Legs collapsing. "Easy—easy!" Hands and arms, capturing me, breaking my fall. "We've got you . . . it's all right. Just lie back for a minute." I gazed up at them in vacuous wonderment. My benefactors were all clad in white!

"You'll be all right," a voice said. "Just stay right here until you regain your strength. We have to go now."

The thought filled me with panic. "No, wait! Don't go!"

"We must," the voice drifted. "Hiroshima is in ruins—everyone dead or dying." The figures were dissolving like ghosts.

"No, don't leave me!" I pleaded and broke into a strange, dry crying, but the crying hurt so much I ceased, groping for rationality. Eventually I got to my hands and knees and struggled to my feet again, still so dizzy I wondered if my ear canals had ruptured.

Days later I learned that my benefactors, the figures in white, were patients from the army hospital who had dived beneath their beds when the explosion occurred, barely escaping destruction themselves. I also learned that I had been buried for approximately six hours.

Gradually, my vision cleared, revealing a spectacle exceeding my most horrifying nightmares—so hideous, my already queasy stomach erupted, and I fell to my knees, retching. Minutes later I was still on all fours, hoping that I had merely been the victim of some gargantuan hallucination. But no, it was all there, far more horrible, in fact, than I had initially realized.

Many have sought to describe Hiroshima following the nuclear holocaust on that fateful day, August 6, 1945, an immense wound in the heart of history that has never fully healed, merely become a throbbing mass of scar tissue. No one has ever succeeded nor will they, for what occurred there was beyond the realm of human experience.

Certain broad pictures remain, however, scorched forever within my memory . . . pictures of a great city reduced to a fiery rubble pit in which approximately 140,000 people had died with an equal number wounded. Some of the former had literally been vaporized or burned to a crisp, and all of it within a few ticks of a watch.

Again, I stood, still swaying, staring dementedly, and now I felt moisture. A black rain was settling from a black sky. Again, lapses of memory. Again, for a time, I could not recall when I had come to this place or why. All about me for miles, the landscape had been virtually leveled, yet it was steadily astir with life and death, like the amorphous agitations in a swamp, steadily becoming more appalling as my vision cleared.

Shiratori Street, I gradually realized, was buried under houses and buildings, folded and smashed like trampled boxes—much of it charred and blackened, portions aflame, periodically flaring up savagely. Bodies were scattered everywhere, some charred and inert, some barely mobile. In the distance, a few of the sturdiest buildings still stood, gray-black and skeletal, a number listing precariously, ready to collapse. Fire and smoke everywhere, rapidly expanding, and at times the smoke drifted my way, blindingly, chokingly.

Groggily I gazed skyward. The sun had been annihilated along with everything else. Despite the hour, night was closing in. I glanced down at the debris nearby and realized that fate had actually worked in my favor. The house under which I was buried had also partially shielded me from the blast. In addition, I had apparently fallen at the base of a large watering trough located against the back wall of the house. The trough, in turn, had helped protect me from the collapsing debris.

Sand, mortar, and litter had nearly filled the trough, forcing it to overflow, and apparently the remaining water had completely evaporated. The awful heat wave had turned nearby grass and other vegetation to ashes, actually melted much of it.

Examining myself more thoroughly now, I discovered a large bruise on the back of my head, lacerations across the side of my face and neck. Both eyes were badly swollen, flowing with tears, and still smarted. My clothing was torn and filthy, with a large rip over my knee. The knee throbbed, sticky with blood and dirt.

Eventually I hobbled away aimlessly, reeling at times like a drunk and within a short distance encountered a pile of bodies, possibly ten or twelve of them. Several were still alive, struggling feebly to extricate themselves. A blackened form rolled from the heap, and a head emerged. The face was singed beef, and its single bloodshot eye blinked at me. The nose was gone, the mouth a lopsided hole.

"Here, here—let me help you," I said, and began dragging free some of the corpses. Tugging at a charred arm, I fell backward. The flesh from the elbow down had sloughed off in my hands like that of a roasted goose. Gorge rising, I continued my task, freeing a man already more dead than alive. One or two people assisted, but others merely stared as though stupefied.

The entire landscape seemed to wreathe with moans and wails, mounting at times to a kind of bedlam. I limped onward, still direction-less, and within seconds I chanced upon a man pinned beneath a beam. Several people were grunting and prying with timbers, struggling to extricate him. Then, as they dragged him free, he emitted an agonized scream and died, blood gushing from his bowels. Hip to ankle, he had been mangled, but the beam's pressure had prevented external bleed-ing.

Bewildered, I wandered on while all about me people were dying, moving aimlessly like half-frozen insects, some clasping their heads other parts of their bodies. Many were naked, and a few—mostly women-sought vainly to cover themselves. Others seemed totally oblivious to their personal nudity. My own clothes were, in fact, more tattered than I had originally realized. One sleeve was missing from my jacket, and one trouser leg, a mere scorched crust, virtually crumbled apart as I brushed against pile of jagged boards.

I reeled onward, a wild, staring animal, bereft of my sanity. Oddly, however, a second part of me, a kind of alter ego, seemed to be moni-toring my responses, somehow detached, from a different perspective. At times, it seemed, that I could actually stand back a bit to observe the strange, haggard creature that I had become, that others were observing. Observing, however, with utter indifference for the great majority were in far worse condition than I.

A short distance ahead someone called feebly, a woman sprawled upon the pavement as though hurled from the sky. Her body was roasted, blackened, and blistered beyond recognition. Her hair had been reduced to charcoal, and patches of her skin and flesh were peeling off.

One side of her throat was scathed and laid open, yet cauterized by the blast, and I could actually see the blood vessels, weakly pulsating with tortured life. Her lips writhed, struggling to form words, but her vocal cords were also dying. Kneeling beside her, I bent low, listening, heard only the dry, hissing buzz of her breath. Then I understood. "Kill me. Please kill me."

Transfixed, I stared at her, my own mouth gaping. The light in those eyes was fading, and suddenly my entire body racked with an immense moan. Clasping my hands to my face, I arose and stumbled off. Innumerable forms lay all about me, some writhing and in their death throes, many afflicted with that same hideous skin condition. Like blackened lepers, they were falling apart. Others, simply wandered in collective confusion.

Slowly, feeble as an old man, I stuggled on throughout the rubble pit that was once Hiroshima for an hour or more, trying at times to be of aid to the wounded and dying but usually with complete futility. Eventually I found myself before the remains of the Yamanaka Girls' High School. Before classwork that morning approximately four hundred girls had assembled in rows on the outer grounds to receive their daily announcements. The blast had cut them down like an enormous scythe, stripping off everything but their belts. Watches, rings and buckles had been embedded in their blackened flesh by the fearsome heat. The school pendants worn about their necks were burned into the sternums between their breasts.

Parents and other family members were examining the bodies. Mothers and sisters were moaning and wailing unlike anything I have ever heard. Some had apparently identified their own, but the efforts in general were futile because most of the girls' faces had been charred beyond recognition. Teeth projected in ghastly grins, and the odor of their bodies cloyed in my nostrils like the reek of manure and decaying fish. Again, I doubled over, holding my stomach and retching, but nothing emerged except for streamers of mucous and saliva flowing from my nostrils and lips, dripping from my chin.

As I turned to leave, a man and woman were huddled before a body, peering into the remains of its face with awful intensity. Many were clinging to each other and weeping as though nothing was left in the universe.

Eventually I spotted an army truck ahead winnowing its way through an expanse of smoldering rubble. "Wait!" I shouted, "wait!" but my voice was the cawing of a crow. The truck lumbered onward, two or three men in the back gaping at me stupidly. "Wait!" The cry tore at my lungs agonizingly, and I stumbled, falling. They could not distinguish me from a civilian, and for a moment I simply sprawled there, face down in the dirt and ashes.

Soon, another truck came grinding my way, and for a time I thought it might run over me. No matter—a blessing, in fact. Nevertheless, by mere instinct, I raised my hand feebly as it rumbled past. Then, a short distance beyond, it halted and began to back up. For the third time that day, I rose from the earth and, surprised at my own strength, began to run. My energy deserted me as I reached the tail gate, however, and I was dragged aboard like the survivor of a ship wreck.

Beyond all feeling now, I stared vacantly at the landscape as it fell behind. Fires still rampaged in many places, smoke stifling the entire area and menacing the sky. We crossed the Ota River upon a bridge miraculously still in tact though precariously near collapse. A human carpet thronged those shores in throbbing blotches. Thousands were sprawled and slowly convulsing along the banks like poisoned lemmings.

Countless numbers wallowed in the shallows, trying to cool themselves. Many had died that way, some from their wounds, others from drowning—bobbing corpses, dozens washing down stream on the current. Mothers, fathers, aged and infant . . . the bomb had not been guilty of discrimination.

Gradually the city fell behind in a ruddy, grit-filled haze, abrading the eyes and nostrils at times like tear gas. Eventually we were passing fields, still green, relatively unchanged, except that the shadows were now lengthening from the west instead of the east.

Chapter Twenty-Nine

The Voice of the Emperor

During the following two days I was restricted to my quarters, exhausted and bedfast. Yet despite my misery and enervation I could find no rest. My body was on fire, my eyes constantly smarting and watering. On August 8, having scarcely slept or eaten, I was detailed to fly a *Shinshitei*, a swift, two-engine reconnaissance plane, over Hiroshima and surrounding area.

From 7,000 feet I peered through my binoculars, down into the city's ravaged heart. Much of it was still burning, and smoke drifted in heavy layers, obscuring large expanses of the area. Everywhere the earth appeared, though, lay havoc, and it was impossible to tell where most of the buildings, even the best known, had stood. Periodically, I detected the bodies of cows and horses, cattle, and dogs along with the mass of human dead. Street cars had been tossed from their tracks, trains flung from their rails like toys.

Flooding the roads in muddy currents were human beings, steadily fleeing toward the mountains and outlying cities: Kaitaichi, Miyajima and Ujina. Occasionally those rivers formed tributaries as military vehicles forded through—truckloads of soldiers, snaking slowly back and forth, evacuating military personnel, fighting fires. What an absurd undertaking it all seemed. The great bomb had utterly demolished the Second General Army Headquarters along with Hiroshima's military supply buildings. Our troops would quickly feel the loss.

Periodically my radio crackled with static, voices, and once for a minute or two, the words whined distinctly: ". . . as yet, authorities have not determined the exact nature of the weapon which . . . new bomb of some kind . . . doctors analyzing the effects but still uncertain."

Then an ongoing blare of static that hurt my ears, and I switched to another station. Strains coming from Light of The Firefly (the melody of Auld Lang Syne). Moments and a familiar voice interrupted: "My dear and esteemed Japanese pilots," it droned, 'This is Saipan, and I am Japanese as you are. At this very moment I am safe from the horror of war—comfortable and well cared for. Are you also?" This was followed by a lengthy pause, so long that I assumed the message had ended.

Then suddenly it continued : ". . . and why, my friends, must you remain the helpless pawns of a senseless war? You gallant and noble *Kamikaze* who daily sacrifice your lives, though now to what avail? Why must you be victimized? Why must you die when those deaths will accomplish no good whatever? When the war is all but over?"

America, the voice continued, would offer but one alternative—surrender or annihilation. "Do you know that your mothers, your wives, your brothers and sisters, your children, are dying by the thousands? That those who survive will soon be starving? Indeed, many are already starving. And why? Because of the enemy—most certainly. But also because of the arrogance and selfishness of your leaders, a comparative few in Tokyo, who insist that their alleged sacred honor is more precious than the suffering and destruction of countless thousands. Ere long, perhaps, millions, of their people. Of you yourselves!"

The voice persisted with painful and relentless logic, much like a surgical procedure without anesthetic. Surrender for our remaining pilots would be relatively easy it promised. We would merely need to waggle our wings upon approaching an American landing field, and the guns would remain silent. We would be given safe haven and good treatment.

"I will be back on the air in two hours," the voice concluded. "My only concern and that of many others who have now joined in our cause is your welfare and happiness. The welfare and happiness of our country."

Then silence, a bit of static and more music. This time, ironically, to the tune of *My Old Kentucky Home* involving the early American Southland yet also very popular throughout Japan in my own time.

Listening now, I was bathed in an immense wave of nostalgia—longing for my own home, for the happy days of childhood. And I felt more powerfully than ever the struggle between hope and fear. It was abundantly clear now that Japan must choose between surrender and destruction. Conceivably surrender could come any day, perhaps any hour. On the other hand, I might yet be flying that mission. My orders were still in force.

Circling over the remains of Hiroshima, I reflected upon the enemy's offer of sanctuary. More than ever, I was thinking of peace. Peace under almost any conditions seemed preferable to my fate at Okinawa. Recently, in fact, I had even pondered the prospect of desertion, heading for Saipan, but limited fuel presented the main problem. As one option, however, I had contemplated sneaking up on the guard by night and knocking him unconscious with one of the ball bats, even rationalizing that it would not be the first time he had felt their hardness. I would then transfer gasoline from the drums to my fighter with buckets. If anyone were to accost me during the process, I would simply explain that a drum was leaking, that I had been ordered to transfer some of the fuel to my *Hayabusa*. Once I was tanked up and heading for Saipan no one could stop me. I was confident of that.

But now . . . staring down into the devastation that had been Hiroshima . . . I was filled with hatred toward the traitor in Saipan. Even though he had spoken the truth, I wanted to lay hold of his throat. Hatred welled also toward the enemy. Had an American plane appeared at that moment, I would have done all within my power to ram it. My own life was of no consequence at the moment.

Two hours of flying had dulled my sight, all my senses, and sleep enveloped me irresistibly. My stomach was queasy, my skin beginning to peel, my hands and face inflamed and puffy. The combination was simply too much; the weariness would drag me under. I radioed in and was granted permission to return.

Upon landing I made my report and sagged off to the barracks feeling as though I had just lost a quart of blood. Inside, several of the radical

Kichigai flyers were arguing with the *Sukebei* about the status of the war. Russia's belated decision to take up arms against us was creating consternation for some. In my own opinion, it made little difference. Russia had played a cunning and avaricious game, like the vulture who arrives to satisfy his gluttony once the eagle has made its kill. Now Russia could share in the spoils of war without the effort and without being hated as the Americans would. Few Japanese a decade or more hence would recall that Soviet boots had helped to trample out our death rattles.

Too enervated to join in the argument, I crumpled onto my cot, oblivious to virtually everything for nearly fifteen hours.

During the next few days my skin grew far worse. The epidermis on all my exposed areas was sloughing off while parts of the remaining layer actually decayed, smelling so bad that people began to avoid me. My face had broken into a rash and was covered with boils, prelude to a lengthy illness that later left me bald for months, and radiation ailments that will linger throughout the rest of my days.

At the medical dispensary, doctors eyed me nervously as though I were afflicted with bubonic plague and offered little help. One of them suggested that my skin condition was simply the result of extreme heat, that my fever was aggravated by a cold. "Just soak your face in a pail of water every hour or so," he advised. "You'll recover soon."

All suicide missions had been temporarily cancelled by the *Daihonei* and, despite the good doctor's unconcern, my condition was now serious enough to prevent me from even flying reconnaissance. Nothing remained but the waiting and wondering. Throughout the base tension was growing. The combination of hope and fear produced a new kind of stress. Our nerves were like fine crystal in a bouncing truck bed, our actions and reflexes spastic. Day and night my body tingled. Whenever I lay down, my muscles twitched, and at times I trembled uncontrollably.

On August 14, a friend rushed into the barracks having just returned from a reconnaissance flight. "Kuwahara!" he exclaimed. "They're saying we'll surrender tomorrow! The Emperor will announce Japan's surrender! The air is full of it!" I stared at him vacantly and offered no reply. The news was utterly mind boggling, momentarily beyond all comprehension.

Swiftly the rumor spread like an invasion of locusts. The tension mounted along with the joy and sorrow, the dejection and euphoria, the incredulity and the inevitability.

At noon the following day all of us, officers and men alike, were assembled in the main mess hall, attention focused upon a large and antiquated radio in front near the serving area. An officer was adjusting the dials, initially generating only squeaks, occasional gibberish, and static. Then came silence except for a faint persistent humming, and at length a voice that none of us, none of our population in general, had ever heard before. High, nasal . . . somewhat eerie . . . almost indecipherable. We listened as though fighting off deafness, cast occasional startled glances at each other, stared at the radio transfixed.

The Emperor, yes! Who else could it be? But the Emperor was speaking in formal Court Japanese, and an officer nearest the front sprang to his feet spontaneously, providing a partial translation as the message quavered onward.

And now the words were taking hold, the incredible yet certain, realization that Japan had accepted the Allied Ultimatum of unconditional surrender.

It was over. Finished. Ended.

For a moment we sat there in silence. The proclamation, like the atomic flash, left everyone stunned. Even though we had sought to condition ourselves mentally, we were still unprepared emotionally. Glancing slowly about, I saw the stricken faces, expressions of growing relief on some, of anger on others. Then, suddenly, one of the *Kichigai* leaped to his feet with a strangled cry. "Those rotten Americans! May God destroy them! Revenge! Revenge! Are we mere feeble women? Let us strike now, this very moment—before it's too late! We are expendable!"

"We are expendable!" rose the cry. A score of men arose and would have rushed to their planes had not the commander intervened.

"You men will return to your seats immediately," he roared, "or face general court martial!" Short, but broad and powerful, with a stern and noble countenance, he was new at Hiro but obviously a man to be reckoned with. "You will obey your Emperor in all things!" He wore a bristling moustache, and his eyes glittered imposingly.

After we had returned to our barracks, however, two aircraft left the runway unexpectedly and circled, passing low overhead with a long, defiant roar. Rushing to the windows and out the doors, we stared as they banked and climbed steeply, heading south. Minutes later, both were circling back at about two thousand feet, and to our amazement, diving vertically at full speed only a hundred yards or so distant. They struck the runway simultaneously in huge, billowing explosions, and the smoke began to rise. Sergeants Hashimoto and Kinoshita had quietly sneaked to their planes and taken off, and become some of the first Japanese to suffer death rather than surrender.

Their demise precipitated additional, even more bitter, argument. Men of my own persuasion contended, naturally enough, that it was not only foolish but treasonable—indeed, sacrilegious, to fight on in defiance of our Emperor's Declaration. Extremists among the *Kichigai*, on the other hand, insisted that life would be hell under the Americans, that they would torture and kill most of us anyway. Furthermore, they argued passionately that we had a moral obligation to avenge the horrible massacre of Hiroshima, and now Nagasaki as well.

A Corporal Yoshida whom I had met only a day or two earlier was among the most bitter and adamant in that regard. After a fiery argument and shoving contest with several others, he rushed from our barracks weeping and cursing. "You filthy, cowardly bastards!" he ranted. Pistol shots ripped through the walls, and we promptly dropped to the floor. Then silence, and before long we peered furtively out the windows to see him sprawled face down on the concrete in a widening pool of blood. His pistol lay only inches beyond one outflung hand. He had used the final bullet upon himself.

A wave of additional suicides followed. Several officers placed loaded pistols in their mouths as Yoshida had done and squeezed the triggers. Men committed *harakiri*, bit off their own tongues and bled to death, a procedure I myself had nearly followed back during those dark times with the Praying Mantis. Others slit their throats or hanged themselves.

That same day Admiral Matome Ugaki, Commander of the Navy's Fifth Air Fleet, and several of his echelon, become some of the war's final *Kamikaze*. Calmly, matter of factly, they taxied their *Suisei* bombers down the strip at Oita and were last sighted heading into the clouds for Okinawa. Vice-Admiral Takijiro Onishi, "Father of the *Tokkotai*," having confessed to an overwhelming sense of guilt, committed *harakiri*. Other high-ranking officials followed his lead.

On the morning of August 18, Hiro's commanding officer announced that the propellers were being removed from our aircraft. All arms and ammunition, except enough for the guards, had been locked away. His face was weary, the lines flanking his mouth deeper, the eyes less glittering.

"You are all aware by now that we have been commanded to refrain from further aggression," he said. "Yet some, to our great sorrow and humiliation, have chosen to disregard that command, thereby heaping dishonor upon themselves, their families, our country, and our esteemed Emperor. Those of you who have accepted his words are to be commended for your faithfulness and loyalty . . . for your courage. As he once commanded you to fight, so now, he has commanded you to cease. As he once commanded you to die, so now, he has commanded you to live. You have obeyed in all these things and shall be crowned with honor."

There followed a lengthy pause wherein his countenance became both fierce and very sorrowful. "Regardless of personal feelings, the time has come for us to accept reality. The war is over." His entire face was atremble, and he bit his lips struggling for control. "Our leaders in Tokyo have accepted the inevitable and rendered their decision. And the Emperor has spoken." The tears were flowing unashamedly down his cheeks. In a moment two hundred broken men were crying.

The ensuing days were among the strangest yet, however. The inequality which had existed so long between officers and enlisted men evaporated. Officers who had dealt unjustly with their subordinates fled and were never heard from again. Others were killed by those same subordinates in their attempts to flee. Anarchy was ripening, and many simply deserted, hoping to gain anonymity among our civilians before the Americans took over. Records, documents, names of air force personnel—all were being destroyed to prevent identification by the enemy.

Heavy guard was posted around warehouses and other installations to avert looting by military personnel and even civilians who ferreted through the barbed-wire fences by night. Violence flared, the *Kichigai* and *Sukebei* bickering and carrying on gang warfare. I refrained from all such involvement, secluding myself for hours in a deserted war-torn barracks, biding my time, wondering. I had seen sufficient conflict to last throughout the eternities.

On August 21, as always, several times each day, since the surrender, I read the reports on our bulletin board near base headquarters. And there, prominently displayed in the very center was a new roster containing a lengthy list of names. My heart lurched. For a moment, I couldn't make sense of the message. Then it took form as though scales were falling from my eyes:

"The following men are to receive full and honorable discharge, effective 23 August 1945." I was breathing fast, heart rate increasing to near fibrillation as my eyes raced down the list of names. And there it was! There it was "Cpl. Kuwahara, Yasuo!"

Again the welling of tears as I struggled to catch my breath. It was as though a great and swirling wind had created a vacuum, sucking the air from my lungs.

I wandered back to the deserted barracks, still riddled with wonderment, light as driftwood. For an hour or more I simply sat there at the remote end of the building, there on the back steps, breathing deeply, still cautiously nurturing that curious sense of wonderment, fearful that it might expand too quickly, that it might explode and vanish like shimmering rainbow colors against the horizon.

Fearful, as well, that it was all a mistake. Wasn't it true that at Kochi and Oita they had yet to remove the propellers from their aircraft? And were not efforts still underway by some of our military fanatics to continue the war? Rumor had it that certain factions were propagating the idea that Japan had not actually surrendered, merely reached a tentative standoff with the Allies. Stupid, blind, abysmal fools! Undoubtedly such individuals had not witnessed the horror of Hiroshima and Nagasaki. Unlike myself, they had not been immersed in the stench that neither time nor place would ever fully eradicate. Part of me was still awaiting my death orders.

More than ten years later I learned that on August 8, 1945, I was to have been part of a final desperation assault, involving thousands of men and planes—all that remained. The great besom of destruction that had swept away so many of my countrymen at Hiroshima had saved me.

Chapter Thirty

The Farewell Cup

Gradually my feelings of paranoia diminished. Still the sense of disbelief, certainly, still a lingering state of shock—but the remaining days passed more tranquilly than I had dared to hope.

Early on the morning of August 23, I donned a new uniform. Then, for a long time I gazed at myself in the shower room mirror—at the golden eagle patches on my shoulders, glowing faintly in gathering light from the open doorway. I was peering into an unfamiliar face, still swollen and inflamed. One of my eyebrows was all but gone, my hair thinning badly. I was looking at an unfamiliar being, a person I scarcely knew. Only age seventeen, yet older than time.

Now, after the long and irredeemable months, I gazed at the image before me pensively, filled with wonderment beyond calculation, at the hand moving of its own volition to trace its fingertips down the scorched and peeling cheek, across a scar at the comer of my lip. "Yasuo Kuwahara," the image whispered, "who are you? What have you become?"

Then I was seeing on through the myself, through the mirror into my past . . . burning cities and dead men, planes, clouds, sky . . . ships and the infinite sea. Voices were calling faintly but ever more persistently, calling my name. I pressed my forehead against the cold hard surface of the mirror, against the forehead of my other self within it, and we closed our eyes.

Tingling strangely, I left the barracks and, as though compelled by another mind, wandered out onto the empty and forsaken airstrip. From somewhere, near yet far, came the sounds of ancient music—music filled with lamentation, yet somehow, faintly welling traces of hope as well.

Hiro's once proud fighter planes huddled together along a remote corner of the air field, emasculated now without their propellers. Instinctively, I began walking toward them, head down, pondering my steps, watching one foot, slowly, persistently succeeding the next like the passage of days.

The nostalgic music continued, flowing with my childhood, my heritage, full of time, tradition, and the land. Yet so very subtly, I could not sense its direction—mere echoes, it seemed, down the corridors of memory. Upon reaching the assembled aircraft, I moved among them slowly, appraisingly, like one who had only observed such things from afar. There, almost in the very center, was my *Hayabusa*, an old and valiant warrior, now consigned to history.

For a while I merely stood there looking at it, unwilling to say farewell. Then, on sudden impulse, I placed my hand upon the patched wing, glanced about to insure my solitude, and climbed into the cockpit. There I remained for some time, perhaps ten minutes, and once I laid my hands upon the controls. Cold and hard, unresponsive like the limbs of a corpse in rigor mortis. Closing my eyes, I listened. The music rose then gradually diminished, infused with the fading drone of motors somewhere along the red horizon . . . a muffled then mounting roar that gradually fell away, simmered, lingered ever more faintly . . . and was gone. Only the most miniscule remnant mingled with the vague, persistent ringing in my ears, within the chambers of my memory. I glanced about, startled. All sound evaporated now, like the final, diminishing tones of an ancient bell. Nothing left but the brightening day. By ten a.m. I had said my last *sayonara*, saluted the riffling flag—still the white flag with its red and rising sun—climbed aboard the waiting bus with several others—and passed beyond the portals of Hiro forever.

Going home. Never before had life been so dreamlike. We were passing among a swelling human throng, gradually being absorbed once more into civilian life. Rolling forward, haltingly among a motley herd of vehicles and bicycles, among the bleats and honks of horns, our driver trying his best to avoid pot holes, bomb craters and other obstructions, past neighborhoods in ruin, crews at work among the debris. The task seemed insuperable, yet there they were, scurrying about with endless and ant-like determination.

I was moving among my people, a population strange yet familiar. Thus far, the enemy had apparently taken no unfair advantage of our surrender. And, surprisingly to many of the Americans, Japan at large was already resigned to a new order. Despite our so-called fanaticism on the field of battle, we were also a people of resignation when it was required. We were the three bamboos of legend that could bend with the wind. Our Emperor had spoken.

The people whom I moved among and my comrades in farewell were a laughing people because of our relief, a crying people because of our defeat and the immensity of our sacrifice . . . a bitter people because of our victimization by many of our trusted leaders . . . a smiling people because of our joy in reunion . . . a grieving people because so many would never return. Many awaited the main invasion with trepidation, others mainly with curiosity. Some, with mere apathy, for the entire gamut of emotion, of fear, pain, and suffering, had grown numb.

Come what may, the war had ended.

The bus rumbled forward, and I heaved an immense, quivering sigh. My skin was still peeling, my eyes still smarting, the fever from August sixth still simmering away, diminishing, alternating with erratic currents of coldness. But the farmland was unfolding now, blending its therapeutic greenery with the growing blue of the sky.

My family was still safe and alive, waiting. And Toyoko? God willing, I would be with her soon. What might happen then? I did not know what the future might hold. Who ever, anywhere, truly knows with certainty from one hour to the next? But I hoped that she might still await and welcome me! That was all I could ask for now.

Idly, I traced my fingers over a tiny cut on my hand, remembering the farewell gathering I had attended the night before. A dozen of us had convened for a *sukiyaki* dinner in the billet of a Lieutenant Kurotsuka. There had been much toasting with *sake*, and each man had cut his own hand and drunk the blood of his comrade's in a token of fidelity. It was a strange and ironic brotherhood—we of the smiling blood-traced lips—yet remarkably real and powerful.

Kurotsuka, an assistant commander for the Second Squadron, had been a man of compassion, one who longed for peace and harmony within the world. He had also been a valiant and exemplary leader, greatly admired by his compatriots and subordinates. I saw now, clearly, his handsome, ruddy visage, highly malleable with its prominent facial muscles. I saw the glow of his dark eyes, caught in the vague incandescence of a light bulb. The lingering blush of red upon his mouth. Most of all, I remembered his parting words as he stood there before us:

"It is true my friends—yes undeniable. There is no turning back. We have lost a great war, lost it at a material and physical level." He paused for some time. "But spiritually . . . we must refuse to be vanquished. Let us therefore covenant together that we shall never lose our spirit of belonging, of brotherhood, the spirit of our heritage and our country.

We are aged men in one sense. We have fought bravely, seen and suffered much. And yet . . . we are very young in years. The future stretches before us, and in time's own due course perhaps we shall become young at heart, in a day to be determined by a power beyond that of our humble mortal reckoning.

"Meanwhile . . . let us dedicate ourselves—not to death, but to life! To life! And to the rebuilding of *Nippon*, that it may one day attain its former power and greatness, yet also stand respected as a force for good among every nation." I glanced at the others, at the intensity of their gaze, the glistening of their eyes. Tears trickled down their cheeks, down my own. "For what men, my brothers, in all this world, will ever know war as we have known it? Or cherish peace as we shall cherish it?"

Our *sake* cups were raised high.